The Kora

A Contextual Reclamation of the African Perspective

First Edition

Edited by Kevin B. Thompson, Ph.D.

 cognella®

SAN DIEGO

Bassim Hamadeh, CEO and Publisher
John Remington, Executive Editor
Anne Jones, Project Editor
Susana Christie, Senior Developmental Editor
Abbey Hastings, Production Editor
Jess Estrella, Senior Graphic Designer
Trey Soto, Licensing Specialist
Natalie Piccotti, Director of Marketing
Kassie Graves, Senior Vice President of Editorial
Jamie Giganti, Director of Academic Publishing

3970 Sorrento Valley Blvd., Ste. 500, San Diego, CA 9212

Contents

Introduction

*T*HE KORA WAS BORN FROM MY desire to showcase the practicality of African-American Studies. The primary resources I use in my Introduction to African-American Studies course are seminal works within the discipline. While they are pivotal in establishing a proper contextual foundation, they are theoretical as opposed to practical. This book is the perfect companion text because it defines and supplements theories and themes often covered in African-American Studies. The volume is composed of articles that examine issues in the following areas: contextual formulation, religion, social sciences, creative production, and education. Each unit ends with critical reflections, which are useful as guideposts for in-person and virtual discussion(s) or as writing prompts for personal reflections on the subject matter.

The text was curated with the student in mind. As educators, we often assume students have a referential understanding of the subject(s) we teach. While this is true in most cases, it is not the norm for African-American Studies. Most of our students' experiences with the discipline center around common "did you know" facts often recited during Black History Month. Given this reality, it is our job to make concepts as simple and clear as possible. The readings provide students with practical examples of Afrocentric approaches to Afrocentric research, which are pivotal in comprehending Sankofa and other concepts taught within African-American Studies.

The discipline is deserving of respect, critique, and analysis. It is also broad and nuanced. Topics concerning African-American life, culture, and spirituality must be approached in a particular fashion to maintain intellectual integrity and rigor. The book differs from other readers because it supplements themes in a strategic fashion, enabling thematic comprehension.

The primary motivation for curating this reader is to provide individuals studying (or investigating) African-American Studies with narrative and qualitative research examples of themes and genres often emphasized within the discipline. A secondary reason involves the author–editor's desire to assist the academician (and the layperson alike) with their recognition and comprehension of the complexities involved within the investigation of phenomena within African-American culture, African-American history, and African-American Studies. Generally, professors and their students would use a book like this within a traditional academic setting. However, it is also a valuable resource to those interested in independently researching the discipline.

Providing a contextual reclamation of the African perspective is the principal motivation for the work. This perspective centers around Dr. Molefi Kete Asante's definition of the term "Afrocentricity," which he created, defined, and implements within his pedagogy, research, and critical analysis. According to Asante (2003, p. 3), "Afrocentricity is a philosophical perspective associated with the discovery, location, and actualizing of African agency within the context of history and culture." Within his explanation of the term, the emphasis rests on the word "agency," which connotes an individual's (or a collective's) power to analyze, investigate, and critique from an internal position. In simpler terms, the book was edited to assist readers in departing from typical Eurocentric perceptions (and opinions) of African and African-American phenomena taught predominantly within academic spaces. The presentation of research on African and African-American phenomena from an African or African-American perspective facilitates *contextual reclamation* which provides readers with contextual clarity concerning African-American culture, African-American history, and the discipline of African American Studies.

As funny as it may sound, readers will not learn about Africans or African-Americans, their history, or their culture. Instead, the editor considered this as an opportunity to dispel rumors commonly perpetuated within society at large and within academic spaces (schools, churches, media, etc.) concerning African-American life and culture. The readings selected vigorously test and critique common misperceptions academicians (and society) have about African and African-American phenomena. Their (the writers selected for this manuscript) work within their respective fields provides us with a counter-narrative to Eurocentric influences on African and African-American research. However, the work encourages readers to entertain alternative perspectives on matters of race, religion, economics, and other areas of interest to the African-American community.

Most readers are not prepared to engage research from this perspective because they have not been taught to seek out (let alone appreciate) African-American perspectives in research given academia's Eurocentric approach to research and inquiry. The readings within these pages will help you identify African-American viewpoints within quantitative and qualitative investigations of religion, sociology, psychology, economics, creative production, and education. You will become more observant of the inclusion or exclusion of African-American perspectives.

The very nature of the discipline requires a thematic approach to inquiry given its breadth. Subsequently, the book employs units as opposed to traditional chapters. The "titles" within this manuscript are themes (as well as titles) used in Dr. Maulana Karenga's *Introduction to Black Studies* (except for "Contextual Foundation" and "Black Education"). The logic behind this decision comes from the discipline's distinctive focus on these areas. Additionally, Karenga's book is a seminal work within the discipline. Honestly, it is often good practice within the discipline to use influential works to inform your work and ensure intellectual integrity.

About the Book

Each unit in the reader plays a significant role in cultivating the reader's comprehension of African-American studies as a discipline. Unit I extends this logic by establishing a contextual baseline of what African-American studies is and how others have used it to analyze and critique subjects commonly associated with African Americans. Unit II deals with the subjects of religion and institution building and underlines their importance within African-American society. Unit III concerns the construction, implementation, and articulation of race and its impact on the American and African-American psyche. Unit IV investigates Black economic power and how its migration encouraged big business to adopt some innovative or racist strategies to attract Black dollars. Black creative production is the focal point of Unit V. Specifically, the unit identifies and presents the complexities associated with the production of Black art in three areas: music, literature, and film. Lastly, Unit VI examines the state of Black education and articulates reasons for educational inequality within Black educational experiences.

Each unit concludes with a critical reflection exercise that encourages readers to deeply think about the material along with any preconceived notions concerning the topic. If one fully engages the text and critical reflection exercises, they will rethink everything they have learned about African-Americans, African-American culture, and history. At the end of this book, students should (and hopefully will) have a deeper appreciation for African-Americans, African-American culture, and African-American history. You should understand that African-American history is American history. Any erasure of African-American contributions to American society discredits the country itself.

Scholars, consider yourselves lucky. You are now agents of change armed with a tool (if correctly used) that will broaden your comprehension of and deepen your appreciation for the multifaceted Black experience. With this information, you can become a valued ally in the fight against the oppression of all people. So, if you are ready to assume the responsibility of eradicating racism, prejudice, injustice, and singleness of thought, read this book, ask questions (of the reading and the topic), and reflect (often). Enjoy!

References

Asante, M. (1980). Afrocentricity: The theory of social change. Africa World Press.

Karenga, M. (2010). Introduction to Black studies (4th ed.). University of Sankore Press.

Unit I

Contextual Foundation

Introduction to Unit I

Historically, narratives concerning Africa and its people (those who remain on the continent and those who are a part of the Diaspora) were written by people who did not resemble them—ethnically or philosophically. As times progressed, African American scholars like W. E. B. Dubois, John Hope Franklin, and Carter G. Woodson presented counternarratives of the African and African American experience to dispel false notions and change academia's perspective concerning the recognition and inclusion of African American intelligentsia within matters concerning African Americans.

Scholars within academia often assume that they know what African-American Studies entails, what it concerns, and the foci of its investigations given its name. Subsequently, it is for this reason that Kevin Gaines's *African American History* serves as the first reading of the book and the sole reading for this unit. Within his article, Gaines directs his focus on literature surrounding three familiar subjects within American and African American history: slavery, segregation, and the Civil Rights Movement. He establishes a contextual baseline for the reader's initial venture into the discipline by highlighting the strengths and weaknesses of intellectual starting points commonly used by traditional academicians to discuss the subjects, while presenting alternative viewpoints within discussions on these topics.

Reading 1.1

African-American History

Kevin Gaines

ACADEMIC HISTORIANS HAVE NO MONOPOLY ON the production of historical narratives. Historians engage in lively public debates about the meaning of the past with many actors, including journalists, politicians, political and religious leaders, and members of civic associations. History is, thus, produced in a set of overlapping sites, including those outside of academia. History is also, as Michel-Rolph Trouillot observed, laden with silences. Academic historians and others with a stake in the matter are often selective in their interests, and not immune to blind spots.

Such overlapping sites of production and silences have shaped the field of African-American history. In its formative period, the history of African Americans was written against the silences, evasions and propaganda of a U.S. historical profession that, until the mid-twentieth century, was dominated by those who had little regard for the humanity of blacks. Early historians of the African-American experience, including W.E.B. Du Bois, Carter G. Woodson, and Benjamin Quarles, confronted either negative depictions of black people or their outright erasure from narratives about the American past. Excluded from the white-dominated academy, these historians recorded the integral contributions of African Americans to the development of constitutional freedom and democracy in the United States. Gaining a doctorate in history at Harvard in 1912, Woodson, the son of former slaves, assumed the vital task of building an infrastructure and audience for African-American history, founding the Association for the Study of Negro Life and History in 1915 and the *Journal of Negro History* the following year, as well as a publishing company. In 1926, Woodson founded

Kevin Gaines, "African-American History," *American History Now*, ed. Eric Foner and Lisa McGirr, pp. 400-420. Copyright © 2011 by Temple University Press. Reprinted with permission.

Negro History Week, initially celebrated during February, now expanded to the entire month. "Negro history," as promoted by Woodson and others, and taught almost exclusively in black schools and colleges, had a dual character as both a public and academic endeavor, taking aim at racial prejudice in American society and the historical profession. The efforts of Woodson and countless others have paid off today, in the transformative impact of African-American history on the writing of U.S. history and through the field's strong global presence within college and university curricula.

The past is always with us, though we often fail to notice. Occasionally it resurfaces, tangibly. In 1991, construction work uncovered the graves of 427 enslaved Africans at the site of a planned 34-story federal office building in Lower Manhattan. The graves were just a portion of what has become known as the African burial ground, a graveyard of approximately 10,000 to 20,000 people paved over as the city expanded northward.

Forensic archaeologists' examination of the skeletal remains suggests the physical suffering of the slaves. In many of the adult skeletons, hollow lesions in the legs, arms, and shoulders offer mute testimony that in life the strain of hard labor severed ligaments and muscle from bone. As Brent Staples wrote in the *New York Times*, "The brutality etched on these skeletons easily matches the worst of what we know of slavery in the South."

Another recent encounter with the past involves the amateur Historian in Chief, Barack Obama, who in July 2009, during a state visit to Ghana, visited the Cape Coast Castle, a massive seaside fortress that served as the seat of Britain's Gold Coast colony and a major transit point for the Atlantic slave trade. Extensive media coverage of the visit of the first African-American president to a major slave-trading fort brought worldwide attention to a place and a history invisible to many Americans. Obama acknowledged the "evil" of the trade, and the tragically double-edged meaning of the place for African Americans, who, like many Caribbean and Latin American people of African descent (but not Obama himself), can trace their origins to places like Cape Coast Castle.

These two events were emblematic of the development of the field of African-American history since the 1990s. Studies of the slave trade and of slavery in the Northern colonies and states have addressed silences in the historical record and in public awareness. These works present U.S. slavery, North and South, as a global system of market relations integral to the development of the American nation-state. Recent scholarship on slavery is noteworthy for its shift away from a prior emphasis on the autonomy of slave culture and on slave "agency" in favor of an emphasis on exploitation and its consequences, including psychological ones, analyzing the impact of slavery's market-driven commodification on the lives of its victims and enslavers alike.

Amid growing public awareness of the foundational significance of Africa and the slave trade, historians have extended their gaze beyond U.S. boundaries, making the African diaspora the key unit of analysis. Moreover, just as the history of slavery in colonial New York disrupts the idea of slavery as a uniquely southern institution, historians of the civil rights movement have expanded their attention to black struggles for equality in the North, as well as those in the South. In this [reading], I will offer an overview of three main periods that reflect significant developments in the writing of African-American history over roughly the last twenty years: slavery and the slave trade; the era of segregation, in both the North and South; and "the long civil rights movement."

Slavery

Slavery was the source of unrivaled political and economic power in the antebellum United States. On the eve of the Civil War, the economic value of slaves in the United States was $3 billion in 1860 currency, a sum that exceeded the combined value of all the factories, railroads, and banks in the country. Members of the merchant and political class in New York City were actively involved in the domestic slave trade, and gleaned profits from the cotton trade as well. Not surprisingly, staunch defenders of the institution could be found among their ranks. According to an 1852 report to Congress, the maritime shipment of the cotton crop was a vast enterprise, with 1.1 million tons of American-bound shipping to eastern and southern gulf ports, employing upward of 55,000 American maritime workers.

An appreciation of the vast profitability of the domestic slave trade and slave-produced cotton is essential for students of U.S. history. But there is another dimension of this history. Inspired by the historian Nell Painter's call for a "fully loaded cost accounting" of slavery, scholars have assessed the psychological toll of slavery's physical and sexual abuse on its victims. Painter challenged historians to ponder slavery's impact as a defining feature of American society, politics, and nation building, past and present. Recent scholars have answered the call by foregrounding the subjectivity and actions of the enslaved, and the impact of slavery's routine violence on its victims, on slave owners, and on American society. They have interrogated the conditions of life within a system of domination that Orlando Patterson has termed "social death."

This scholarship shows how far the field has come since the late 1960s. Then, almost without exception, male historians studied male slaves. And the question of that generic male slave's personality loomed large, as historians shied away from issues of political economy raised by Eric Williams in *Capitalism and Slavery* (1944). Stanley Elkins set the terms of debate in 1959, when, in describing the crippling impact of slavery, he portrayed slaves as too traumatized to resist their lot. Elkins's view of the slaves' child-like, compliant personality was based on studies of the inmates of Nazi concentration camps. To be sure, Elkins's account of the brutality of slavery and its traumatized victims countered enduring myths of the plantation legend that portrayed slavery as a benevolent institution. At that time, by a similar logic of paternalism, segregationists parried rising demands for equality by asserting that Jim Crow society bestowed upon

African Americans a higher standard of living than most of the world's peoples. The damage-victimization thesis invoked by Elkins and others was subjected to critical analysis by Daryl Michael Scott's study *Contempt and Pity* (1997), but in Elkins's time the idea of blacks damaged by racial segregation was a staple of liberal demands for civil rights and was endorsed by black and white scholars alike. No less than E. Franklin Frazier and Howard Zinn lauded Elkins's account of the crippling impact of the "closed system" of plantation slavery on the personality of the slaves.

The most influential challenge to Elkins came from Sterling Stuckey's 1968 essay "Through the Prism of Folklore: The Black Ethos in Slavery." Stuckey's essay called for more rigorous investigation of African-American culture as a site of resistance. Stuckey's subsequent work on the salience of the African past for the study of African-American history and culture helped inspire among scholars of slavery an increased emphasis on the African diaspora as the central unit of analysis. Over the past twenty years, Michael A. Gomez, Dylan Penningroth, Sharla Fett, Stephanie Smallwood, and others explored the West African social and cultural roots of the Afro-American experience of slavery.

Rejecting Elkins's thesis of slave docility, such scholars as John Blassingame, Herbert Gutman, Stuckey and others emphasized the survival of family, community and autonomous cultural identities, and practices of resistance. But claims of community strength and resistance, and an emphasis on Africanity, while important in their time, deferred consideration of slavery as a sociopolitical and legal system with gender as a defining feature of its power relationships. The pioneering work of Deborah Gray White and subsequent studies of slavery informed by women's and gender history, including the work of Stephanie Camp, Thavolia Glymph, and Stephanie McCurry, have deepened our understanding of resistance, moving away from the limited, all-or-nothing, male-centered image of slave revolts at the heart of the dispute between Elkins, on one side, and his critics, on the other.

Jennifer Morgan has been especially influential in employing gender analysis to complicate issues of resistance. In *Laboring Women*, Morgan writes of the intolerable burden of enslaved women forced to bear children in addition to the agricultural labor they performed. Slave owners in the colonial Bahamas referred to their female slaves as "increasors." Besides physical and sexual abuse, these women endured the constant threat of separation from their offspring through sale. Morgan warns us of the difficulty of defining resistance in this degrading situation rife with contradictions. Enslaved women enriched their captors while at the same time playing a vital role in creating the communities that would foster a complex dynamic of opposition to and compliance with racial slavery. Under such abject conditions, the meanings enslaved women might ascribe to their fertility or infertility defy generalization. Morgan cautions historians against imposing modern assumptions about resistance or motherhood in assessing the behavior of enslaved women.

While historians have written extensively about the slaves' culture and resistance, some have focused their attention on the slave trade. Since the publication of Philip Curtin's classic study *The Atlantic Slave Trade*, historians have debated estimates of the number of Africans caught up in this forced mass migration. In *Saltwater Slavery*, Stephanie Smallwood goes beyond this quantitative approach by focusing on the experience of the captives. Inventively mining the records of the Royal African Company, Small wood follows the captives from enslavement on the Gold Coast in Africa and detention in the dungeons of Cape Coast and Elmina to the crossing of the ocean in the so-called Middle Passage and, finally, to sale in the British colonies of the Americas. Smallwood describes how the Atlantic slave trade and forced migration across the water transformed people into commodities. Smallwood not only attends to the subjectivity and actions of enslaved Africans, but also seeks to understand the traders themselves, along with the world that produced them. Smallwood demonstrates how African captives made meaning of the terror, death, and suffering that underwrote the destruction of the bonds of community and kinship, in sum, their social annihilation. In so doing, she succeeds in bringing the captives aboard slave ships to life as subjects of American social history.

Focusing on a different site of commodification, the antebellum slave market, Walter Johnson examines the internal slave trade in his influential work *Soul by Soul*. Johnson lays bare the dehumanizing market logic of slavery and the racial and ideological assumptions, transmogrified into notions of value and worthlessness, that underlay its mundane transactions. He writes vividly of the moral, spiritual, and physical annihilation of the bodies and souls of the enslaved that took place in the slave pen. The negotiations between traders and buyers and the inspections of the bodies of the enslaved enacted racial theories positing the disobedience of slaves as evidence of biological depravity and reinforcing invidious distinctions between blackness and whiteness. Johnson, like Morgan, writes of the limits of notions of agency and resistance for those subject to the violent logic of the slave market. Johnson nevertheless shows the slaves as thinking, even calculating, beings, who sought to gain whatever leverage they could, attempting to manipulate the decisions of buyers and sellers to their potential advantage.

In addition to work that reads the records of slave traders and planters against the grain to recover the experience of those reduced to property by the market relations of slavery, recent studies have expanded our understanding of the scope of the institution. Tiya Miles's groundbreaking *Ties That Bind*, a study of an Afro-Cherokee family shaped by antebellum slaveholding among Native Americans, challenges popular assumptions about race, exploitation, and community. Writing the largely untold history of black slaves in Cherokee country, Miles pieces together the story of Doll, the African-American concubine of the Cherokee war hero Shoe Boots. Mobilizing secondary literature on the sexual oppression of enslaved women, Miles writes with sensitivity about Doll's likely feelings regarding the narrow range of choices she faced as Shoe Boots's slave and mother of his children.

Miles's study locates the genesis of present-day conflict between the Cherokee nation and Afro-Cherokees in the nineteenth-century trauma of removal from Georgia. The forced separation from Cherokee ancestral lands destroyed a shared past of personal and communal ties between native and black Cherokees. Miles foregrounds the "psychological and spiritual reverberations" of Indian removal. She contends that it "was more than the relocation of bodies and possessions. It was the tearing of the flesh of the people from the same flesh of the land, a rupture of soul and spirit. ... [R]emoval created a legacy of detachment between Cherokees and blacks that would lessen potential for cross-racial alliances and narrow the possibility of subverting racial hierarchies."

Annette Gordon-Reed provides still another rich portrait of enslaved women's experience in her magisterial work the *Hemingses of Monticello: An American Family*, the definitive history of the Hemings family *and* the family of Thomas Jefferson, whose blood ties to the Hemingses belie the racial fiction of separateness. Making a powerful case for Hemings's historical importance, Gordon-Reed ultimately provides an account of American slavery worthy of Painter's injunction to study the inner lives of the enslaved, in Gordon-Reed's words, "to see slavery through the eyes of the enslaved." At the same time, Gordon-Reed's study of the Hemings family breaks with Patterson's view of slavery as social death, a view which, while theoretically compelling, is also challenged by Penningroth's study of property ownership among slaves and Fett's book on slave healing practices, both of which suggest that the lives of slaves were defined by creativity and resiliency as much as social and spiritual annihilation. It does not mitigate the horror of slavery to write, as Gordon-Reed does, "That the Hemingses were enslaved did not render them incapable of knowing who they were, of knowing their mothers, fathers, sisters and brothers. Slavery did not destroy their ability to observe, remember and reason."

Gordon-Reed's chapters on the genesis of the relationship between Sally Hemings, a girl of sixteen, and the widowed Jefferson, thirty years her senior, while the latter was on a diplomatic mission in France, are a tour de force. Seeking to unlock the "mystery" of what transpired between them from the record of Jefferson and Hemings's five years in Paris, Gordon-Reed mines numerous sources, including the vast biographical record of Jefferson's actions and temperament, the historiography of courtship and marriage in early America (whose legal status and protections were unavailable to Hemings), and the reminiscences of Madison Hemings, the son of Jefferson and Hemings.

The work of Leslie Harris, Joanne Melish, and others reminds us that slavery, though largely domestic in the North, was hereditary and permanent. As Melish shows for New England and Harris for New York City, the racial and gendered hierarchies at the core of the system survived its abolition in northern states, constraining the lives of emancipated and free blacks. As a buffer against this stark prejudice and discrimination, free blacks in the antebellum North and many areas of the South developed vibrant communities of their own, replete with churches, schools, and mutual aid institutions. By 1830, America's free black population had grown to almost a quarter of a million. Roy E. Finkenbine and Richard S. Newman have written of the outspoken leadership of "black founders" of the early republic, who condemned slavery and the exclusion of blacks from northern white churches, schools, and civic organizations, laying a solid foundation for the abolitionist and civil rights movements of the nineteenth and twentieth centuries. As the work of Julius Scott and Maurice Jackson has shown, the Haitian Revolution loomed large in the political imagination of these "black founders," enslaved and free persons throughout the Atlantic world, and less renowned African-American seamen.

After Slavery: African-American Political Behavior in the Era of Segregation

As W.E.B. Du Bois wrote of emancipation and Reconstruction in 1935, "The slave went free, stood a brief moment in the sun, then moved back again towards slavery. The whole weight of America was thrown to color caste." Reconstruction revolutionized the South's and the nation's politics, outlawing slavery and enfranchising black male citizens. Black men were elected to office in substantial numbers, serving in Congress, state legislatures, and municipal governments throughout the South. African-American elected officials, in tandem with white Republicans, redefined the scope of government for the South and the entire nation, enacting a broader vision of freedom. Reconstruction state governments throughout the South supported free public education and universal male suffrage, outlawed racial discrimination, and expanded the public infrastructure.

But the defeated slave owners and their political representatives waged incessant war against Reconstruction governments and the voting rights of blacks. With the withdrawal of federal troops from the South in 1877, antiblack violence escalated in the region. Blacks were deprived of the suffrage and barred from juries, police forces, and electoral offices. Silences and willful acts of forgetting continue to define the violent legacy of post-Reconstruction. In recent years, some states have conducted official investigations into atrocities of the era of segregation and disfranchisement, seeking some measure of civic healing. In 2006, the 1898 Wilmington Riot Commission appointed by the state of North Carolina concluded that the overthrow of Wilmington's Republican interracial "fusion" government was an insurrection planned for months by white supremacists. Following a spate of inflammatory newspaper articles demonizing black political power as a threat to white womanhood, an unknown number of blacks were killed in broad daylight, in the words of the report, as "part of a statewide effort to put white supremacist Democrat[ic Party members] in office and stem the political advances of black citizens."

After the violence, white Democrats enacted laws that disfranchised blacks until the Voting Rights Act of 1965. Noting the continuing debate over voting rights in Congress and the courts, the state archivist who helped research the report noted, "More than a hundred years later, we're still trying to resolve the issues."

Investigative commissions on events like the Wilmington massacre are much-needed attempts to educate the public. It is also true that African Americans were not simply the passive victims of the post-Reconstruction onslaught against their political and civil rights, a period termed "the Nadir" by historian Rayford Logan. Following Logan, scholars often centered their accounts on the rise of segregation, the coerced labor of the share crop ping system, disfranchisement, and lynching. Sexual violence against women, neglected until recently, has been studied by Darlene Clark Hine, Hannah Rosen, and Crystal Feimster. If works on slavery have moved from highlighting agency to a recent concern with exploitation, since the late 1990s the trend seems to have gone in the opposite direction for historians of the era of segregation. Their earlier narratives of antiblack oppression have given way to accounts of agency, resistance, grassroots organization, and mass activism.

Over the last three decades, historians have grappled with the problem of defining the political behavior of African Americans reduced to statelessness by the systematic repeal of their civil and political rights. Shane and Graham White have explored the bodily displays and comportment of African Americans in urban public spaces as acts of individual and collective transgression of white expectations of deference under slavery and Jim Crow. "From Reconstruction through the early decades of the twentieth century," they write, "African-American parades became an established feature of the southern urban landscape," with a plethora of black civic associations staging processions on Emancipation Day and the Fourth of July, using these occasions to express a sense of unity and pride. But such manifestations were impossible for African Americans in besieged rural areas. Under such dire conditions, migration to southern cities, and later, to the relative freedom of the urban North during World War I, constituted the most viable means of escape from poverty and the constant threat of violence through lynching and rape.

Nell Painter's *Exodusters*, a study of the mass migration of some five to seven thousand blacks from the Louisiana and Mississippi Delta to Kansas in 1879, enriched our understanding of the political behavior of poor and working African-American people. The immediate causes of the Kansas Exodus were chronic poverty and a surge of political violence against rural blacks in Louisiana. But the Exodus also reflected the freedpeople's enduring aspirations for economic independence and freedom from white dominance. Painter's study highlighted the importance of emigration and an African diaspora perspective, along with the black folk religion derived from the Old Testament

Exodus story, for blacks in the rural South. The initial destination of the migrants had been Liberia, which soon proved beyond their resources.

For impoverished African Americans, migration—voting with one's feet—was their strongest collective protest against exploitation and terror. The journalist and anti-lynching activist Ida B. Wells understood this fact when she convinced many blacks in Memphis to punish white civic and business leaders who condoned lynching by leaving the city, taking with them their labor and purchasing power. Equally aware of the stakes for employers, Booker T. Washington rejected migration, famously urging the southern black masses in 1895 to "cast down your bucket where you are." Painter contrasts grassroots black leaders such as Henry Adams and Joseph "Pap" Singleton, both of whom supported the Exodus, with Frederick Douglass and less renowned "representative colored men" who implored would-be migrants to stand their ground against rampant political terror, lest the depletion of their numbers erode the strength of the Republican Party.

Painter's study, along with subsequent scholarship on the era of Jim Crow segregation, brought into focus an indigenous black politics as a defining feature of African-American life. In much of this work, the class dynamics of African-American leadership and politics are a central concern. All told, recent scholarship on the Nadir points to a varied repertoire of African-American political activism, both within and outside the formal domains of party, electoral, and trade union politics, and reflecting assertions of economic and cultural citizenship that were often inseparable from the quest for political and civil rights.

A Nation under Our Feet, Steven Hahn's study of the grassroots thought and politics of southern African Americans from Emancipation to the Great Migration to the North during World War I, builds on Painter's work and Robin D. G. Kelley's study of African-American Communists in Alabama during the 1930s. For Hahn, emancipation and aspirations for economic independence and the redistributive justice of "forty acres and a mule" were integral to African-American politics over generations. Labor concerns were at the core of black aspirations, nurtured despite the constant threat of white violence within a vibrant black civil society. During the late 1880s and 1890s, after the violent ouster of Reconstruction and fusion interracial coalitions, populist and labor challenges to white landowners reached a crescendo throughout the region. Excluded from white agrarian organizations, African Americans organized Colored Farmer's Alliance locals all over the Deep South. The Knights of Labor, which recruited blacks, spread from such cities as Richmond, Raleigh, Birmingham, and Little Rock to nearly two thousand local assemblies in small towns, more than two-thirds in rural counties in the former Confederacy. These organizations "appear to have tapped and fed on an institutional infrastructure of benevolent, church, and political associations commonly known to African Americans as 'secret societies,' which had been developing in the countryside for years." Secrecy was essential, as landowners and authorities organized white militias and "regulators" with the aim of intimidating black labor insurgencies and their leaders into submission.

Undaunted, African Americans demanded justice at public assemblies, with black women often playing prominent roles. The assault on black electoral politics and labor insurgency led to the rise of separate black neighborhoods and enclaves and the rise of an extensive black civil society, with scores of benevolent societies, schools, churches, and associations, and an explosion of black newspapers in cities and towns across the South. "It may well have been," writes Hahn, "that the exclusion of black men from the official arenas of politics in the 1890s and early 1900s" helped give "new voice and authority … to black women who, for years had been actively involved in community mobilizations through churches, schools, charitable organizations, and auxillaries, not to mention Union Leagues, Republican Parties, and benevolent societies."

The prominence of African-American women within the intraracial politics of class, gender, and sexuality is an even more central theme in Michele Mitchell's analysis of the discourse of racial destiny of African Americans, from the post-Reconstruction South to the Garvey movement of the 1920s. Racial destiny was the preoccupation of black reformers and spokespersons of middle- and striving-class status. In a bid for cultural citizenship, these reformers voiced an intense concern with the race's biological reproduction, viewed as synonymous with its social well-being. Mitchell analyzes a neglected archive of frank public discussions of sexuality and hygiene. Breaking with late Victorian norms of reticence about sexuality, these "race activists" opposed the ubiquitous racial and sexual stereotypes that justified the oppression of black men and women, while openly confronting threats to the community's well-being posed by a lack of instruction in sexual matters and by self-destructive sexual behaviors. Mitchell surveys their efforts in a number of gendered sites: late-nineteenth-century emigrationist movements, scientific and popular discourses on eugenics, anthologies of race progress, "better baby" contests, conduct manuals, tracts asserting the importance of homes for black progress, and black nationalist discourses of motherhood and child rearing. For Mitchell, the activities of domestic reformers, particularly women, constituted an ephemeral grassroots politics. Mitchell's study illuminates how perennial concerns about sexuality, well-being, and the role of patriarchy mitigated an effective response to public health problems in African-American communities.

Taken together, these studies expand the purview of black politics during the ordeal of racial segregation, North and South, indicating a departure from narratives about the integration of black people into the U.S. nation. Instead of a focus on black participation in the mainstream areas of electoral politics, civil rights activism, the labor movement, and military service in domestic and foreign wars, with pride of place given to the thought and actions of educated elites, the work of Painter, Hahn, and Mitchell, among others, offers examples of indigenous and grassroots politics emerging from a black civil society suffused with the long memory of postemancipation struggles for economic independence and full citizenship. In these accounts, African Americans confront the barriers of segregation by seeking inclusion into the American nation on their own terms.

Just as one almost suspects that all the stories have been researched and told, one is startled by the seeming infinity of the past and its enduring silences. Mary Frances Berry tells the remarkable story of an indigenous black mass movement led by an unlettered black woman who petitioned the U.S. government for ex-slave pensions and was undone by federal agencies in her quest for justice. In recounting the activism of the former slave and Nashville washerwoman Callie House, Berry recovers a neglected strain of grassroots politics that illustrates the simultaneous production of scholarship and silences. Inspired by the payment of pensions to Civil War veterans and a pamphlet and proposed legislation for a pension for ex-slaves during the 1890s, House and others organized the Ex-Slave Mutual Relief, Bounty, and Pension Association, backing legislation proposed in Congress that would provide pensions for former slaves. As one of the officers of the organization, House traveled throughout the South, gaining the support and dues of thousands of former slaves and their relatives. As House and others gathered names on petitions in support of the ex-slave pension bill, the association provided mutual aid for its impoverished members and held national conventions. But House ran afoul of the Justice Department, which enlisted the Post Office to seek the destruction of the organization through accusations of mail fraud. Despite the lack of support, if not outright contempt, of middle-class black leaders and journalists, House and her organization withstood the hostility of the federal government for years, a testament to the popularity of the cause with southern blacks. House was released from federal prison in 1918, and the association was largely forgotten at the time of her death in 1928. But elderly ex-slaves had not forgotten, writing letters to Presidents Herbert Hoover and Franklin D. Roosevelt inquiring about pensions for ex-slaves. Berry views Callie House and her movement as a precursor for the contemporary reparations movement.

Berry's study, along with other studies of the era of segregation, suggests the varied nature of black struggles, often against difficult odds. Diverse expressions of indigenous politics, including migration and emigration, civil society reform efforts, parades and public commemorations, and claims for reparations, defy normative generalizations or teleological assumptions about integration into the U.S. nation. Of course, state-centered approaches have generated much important work on the legal, constitutional, and legislative dimensions of the struggle for equality, and much more work remains to be done in these areas. But what seems to have emerged is a composite view of black struggles that foregrounds the economic and cultural dimensions of the struggle for full citizenship and views internationalism and "overlapping black diasporas," in Earl

Lewis's phrase, as resources for African Americans against the constraints imposed by the U. S. government and civil society.

For example, Beth Bates's study of A. Philip Randolph and the Brotherhood of Sleeping Car Porters reminds us that the brotherhood's conception of "manhood rights" was more than a struggle for the suffrage, but held at its core a vision of economic justice dating back to Reconstruction. Winston James's *Holding Aloft the Banner of Ethiopia*, a study of Caribbean radicalism in the early twentieth century, highlights the diasporic cosmopolitanism of black public culture, particularly in a Harlem shaped by immigration from the West Indies as well as urban migration from the South. Brenda Gayle Plummer produced the first comprehensive study of African Americans' engagement with foreign affairs over the course of the twentieth century. African Americans across the political spectrum, from civil rights leaders and organizations to left-wing activists and grass-roots nationalist groups, were intensely engaged in foreign affairs, seeking to influence U.S. policy toward Africa and Haiti, forging alliances between anticolonial movements and U.S. black struggles for equality, and using the United Nations as a forum for crafting a vision of global order that would encompass the democratic aspirations of blacks and colonized peoples. More recently, Clare Corbould has argued that a central theme in black public life in Harlem during the interwar years was a formative engagement with African art, history, and expressive cultures. The search for a usable African past and present was manifested in the New Negro Renaissance, the Garvey movement, protests against the U.S. occupation of Haiti, and Italy's invasion of Ethiopia in 1935.

The Long Civil Rights Movement

The outpouring of work over the past three decades on the history of the black freedom struggle defies easy summation. Scholars in the last decade have adopted the term "the long civil rights movement," to describe this proliferation of scholarship, but also to register qualms about mass-media representations of the movement. Nikhil Singh and Jacquelyn Hall use the phrase to refer to the blossoming of studies whose overall impact challenges a narrow master narrative of the movement. That narrative chronicles a "short" civil rights movement beginning with the 1954 *Brown v. Board of Education* decision and concluding with the passage of the Civil Rights Act of 1964 and the Voting Rights Act of 1965. Subsequent events—urban riots, the Vietnam war, black militancy, feminism, student revolts, busing, and affirmative action—signal the unraveling of America and the decline of the movement. Martin Luther King, Jr., remains fixed at the Lincoln Memorial in 1963, his dream of a color-blind America endlessly replayed while his opposition to the Vietnam War and support of campaigns for economic justice are expunged from popular memory.

This triumphant but diminished image of the movement prevents it, Hall writes, "from speaking effectively to the challenges of our time." Against this distortion of the movement, Hall emphasizes "a more robust, more progressive and truer story" of a "long civil rights movement" that took root during the New Deal and the Popular Front, accelerated during World War II, extended far beyond the South, was hotly contested, and persisted with considerable force into the 1970s. By situating the post-*Brown* struggle for civil rights legislation within that longer story, Hall not only reinforces the moral authority of those who fought for change, but also seeks to "make civil rights harder. ... [H]arder to simplify, appropriate and contain."

But the "long civil rights movement" thesis has not gone unchallenged. Sundiata K. Cha-Jua and Clarence Lang argue that the thesis expands the time period and regional scope of the movement beyond all recognition. These critics seem most concerned with the potential marginalization of the southern struggle for civil and voting rights during the 1960s, which for many Americans retains an unquestioned moral authority. As the work of John Dittmer, Tim Tyson, and others has shown, however, the southern freedom movement encompassed the local and the global, and rested on the shoulders of traditions of black resistance that predate the modern civil rights movement. It did not burst onto the scene, sui generis, in splendid historical or regional isolation. Rather, its possibilities were forged in the immediate aftermath of the eclipse of a wartime liberal-left alliance between labor, civil rights, and anticolonial activists.

Several influential studies viewing the southern movement from the vantage point of indigenous and grassroots politics have challenged accounts centered on high-level administration officials and such national civil rights leaders as King. Taking issue with the view of the 1954 *Brown* decision as the catalyst for the movement, Aldon Morris emphasized the indigenous resources that gave rise to the modern struggle for equality, with the black church supplying crucial leadership, organization, and fundraising. Breaking from top-down approaches to the movement, Clayborne Carson's book on the Student Nonviolent Coordinating Committee (SNCC) foregrounded the southern movement's radical wing, with SNCC organizers Robert Moses, John Lewis, and Fannie Lou Hamer, under the inspiration of veteran civil rights organizer Ella Baker, adopting the strategy of grassroots organizing for voting rights in Mississippi. Laboring in rural communities far from the media spotlight and facing the constant threat of violence, SNCC sought to empower the most downtrodden blacks in the Deep South. In a somewhat different vein, Charles Payne's magisterial study of the "organizing tradition" in Mississippi recounts the deep egalitarian and democratic structures of black southern life that informed SNCC's ethos and efforts, rooted in generations of struggle. Through their voter education efforts, the young activists in SNCC "were bringing back to the rural Black South a refined, codified version of something that had begun there, an expression of the historical vision of ex-slaves, men and women who understood that, for them, maintaining a deep sense of community was itself an act of resistance." Eschewing triumphalism, Payne explores the limits of liberal consensus. He notes SNCC's fraught relationship with liberalism and the Democratic Party. The activists' faith in government as an ally and their own ideals of interracial cooperation were tested by their mounting frustration at the nation's apparent indifference to the loss of black life. Particularly telling is Payne's discussion of the impact of the news media, which, by focusing on Dr. King's nonviolent direct action campaigns and largely ignoring SNCC's undramatic grassroots organizing, set the tone for histories of the movement that rendered indigenous mass activism invisible.

A similar interest in recovering traditions of resistance and struggle obscured by "mainstream" perspectives has guided the efforts of scholars working at the juncture of African-American, southern, and labor history, focusing on what Robert Korstad has called civil rights unionism. As Patricia Sullivan has shown, the New Deal's federal relief programs and pro-labor policy opened the solid South to labor organizing and voting rights campaigns mounted by black labor and civil rights activists and southern liberals and progressives. This revival of mass activism shocked those convinced of black acquiescence to Jim Crow. In Theodore Rosengarten's *All God's Dangers*, Ned Cobb, an Alabama sharecropper and organizer with the Southern Tenant Farmer's Union, recalled a white employer's alarmed response to the union's popularity among blacks: "The Lord is bringing down the world." Whether or not African-American workers believed their fight against workplace discrimination enjoyed a divine sanction, the wartime mood of antiracism and rights consciousness fueled the alliance between civil rights organizations and the Congress of Industrial Organizations (CIO). The vibrant labor–civil rights pact recounted by Sullivan, Korstad, Michael Honey, and others became a casualty of the red scare's campaign against liberal-left unionism in northern bastions such as Detroit and southern cities including Memphis and Winston-Salem. While the Supreme Court's majority opinion in *Brown v. Board of Education* (1954) cited the importance of desegregation as an asset in the cold war struggle against the Soviet Union, cold war anticommunism also provided segregationists with a formidable weapon in their opposition to Court-ordered desegregation. The cold war consensus in national politics pressured civil rights leaders to jettison demands for economic justice for the pursuit of formal equality through legal and legislative remedies.

Martha Biondi's *To Stand and Fight* brings together several aspects of the approach to the long civil rights movement, writing the history of the movement from the standpoint of postwar northern liberalism. Moving beyond an exclusive emphasis on the Jim Crow South, Biondi shows that discrimination in public accommodations, housing, and the workplace, as well as police brutality, were deeply entrenched in New York City. Biondi's account of racial apartheid in the North leads her to debunk the notion of "de facto segregation," an argument reinforced by the work of Matthew Countryman on Philadelphia and Thomas Sugrue on Detroit. Public policies of real estate, banking, and insurance companies; federal, state, and local governments; and members of the judiciary promoted and upheld segregation in New York and other northern cities. Black mobilizations against discriminatory practices and policies gained momentum from the antiracist thrust of wartime popular sentiment and from a vibrant liberal-left political culture that Biondi terms a "Black popular front." These mobilizations, in which trade unions played a crucial role, influenced the national Democratic Party and served as incubators for political leadership and legal support for the southern civil rights movement. Although the movement in New York and many of its left-wing and labor activists were casualties of the cold war, Biondi concludes that their campaigns against discrimination in housing and employment were influential in providing the basis for such national reforms as affirmative action and the Great Society. Biondi highlights the global consciousness of local black activists, some of them products of multiple histories of racism and colonialism, migrating from the Caribbean and the Panama Canal Zone to societies differently structured in racial dominance in Harlem and New York City.

Indeed, African Americans' interactions with the broader colonial world has been an important dimension of African-American historiography as well as politics, stretching back to the early work of W.E.B. Du Bois, Carter Woodson, and C.L.R. James, to name just a few. As Nikhil Singh has shown, black radical and liberal intellectuals responded to the crises of segregation, depression, and war with a critical discourse of "Black worldliness" that framed U.S. black demands for equality within the democratic aspirations of colonized and oppressed peoples on a global scale. As Rayford Logan phrased the issue in *What the Negro Wants* (1944), a collection of essays by fourteen black intellectuals, "We want the Four Freedoms to apply to black Americans as well as to the brutalized peoples of Europe and to other underprivileged peoples of the world."

Since the mid-1990s, such scholars as Brenda Gayle Plummer, Penny Von Eschen, and James Meriwether have explored the fluid wartime order defined by the collapse of Europe's colonial empires, decolonization, and African and Asian nonaligned movements. What Von Eschen has termed "the politics of the African Diaspora," took shape in the form of African-American activists' linkage of their struggle against U.S. racism with accelerating anticolonial movements in Africa and Asia. Led by stalwarts of the black left—W.E.B. Du Bois, Paul Robeson, and Alphaeus Hunton—the broad-based advocacy of African anticolonial struggles and international labor was grounded in such institutions as the nationally circulated black press, labor unions, and churches, and attracted broad support from African Americans of all political persuasions. As civil rights organizations and black civil society institutions sought representation at the United Nations to lobby on behalf of anticolonial causes, and amid the global war against fascism, internationalism seemed to be a viable strategy for opposing Jim Crow and campaigning for political and economic rights. However, with the advent of the cold war, such figures as Rayford Logan, Walter White, and A. Philip Randolph opposed discrimination within the framework of anticommunism, rather than anticolonialism. Cold war ideology demanded that African Americans limit their political and civic affiliations to the American nation, discrediting wartime expressions of solidarity with African and Asian anticolonial struggles.

Although the cold war's rollback of progressive labor–civil rights–anticolonial projects blocked hopes for a more democratic global order, a dissident black worldliness persisted among a younger generation of black radicals critical of cold war liberalism and U.S. foreign policy toward Africa. Such diverse figures as Du Bois, James Baldwin, Lorraine Hansberry, Malcolm X, and others wondered how African Americans on the threshold of full citizenship would define themselves in relation to political change in Africa and the colonized world. In 1959, while visiting India, Martin Luther King himself declared that "the strongest bond of fraternity was the common cause of minority and colonial peoples in America, Africa, and Asia struggling to throw off racism and imperialism." Whether as expatriates in Ghana or as part of the Harlem-based activist community, some African Americans reserved the right to define their U.S. citizenship in affiliation with Africa and its diaspora, breaking from the ideological tenets of U.S. cold war liberalism. As hopes for nonviolent change in the United States and Africa yielded to the bloodshed that in the minds of many would join Mississippi and Birmingham with South Africa and the Congo, black Americans critical of cold war liberalism declared themselves Afro-American nationalists, fending off reflexive accusations of communism. The former Nation of Islam minister Malcolm X's meeting with voting rights activists in Selma, Alabama, signaled, according to Clayborne Carson, a transformation of his politics from racial-religious separatism to militant political engagement. Malcolm's interactions with young SNCC activists and the high esteem in which they held him indicate the growing influence of his radical pan-African internationalism.

To date, the scholarship produced under the banner of the long civil rights movement tends to cluster around locating the movement's origins in the decades spanning the New Deal and World War II. But the long civil rights movement also includes a growing number of studies of the black power movement. Some of this scholarship challenges the master narrative's declension story by blurring the line between civil rights and black power. Such a view can be seen in Tim Tyson's study of Robert F. Williams, the militant North Carolina NAACP official whose advocacy of armed self-defense during the late 1950s led to his ouster from that organization and his increasingly radical critique of cold war liberalism. Recent scholarship on northern struggles for equality, such as Matthew Countryman's work on Philadelphia, views black power activism in that city not as a rupture, but as an outgrowth of the limited gains of civil rights organizations in the face of persistent discrimination in the workplace and public schools. Historian Peniel Joseph has been a leading contributor to the emerging field of "Black Power studies."

The work of Joseph, William Van Deburg, and Jeffrey Ogbar has emphasized the transformative cultural significance of black power. Though not focused on black power per se, Rhonda Williams, Premilla Nadasen, and Annelise Orleck have studied black women's involvement in public housing and welfare rights activism, both key expressions of black power's shift to struggles for economic and social justice after the passage of civil rights reforms. Komozi Woodard's groundbreaking study of Amiri Baraka and black power politics in Newark suggests the need for more local studies of black power.

Scholarship on black power faces its sternest challenge not from the "normative" studies of liberal consensus historians of the "short civil rights movement," but from such scholars of the southern movement as Clayborne Carson and Charles Payne. Carson notes a deep disconnect between black power leaders and mass mobilizations. In his view, black power spokespersons gained national status through media coverage, but they could only react to spontaneous urban rebellions and were unable to deliver any tangible results to the masses they purported to lead. For his part, Payne views the "radical-nationalist thrusts" after the mid-1960s as diametrically opposed to the nonhierarchical assumptions of the organizing tradition. "While their analysis was in fact growing sharper in many ways," according to Payne, "movement activists lost the ability to relate to one another in human terms." The growing number of studies of local black struggles during the 1960s and 1970s that might perhaps be grouped under the heading of Black Power studies seems analogous to the aforementioned trend of scholarship on grassroots black struggles during the era of segregation, more legible as an efflorescence of local struggles rather than as a full-fledged national movement with dedicated leadership.

As with studies of slavery, a focus on women, gender, and sexuality has transformed the study of the civil rights movement. Barbara Ransby's *Ella Baker and the Black Freedom Movement: A Radical Democratic Vision*, along with other studies of women in the movement, greatly enhances our understanding of the movement's gendered dimension. Ransby grounds Baker's long career as an activist for civil and women's rights, from the Popular Front era to the 1970s, in her rural North Carolina origins and the traditions of black southern resistance that were bequeathed to her and many others. Baker, who had contended with the sexism of male-dominated leadership during her brief tenure as executive director of the Southern Christian Leadership Conference, inspired SNCC workers with her democratic vision of grassroots organizing and an ideal of social change that transcended struggles for civil and political rights. Biography appears to be a fruitful means of exploring issues of gender and sexuality. Like Ransby's book on Ella Baker, John D'Emilio's biography of Bayard Rustin complicates triumphalist narratives of the movement, illuminating the dilemma of Rustin, the African-American pacifist and gifted organizer of the 1963 March on Washington, whose homosexuality made him a convenient target of segregationists and often estranged him from his ostensible allies in the movement.

African-American history continues to thrive as a vital subfield of U.S. history. Its subject matter continues to provide occasions for scholarly and public debate, some measured, others strident, on the nation's tortured history of racial and social conflict. In a nation that continues to be afflicted by racial segregation, scholarship outstrips understanding. Many continue to deny the wide gulf separating America's promises and its practices, resulting, for example, in cumulative wealth disparities between blacks and whites. African-American history offers all Americans a unique opportunity for understanding past and present inequalities and ultimately, reconciling differences. Indeed, reconciliation and humanism are central themes of the African-American story. That much is illustrated by those who have experienced the worst treatment at the hands of whites in Jim Crow Mississippi and yet concluded, as did Lou Emma Allen, "Of course there is no way I can hate anybody and hope to see God's face." In addition, one cannot fail to notice African Americans' unmatched fidelity to ideals of freedom and citizenship, grounded in a long memory of generations of struggle and the sacrifices of millions. Darrell Kenyatta Evers once argued with his mother, claiming that he did not see the point of voting. Myrlie Evers ended the discussion by showing her son the bloodied poll-tax receipt his father, Medgar Evers, had been carrying when he was gunned down in his driveway in 1963. At a moment when the progress and legacy of the civil rights movement remain hotly contested, a final lesson that we can derive from African-American history is the extent to which past social and political advances of African Americans have been subject to backlash and reversal by the forces of reaction. That final lesson raises the stakes for the production of future scholarship that advances the field and meaningfully engages public audiences.

Bibliography

Bates, Beth. *Pullman Porters and the Rise of Protest Politics in Black America, 1925–1945*. Chapel Hill: University of North Carolina Press, 2001.

Berry, Mary Frances. *My Face Is Black Is True: Callie House and the Struggle for Ex-Slave Reparations*. New York: Knopf, 2005.

Biondi, Martha. *To Stand and Fight: The Struggle for Civil Rights in Postwar New York City*. Cambridge, MA: Harvard University Press, 2003.

Blassingame, John. *The Slave Community: Plantation Life in the Antebellum South*. New York: Oxford University Press, 1972.

Camp, Stephanie. *Closer to Freedom: Enslaved Women and Everyday Resistance in the Plantation South*. Chapel Hill: University of North Carolina Press, 2004.

Carson, Clayborne. "African American Leadership and Mass Mobilization." *The Black Scholar* 24 (Fall 1994): 2–7.

_____. *In Struggle: SNCC and the Black Awakening of the 1960s*. Cambridge, MA: Harvard University Press, 1981.

Cha-Jua, Sundiata Keita, and Clarence Lang. "The 'Long Movement' as Vampire: Temporal and Spatial Fallacies in Recent Black Freedom Studies." *Journal of African American History* 92 (Spring 2007): 265–288.

Corbould, Clare. *Becoming African Americans: Black Public Life in Harlem, 1919–1939*. Cambridge, MA: Harvard University Press, 2009.

Countryman, Matthew. *Up South: Civil Rights and Black Power in Philadelphia*. Philadelphia: University of Pennsylvania Press, 2006.

Curtin, Philip. *The Atlantic Slave Trade: A Census*. Madison: University of Wisconsin Press, 1969.

D'Emilio, John. *Lost Prophet: The Life and Times of Bayard Rustin*. New York: Free Press, 2003.

Dittmer, John. *Local People: The Struggle for Civil Rights in Mississippi*. Urbana: University of Illinois Press, 1995.

Du Bois, W.E.B. *Black Reconstruction*. New York: Oxford University Press, 2007 [1935].

Elkins, Stanley M. *Slavery: A Problem in American Institutional and Intellectual Life*. Chicago: University of Chicago Press, 1959.

Feimster, Crystal. *Southern Horrors: Women and the Politics of Rape and Lynching*. Cambridge, MA: Harvard University Press, 2009.

Fett, Sharla. *Working Cures: Healing, Health, and Power on Southern Slave Plantations*. Chapel Hill: University of North Carolina Press, 2002.

Finkenbine, Roy E., and Richard S. Newman, "Black Founders in the New Republic: Introduction." *William and Mary Quarterly* 64 (January 2007): 83–94.

Frazier, E. Franklin. *Black Bourgeoisie*. New York: Collier, 1962.

Glymph, Thavolia. *Out of the House of Bondage: The Transformation of the Plantation Household*. New York: Cambridge University Press, 2008.

Gomez, Michael A. *Exchanging Our Country Marks: The Transformation of African Identities in the Colonial and Antebellum South*. Chapel Hill: University of North Carolina Press, 1998.

Gordon-Reed, Annette. *The Hemingses of Monticello: An American Family*. New York: W. W. Norton, 2008.

Gutman, Herbert. *The Black Family in Slavery and Freedom*. New York: Pantheon, 1976.

Hahn, Steven. *A Nation under Our Feet: Black Political Struggles in the Rural South, from Slavery to the Great Migration*. Cambridge, MA: Belknap/Harvard University Press, 2003.

Hall, Jacquelyn. "The Long Civil Rights Movement and the Political Uses of the Past." *Journal of American History* 91 (March 2005): 1233–1263.

Harris, Leslie. *In the Shadow of Slavery: African Americans in New York City, 1626–1863*. Chicago: University of Chicago Press, 2003.

Hine, Darlene Clark. "Rape and the Inner Lives of Black Women in the Middle West: Preliminary Thoughts on the Culture of Dissemblance." In Beverly Guy-Sheftall, ed., *Words of Fire: An Anthology of African-American Feminist Thought*, 380–388. New York: New Press, 1995.

Honey, Michael. *Southern Labor and Black Civil Rights: Organizing Memphis Workers.* Urbana: University of Illinois Press, 1993.

Jackson, Maurice. "'Friends of the Negro! Fly with Me, the Path Is Open to the Sea': Remembering the Haitian Revolution in the History, Music, and Culture of the African American People." *Early American Studies* 6 (Spring 2008): 59–103.

James, Winston. *Holding Aloft the Banner of Ethiopia: Caribbean Radicalism in Early Twentieth-Century America.* London: Verso, 1998.

Johnson, Walter. *Soul by Soul: Life inside the Antebellum Slave Market.* Cambridge, MA: Harvard University Press, 1999.

Joseph, Peniel. *Waiting 'til the Midnight Hour: A Narrative History of Black Power in America.* New York: Henry Holt, 2006.

Kelley, Robin D. G. *Hammer and Hoe: Alabama Communists during the Great Depression.* Chapel Hill: University of North Carolina Press, 1990.

Korstad, Robert. *Civil Rights Unionism: Tobacco Workers and the Struggle for Democracy in the Mid-Twentieth-Century South.* Chapel Hill: University of North Carolina Press, 2003.

Lewis, Earl. "'To Turn as on a Pivot': Writing African Americans into a History of Overlapping Diasporas." *American Historical Review* 100 (June 1995): 765–787.

Logan, Rayford. *The Betrayal of the Negro, from Rutherford B. Hayes to Woodrow Wilson.* New York: Da Capo Press, 1997.

————. *What the Negro Wants.* Notre Dame, IN: University of Notre Dame Press, 1944.

McCurry, Stephanie. *Masters of Small Worlds: Yeoman Households, Gender Relations, and the Political Culture of the Antebellum South Carolina Low Country.* New York: Oxford University Press, 1995.

Melish, Joanne Pope. *Disowning Slavery: Gradual Emancipation and "Race" in New England, 1780–1860.* Ithaca, NY: Cornell University Press, 1998.

Meriwether, James. *Proudly We Can Be Africans: Black Americans and Africa, 1935–1961.* Chapel Hill: University of North Carolina Press, 2002.

Miles, Tiya. *Ties That Bind: The Story of an Afro-Cherokee Family in Slavery and Freedom.* Berkeley: University of California Press, 2005.

Mitchell, Michele. *Righteous Propagation: African Americans and the Politics of Racial Destiny after Reconstruction.* Chapel Hill: University of North Carolina Press, 2004.

Morgan, Jennifer. *Laboring Women: Reproduction and Gender in New World Slavery.* Philadelphia: University of Pennsylvania Press, 2004.

Morris, Aldon. *The Origins of the Civil Rights Movement: Black Communities Organizing for Change.* New York: Free Press, 1984.

Nadasen, Premilla. *Welfare Warriors: The Welfare Rights Movement in the United States*. New York: Routledge, 2005.

Ogbar, Jeffrey. *Black Power: Radical Politics and African American Identity*. Baltimore: Johns Hopkins University Press, 2005.

Orleck, Annelise. *Storming Caesar's Palace: How Black Mothers Fought Their Own War on Poverty*. Boston: Beacon Press, 2005.

Painter, Nell Irvin. *Exodusters: Black Migration to Kansas after Reconstruction*. New York: W. W. Norton, 1977.

———. "Soul Murder and Slavery: Toward a Fully Loaded Cost Accounting." In *Southern History across the Color Line*, 15–39. Chapel Hill: University of North Carolina Press, 2002.

Patterson, Orlando. *Slavery and Social Death: A Comparative Study*. Cambridge, MA: Harvard University Press, 1982.

Payne, Charles. *I've Got the Light of Freedom: The Organizing Tradition and the Mississippi Freedom Struggle*. Berkeley: University of California Press, 1995.

Penningroth, Dylan. *The Claims of Kinfolk: African American Property and Community in the Nineteenth Century South*. Chapel Hill: University of North Carolina Press, 2003.

Plummer, Brenda Gayle. *Rising Wind: Black Americans and U.S. Foreign Affairs, 1935–1960*. Chapel Hill: University of North Carolina Press, 1996.

Quarles, Benjamin. *Black Mosaic: Essays in Afro-American History and Historiography*. Amherst: University of Massachusetts Press, 1988.

Ransby, Barbara. *Ella Baker and the Black Freedom Movement: A Radical Democratic Vision*. Chapel Hill: University of North Carolina Press, 2003.

Rosen, Hannah. *Terror in the Heart of Freedom: Citizenship, Sexual Violence, and the Meaning of Race in the Postemancipation South*. Chapel Hill: University of North Carolina Press, 2009.

Rosengarten, Theodore. *All God's Dangers: The Life of Nate Shaw*. New York: Knopf, 1974.

Scott, Daryl Michael. *Contempt and Pity: Social Policy and the Image of the Damaged Black Psyche*. Chapel Hill: University of North Carolina Press, 1997.

Scott, Julius. "'Negroes in Foreign Bottoms': Sailors, Slaves, and Communication." In Laurent Dubois and Julius Scott, eds., *Origins of the Black Atlantic: Rewriting Histories*, 69–98. New York: Routledge, 2010.

Singh, Nikhil Pal. *Black Is a Country: Race and the Unfinished Struggle for Democracy*. Cambridge, MA: Harvard University Press, 2004.

Sitkoff, Harvard. *A New Deal for Blacks: The Emergence of Civil Rights as a National Issue*. New York: Oxford University Press, 1978.

Smallwood, Stephanie. *Saltwater Slavery: A Middle Passage from Africa to American Diaspora*. Cambridge, MA: Harvard University Press, 2007.

Staples, Brent. "History Lessons Learned from the Slaves of New York." *New York Times*, January 9, 2000.

Stuckey, Sterling. *Slave Culture: Nationalist Theory and the Foundations of Black America*. New York: Oxford University Press, 1987.

————. "Through the Prism of Folklore: The Black Ethos in Slavery." *Massachusetts Review* 9 (Summer 1968): 417–437.

Sugrue, Thomas. *Sweet Land of Liberty: The Forgotten Struggle for Civil Rights in the North*. New York: Random House, 2008.

Sullivan, Patricia. *Days of Hope: Race and Democracy in the New Deal Era*. Chapel Hill: University of North Carolina Press, 1996.

Trouillot, Michel-Rolph. *Silencing the Past: Power and the Production of History*. Boston: Beacon Press, 1995.

Tyson, Timothy B. *Radio Free Dixie: Robert F. Williams and the Roots of Black Power*. Chapel Hill: University of North Carolina Press, 1999.

Van Deburg, William. *New Day in Babylon: The Black Power Movement and American Culture, 1965–1975*. Chicago: University of Chicago Press, 1992.

Von Eschen, Penny. *Race against Empire: Black Americans and Anticolonialism, 1937–1957*. Ithaca, NY: Cornell University Press, 1997.

White, Deborah Gray. *Ar'n't I a Woman: Female Slaves in the Plantation South*. New York: W. W. Norton, 1985.

White, Shane, and Graham White. *Stylin': African American Expressive Culture from Its Beginnings to the Zoot Suit*. Ithaca, NY: Cornell University Press, 1998.

Williams, Eric E. *Capitalism and Slavery*. New York: Capricorn Books, 1966 [1944].

Williams, Rhonda. *The Politics of Public Housing: Black Women's Struggles against Urban Inequality*. New York: Oxford University Press, 2004.

Wilmington Race Riot Commission. Final Report. May 31, 2006. www.history.ncdcr.gov/1898-wrrc/report/report.htm.

Woodard, Komozi. *A Nation within a Nation: Amiri Baraka (LeRoi Jones) and Black Power Politics*. Chapel Hill: University of North Carolina Press, 1999.

Zinn, Howard. *The Southern Mystique*. New York: Knopf, 1964.

- Do you think being exposed to different perspectives and narratives make history more confusing? Please share your thoughts.
- Is America's history complete or redacted without recognition of African-American achievement and intellectual perspective? Please list three reasons for your perspective.

Unit II

Black Religion and Black Institutions

Introduction to Unit II

Religion is a global phenomenon with many professing a belief in the systematic veneration of one or more deities. And, like most, Africans hold similar views on the topic of religion. However, African religion (or African religious systems) are often viewed as primitive, pagan, and of ill-repute. Traditional African healers are often depicted as "witch doctors," conjuring spirits and casting spells on their enemies and the unsuspecting. These depictions have been played out in movies, written in books, and communicated across various platforms.

When the continent was invaded, the trespassers believed that the people were primitive and not capable of creating sophisticated systems such as religion. As a result, many of them tried to convert the Africans to Christianity or to other "civilized" religions. So, in order to right the wrong, early theologians and academicians made in describing African religions, African scholars and theologians took it upon themselves to tell their story. Within this unit, Ibigbolade Simon Aderibigbe, author of "African Traditional Religion, Nature, and Belief, argues that the constructed perception of African religion is totally false. Within the chapter, the author explains the importance of religion within African society and breaks down ways in which their traditional beliefs are expressed. Lastly, Dr. Anthony Pinn, the author of *Africans in the Americas* supports this counter-narrative with discussions on the African American presence within the Americas, which was heavily influenced by their spiritual practices.

African Traditional Religion, Nature, and Belief Systems

Ibigbolade Simon Aderibigbe

Introduction

Religion is found in all established human societies in the world. It is one of the most important institutional structures that make up the total social system. There is hardly a known race in the world, regardless of how primitive it might be, without a form of religion to which the people try to communicate the divine. This religion becomes inseparable with the total life experience of the people. It thereby permeates into every sphere of the people's lives, encompassing their culture, the social, the political, and the ethical, as well as the individual and societal expectations in their ups and downs. As is the case of nearly every other people in the world, religion is one of the keystones of African culture and is completely entwined in the people's lifestyle. A basic understanding of African religion will provide an awareness of African customs and belief systems.

Perhaps no religion has been so confused in the minds of Western audiences as the African Traditional Religion. The images of this religion have been presented as hopelessly savage and full of ugly superstition. This is solely because the earliest investigators and writers about the religion were mostly European and American anthropologists, some missionaries, and colonial administrators who had no knowledge of the true African spiritual situation. Their works portrayed a distorted image of a religion drawn from half-truths and fertile imaginations. However, an increasing number of African theologians are conducting valuable studies in the African Religion. They have been able to unveil the position that the tenets, spiritual values, and satisfaction which are found in the other world religions—namely, Christianity, Islam, and Buddhism, to mention a few—could also be found in African Traditional Religion. Furthermore, it is imperative to say that these researches have left a positive impact, in the sense that they have helped highlight the general truths, concepts, and trends about the religion, thereby dispelling most of the popular misconceptions about the religion.

The emphasis of this [reading] will be on the basic concepts of African Traditional Religion. These are its nature, characteristic features, and its conceptual framework.

The Nature of African Traditional Religion

The African Religion is the religion of the Africans and strictly for the Africans. It is not a religion preached to them, but rather a part of their heritage that evolved with them over the years. They were born and not converted into it. It has no founder, but rather a product of the thinking and experiences of their forefathers who formed religious ideas and beliefs. Therefore, its existence cannot be attributed to any individual as in other world religions, such as Christianity, Islam, Confucianism, Buddhism, Hinduism, and so on.

Through the ages, the Africans have worshipped without being preoccupied with finding names for their religions. It was the investigators of religion who first supplied labels such as paganism, idolatry, and fetishism, to mention a few. In order to correct the misconception of such derogatory terms, it became important to designate the religion with a name that describes its true and real nature.

The name African Traditional Religion has been used by scholars to describe the religion. The name was not coined in order to brandish the religion as primitive, local, or unprogressive—rather, it is employed to reflect its location in geographical space and to underscore its evolution from the African personal experience (Aderibigbe, 1995). Furthermore, it is used to distinguish the religion from any other type of religion, since there are other religions in Africa that did not grow out of the African soil but were brought from outside. This shows that the religion is particular to the people, and it would be meaningless and useless to try and transplant this religion to an entirely different society outside of Africa (Mbiti, 1975).

To the African, religion is a hidden treasure secretly given by the Supreme Being solely to the African as a vehicle of communicating and for expressing himself before the sacred entity. In order for a non-African to see and appreciate the wealth of spiritual resources embedded within the religion, he needs to actively participate in order to unveil the nature of the religion, which cannot be understood by mere casual observation. This is why the true nature of the African Religion has been wrongly described and expressed by many, particularly foreign writers and scholars who were outsiders and had no deep knowledge of the experience of the true African spiritual dynamics. These unfortunate misconceptions have been variously demonstrated in derogatory terms for the religion, the denial of African concepts of God (Aderibigbe, 1995), and as ugly superstition that is demon-oriented. It therefore lacks the spiritual fulfillment necessary for the salvation of the soul. Consequently, their works are full of fabrications, exaggerations, half-truths, and biases against the religion and its adherents.

Nevertheless, their works have left a significant impression on most Westerners. Most people remember the African Religion with the image of a missionary in a cannibal's pot about to be cooked and eaten or an evil witch doctor trying to cast a voodoo spell upon a victim. However, with the increase of scholars in the field of African theology such as E. B. Idowu (1962) and Mbiti (1975), there have been some successful attempts to correct some erroneous ideas about African Religion and its belief systems, thought patterns, rituals, and culture generally. The true nature of African Religion cannot be based on erroneous claims of the Europeans concerning the Religion, but rather on what the Africans think and feel about their religion. The true nature of African religion is hinged on the embodiment of the religion in a belief system and functionalism that are actualized in the everyday life of the indigenous African.

A basic understanding of the religion will provide an awareness of African customs, belief systems, concept of God, relationship with the divinities, spirits, ancestors, and the view of death and life beyond death.

Characteristic Features

The fact that African Traditional Religion has no sacred scriptures like other world religions does not necessarily mean that it is devoid of organized religious beliefs and practices. The religion is characterized by a belief system which consists of the totality of the African beliefs, thought patterns, and ritual practices. The religious beliefs of African Religion are in two inclusive categories: the major beliefs and the minor beliefs. The major beliefs are in a fivefold classification. The major beliefs in their hierarchical order have significant relevance on the totality of African religious belief systems.

The [...] diagram represents an overview of the belief system in a hierarchical order.

Belief in the Supreme Being

In the religious belief system, the belief in the Supreme Being is fundamental to all other beliefs and is firmly entrenched in African belief and thought. This is contrary to the Western view that the primitive African is not capable of having any conception of a single Supreme Deity. As Idowu points out:

Those who take one look at other people's religion and assert glibly that such people have no clear concept of God or no concept of God at all should first look within themselves and face honestly the question, "How clear is the concept of God to me ..." (Idowu, 1973).

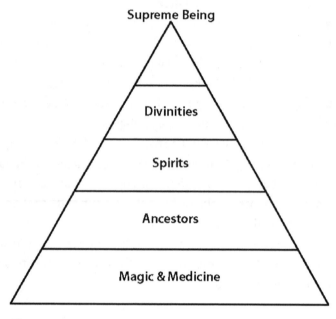

Figure 2.1.1

The Africans believe in the Supreme Being and recognize Him as the ultimate object of worship. He is not an abstract power or entity, neither is He an idle Negro king in a sleep of idleness occupying Himself only with His own happiness (Baudin, 1885). Rather He is actively involved in the day-to-day affairs of the people. The people strongly attest to the fact that He is the creator and author of all things in heaven and on earth. The names and attributes of God clearly connote the people's belief in Him. He is regarded as omnipotent, holy, the creator and source of all other beings that originate from Him and are in turn responsible to Him. The exalted place of the Supreme Being as above other creatures gives rise to His worship in various African societies, either fully as is the case of the Ashanti of Ghana and the Kikuyu tribe of Kenya, or with partial worship as the Ewe and Abomey peoples of Togo do. Among the Yoruba and Igbo of Nigeria, the lack of an organized cult such as temples, shrines, altars, or priests for Him does not in any way diminish His presence and significance. He is believed to be present everywhere. At the same time, this is why He is not limited to a local shrine or represented in images or symbols. God is real to the Africans—His name is constantly on their lips. Each people have a local name which uniquely belongs to Him. The names by which the Deity is called in Africa are descriptive of His character and emphatic of the fact that He is a reality and that He is not an abstract concept (Idowu, 1973). As Westermann (1937) observes:

> The figure of God assumes features of a truly personal and purely divine Supreme Being ... it cannot be overlooked that he is a reality to the African who will admit that what he knows about God is the purest expression of his religious experience.

The Yoruba people refer to Him as Olodumare—Almighty God; Olorun—owner or Lord of Heaven; Aterere Kari aye—Omnipresent God. The Igbo refer to Him as Chukwu—the Great Source Being or Spirit; Chineke—the Source Being who created all things. The Akan of Ghana refer to Him as Onyame—the Supreme Being, the Deity. The Memde of Sierra Leone refer to Him as Ngewo—the Eternal One who rules from above. These various names and their meanings give us a vivid understanding of the African concept of the Supreme Being. To Africans, God is real, the Giver of Life and the All-Sufficient One.

Belief in Divinities

The belief in divinities form an integral part of the African belief system. The divinities were created for specific functions and do not exist of their volition. The relationship of the divinities to the Supreme Being is born of African sociological patterns. Most African countries have a king or chief as the head of the society, and he is always approached by other chiefs who are lesser in rank to the king. This is due to the belief that the king is sacred and must not be approached directly. The role of the divinities like the lesser chiefs as intermediaries between the Supreme Being and man is that of serving as a conventional channel of communication, through which man believes he should normally approach the Supreme Being. This distinctive role of the divinities led to the erroneous conclusion of the Europeans that the Supreme Being is never approached directly by Africans.

To the African, divinities are real, each with its own definite function in the theocratic government of the universe. The divinities are halfway as a means to an end and can never be ends in themselves. The real and final authority comes from the Supreme Being. This is why after each prayer and supplication before the divinities the Yoruba end the devotions with -ase, meaning "may it be sanctioned by the Supreme Being." The divinities have different names in different African societies. The Yoruba call them Orisa. To the Igbos, they are known as Alusindiminuo. The Akan address them as Abosom. There are numerous divinities in Africa, and their number varies from one community to another or from one locality to another. Their number ranges between 201 and 1,700 in various Yoruba localities. The names of divinities depict their nature or natural phenomenon through which they are manifested. For example, the divinity first associated with the wrath of God among the Yoruba was Jakuta, meaning "he who fights with stones." The same god among the Igbos is known as Amadioha. Among the Nupe the same divinity is called Sokogba—Soxo's ax.

The divinities in African concept can be classified into three categories. First are the primordial divinities. These are believed to have been in existence with the Supreme Being before and during the creation of the world. They are believed to have partaken in the creative works of God. Their origins are not known and are beyond man's probing. One of such divinities is Obatala, a Yoruba divinity believed to have been entrusted with the creation work of the physical part of men. Consequently, he is popularly referred to as Alamorere (the fine molder). He is also called Orisa-nla and designated as an arch-divinity; he is believed to be the deputy of Olodumare, deriving his attributes from those of the Supreme Being.

The second are the deified ancestors—those who were heroes during their lifetime by living extraordinary and mysterious lives are deified after their death. They are no longer mere ancestors, but absorb the characteristics of an earlier divinity. A vivid example is Sango, the deified Alaafin of Oyo, who assumed the attributes of Jakuta, the erstwhile thunder divinity in Yoruba land.

There are also divinities that found expression in natural phenomena. Such divinities are spirits associated with natural forces such as rivers, lakes, trees, mountains, forests, etc. Their habitations are considered sacred, and there are usually priests who are custodians of such places and through whom the spirit may be consulted. An example of this is the Olokun (water divinity), which is common among the Yoruba and Edo people.

Finally, divinities are believed to be ambidextrous. With this nature, they are capable of being good and bad simultaneously. Positively, they help in solving people's various problems by helping in procreation, fertility, increasing man's prosperity, and so on. On the other hand, when denied veneration, they could inflict misfortunes on a community.

Belief in Spirit

Africans believe in and recognize the existence of spirits referred to as apparitional beings who inhabit material objects as temporary residence. According to African belief, spirits are ubiquitous and can inhabit any area of the earth because they are immaterial and incorporeal beings. Though divinities and ancestors are sometimes classified as spirits, they are, however, different from the kinds of spirits being discussed here, in the sense that they are more positively associated with the people. They are, in fact, described as "domesticated" spirits. While men venerate, respect, and communicate positively with the divinities, he associates with the spirit out of fear and awe. Spirits are normally synonymous with inimical activities detrimental to man's prosperity, so the people try to placate them so that their progress may not be hindered. Spirits inhabit such places as rivers, hills, water, bushes, and trees. Such places are naturally sacred. For instance, among the Yoruba, the Akoko (known by the Igbo as Ogilisi) is reputed to be an abode for spirits.

Spirits have been classified into groups. Among the Yoruba, there are spirits known as Abiku or Ogbange. The Igbo refer to them as born-to-die children. These are considered sadistic spirits that specialize in entering into the womb of women in order to die at a specific period, thereby causing their victims pain and anguish. Such spirits could plague a particular woman several times if treatment is not applied. This is why in Yoruba land pregnant women are not allowed to walk about at noontime, because it is believed that this is the time the spirits roam about and they are capable of ejecting the original fetus of the pregnant woman and implant themselves as substitutes for the ejected fetus.

The second category of spirits is believed to be spirits of the dead whose souls have not been reposed. These are spirits the dead whose bodies have not been buried with due and correct rites. It is believed that their spirits will not be admitted to the abode of the departed. Thus, until they are properly buried, they will continue to wander about. Such spirits could also belong to those who engaged in wicked works while alive and also died wicked. Such spirits could haunt the community, wreaking havoc if not continually appeased.

The spirit of witchcraft belongs to the third category of spirits. It is a human spirit, and it is believed it can be sent out of the body on errands of havoc to other persons or the community in body, mind, or estate. Such spirits may cause diseases, miscarriages in women, insanity, or deformity in human beings.

Finally, Africans recognize spirits in anthropomorphic terms since they are believed to possess the same human characteristics such as tastes, emotions, and passions.

Belief in Ancestors

This belief is based on the concept that the world is dual: it is comprised of the physical world and the spiritual world. The spiritual world is recognized as an extension of the physical, thereby controlling it. Africans have a strong belief in the continued existence of their dead. The communal and family bonds are held to continue even in the next world. They are usually referred to as ancestors or the living dead. They are closely related to this world, but are no longer ordinary mortals. The Africans believe they can come to abide with their folks on earth invisibly to aid or hinder them to promote prosperity or cause adversity. This is why belief in them is not only taken seriously, but is also one of the most important features of the African Religion. The ancestors are factors of cohesion in the African society. This is because of the respect and honor given to them as predecessors who have experienced the life the living are now treading.

However not all the dead are ancestors. There are conditions laid down that must be fulfilled before assuming the exalted status of an ancestor. The first condition is that the dead person must have lived a good and full life. Second, he must have died a good death and not an abominable death caused by accident, suicide, or a violent or unusual death such as from chronic diseases. Finally he must have died in old age and be survived by children and grandchildren. When these conditions are fulfilled, he automatically becomes an ancestor and receives veneration so intense as to be erroneously regarded as worship. Idowu has this to say of the African belief in ancestors:

> To some extent, they are believed to be intermediaries between the Deity or the divinities and their own children; this is a continuation of their earthly function of ensuring domestic peace and the well-being of their community, to distribute favors, to exercise discipline or enforce penalties, to be guardians of community ethics and prevent anything that might cause disruption (Idowu, 1973).

Based on this belief, the Africans bury their dead in the family compound in the hope that they will continue to influence their lives. In the African societies, there are various ways of venerating the ancestors. It may be by pouring a libation of food and drinks and/or by prayers. It may be carried out by individuals or on a communal basis. Furthermore, there are also religious festivals which are usually carried out in the ancestral cult. In Yoruba land, the Oro and Egungun festivals are the symbolical representations of the ancestral cult.

Almost all the tribes in Africa have one form of ancestral cult with festivals associated with it for the veneration of the ancestors. An example is the Ashanti of Ghana, where we have the sacred Golden Stool, which is the ancestral symbol of the Ashanti. Other tribes in Africa with ancestral cults are the Mende of Sierra Leone, the Lugbara of Central Africa, and the Ovambo of Southern Africa.

Belief in Magic and Medicine

Magic and medicine form a significant part of the traditional beliefs of Africans. By definition, magic is an attempt on the part of man to tap and control the supernatural resources of the universe for his own benefit (Idowu, 1973). Through the use of supernatural powers, he tried to achieve his own desires through self-effort. Man's use of this power could either be positive or negative, depending on his conception of the power. Medicine, however, is the science or art of the prevention, treatment, and cure of disease. The art of medicine is important because man recognizes that health can be lost and medicine helps the body return to its normal state.

Basically, the difference between magic and medicine is that in the use of magic, man tries to enforce his will by using supernatural powers at his disposal; while through the use of medicine, man tries to utilize the powers at his disposal to prevent or cure any form of misfortune which might befall his body or estate. This is clearly seen in the words of R. S. Rattray, concerning the Akan belief about medicine:

> If God gave you sickness, he also gave you medicine (Rattray, 1923).

This is why medicine men, known as traditional doctors, abound in Africa. They regard their powers as a gift from God through the divinities. They claim they are given the art of medicine by divinities through dreams or through spirit possession. Among the Yoruba, the tutelary divinity of medicine is Osanyin. The divinity is believed to be the custodian of the art of medicine. Though magic is negatively viewed, when it is associated with medicine, the two become so interlinked that it becomes difficult to know where one ends and the other begins. This is because both employ supernatural powers and can be employed for both evil and good, depending upon the individual involved.

Another common trait about magic and medicine highlighted by Awolalu and Dopamu in writing about the religion of West Africa is that some tribes in Africa have a common name for magic and medicine. For example, the Yoruba call oogun, *egbogi*, and *isegun*. The Igbo call them *ogwu*, while the Akans of Ghana call them *suman*.

Finally, it is essential to point out that both magic and medicine constitute a part of the mysteriousness of the African Religion. This is because they derive their supernaturalness, efficacy, taboos, and custodians from the religion. This is why incantations and rituals are common features of magic and medicine in the African Religion.

Other Beliefs in African Religion

There are some other beliefs within the African Religion that are basically derived from the five major beliefs discussed above. They complement the major beliefs, and together they form the totality of the African Religious Belief. They are referred to as minor beliefs.

Belief in the Hereafter

Like all other world religions, the concept of a life after death is firmly entrenched in the people's belief: African Religion also holds the view that life exists beyond this physical world, which is considered the temporary abode of men while heaven is the spiritual and real home of man. Africans believe that man is made up of both body and soul. The soul does not die like the physical body, but rather it returns to the Supreme Being, who is believed to reside in heaven. The Supreme Being is the final destination of man to whom he belongs and must return. This belief is clearly illustrated in the Yoruba adage *Aye loja orun nile*—that is, the world is a marketplace and heaven is home. No one sleeps in the marketplace. After each day's transactions he or she returns home to rest.

However, not everyone is qualified to enter into heaven. Only those who have engaged in good works while on earth would be granted eternal rest with the Supreme Being, the Supreme Judge of all men. Among the Yoruba there is a saying which encourages man to do good while on earth in order to earn eternal life: *Serere to ri ojo ati sun*—do good so you can earn eternal life. It is believed that those who live an ungodly life on earth will be banished and separated from the Supreme Being.

Belief in Morality

Morality in African Religion is religiously based, since every sphere of the African life is closely associated with being religious. This is why Adewale (1988) asserts that the ethics (morality) of Africans from one to another is religious. Africans have a deep sense of right and wrong, and this moral sense has produced customs, rules, laws, traditions, and taboos which can be observed in each society (Mbiti, 1975).

Morality deals with human conduct, and this conduct has two dimensions, the personal and the social. It guides people in doing what is right and good for both their sake and that of their society. It evolved in order to keep society in harmony, which is achieved through the system of reward and punishment. African morality is centered around some basic beliefs. It is believed that morals are God given and were instituted simultaneously with creation. Therefore, its authority flows from God and must not be challenged. For his part, man is compelled to respond appropriately to these moral demands; failure to comply could incur the wrath of God. This is why certain calamities which may befall a community or person are often interpreted as a punishment from God.

Furthermore, Africans believe that some supernatural beings like the ancestors and the divinities keep watch over people to make sure they observe moral laws. They could punish or reward moral behavior. This further strengthens the authority of the morals. Human beings also play an active role in controlling the morality of the people. The individuals keep a close watch on those with bad moral attitude and often uproot them before they turn the society into an immoral one. This is based on the belief that the welfare and solidarity of the people are closely related to the moral action of individuals. Good deeds are normally encouraged, for these bring harmony, peace, and prosperity. On the other hand, misdeeds could bring calamities of all kinds.

Finally, the importance of morality to Africans cannot be overemphasized. It is evident in their myths, legends, and proverbs, which stress the need to keep the moral demands of human conduct.

Belief in Worship

The act of worship is an integral part of any religion and African Religion is not excluded. It is believed that through worship, one turns to his object of worship in adoration and supplication. Worship in African Religion is directed to the Supreme Being and veneration to the divinities. It is believed that if there is effective worship of both, there will be peace and harmony between the supernatural beings and man.

There are various forms of worship in African Religion. There is the formal and also the informal, the direct and the indirect. In parts of Africa with a direct form of worship, it is characterized by altars, priests, and sacrifices. This is especially so with the worship of the Supreme Being. In the case of indirect worship, there are no temples or priests specially designed for the Supreme Being.

The veneration of divinities could be done regularly on a communal level or individually. This is because they are frequently called upon for one favor or another. On the individual level, the informal type of veneration is carried out privately at the personal shrine normally located in the compound. At the communal level, the formal kind of veneration is carried out at the public shrine, where everyone within the community participates, including family heads, clan heads, priests, priestesses, and traditional rulers.

The main components of worship and veneration are prayers, songs, libations, invocations, and offerings. On the whole, worship or veneration in African Religion is employed to show adoration of and communication with the supernatural beings. It is believed that when these beings are adequately worshipped or venerated, they will bestow upon man the necessary blessings required for successful living on earth.

Sources of Information on African Traditional Religion

Africans have a rich cultural heritage, which has been handed down from one generation to another. The richness of their heritage reflects in all spheres of their lives, especially in the area of the Traditional Religion. Though the religion does not have a sacred scripture like other world religions, it has means by which its religious beliefs and practices can be known and appreciated. These devices are categorized into oral and non-oral. The oral devices are proverbs, myths, pithy sayings, legends, liturgy, everyday speech, songs, and Theocratic names. The non-oral devices consist of artistic expression.

Oral Traditions

This is regarded as the scriptures of African Traditional Religion. The lack of knowledge in the art of reading and writing caused the African society to employ a means of preserving and transmitting their religious beliefs and practices through oral traditions. They are testimonies of the past, which are transmitted from person to person over the ages. Some of them are records of actual historical events memorized by the people. Others are created by the people's imagination. Consequently, some are regarded to be more reliable than others. For example, proverbs, pithy sayings, and names are believed to be more reliable than legends, myths, daily speeches, and folktales, which are often distorted and cannot be regarded as authentic for grasping the people's beliefs and practices. Here are some forms of oral traditions and their functions:

Myths

In the African traditional society, storytelling at night is the most common recreation in many homes enjoyed by the children and young people. Myths attempt to explain certain things, especially the origin of man and the world. They are vehicles for conveying certain beliefs about man's experience in his encounter with the created order and with regard to man's experiences in the supersensible world. Through myths, man tries to find explanations for certain things. For example, how death came into world; why only women conceive; why they must labor before giving birth to children; why different languages in Africa came into being. Answers to such questions are conveyed in stories which help to preserve them in the memory, making it easier for retention. Myths give us an insight into some of the religious concepts of the Africans who evolve them. Myths are variable sources of information in African Religion because they serve as practical ways of preserving the nonliterate beliefs for possible transmitting without losing their theological themes, since most of these myths are popular stories that draw from beliefs and ideas familiar to the people. Some myths, especially those used during rituals, may enjoy a high degree of authenticity. Such myths could provide the basis for the scriptures of African Religion.

Proverbs

Proverbs are a major source of African wisdom and a valuable part of her heritage. They are a rich deposit of the wisdom of many generations and are held in high esteem. There are hundreds of such proverbs in different African societies which carried with them theological instructions, moral teachings, and metaphysical significance (Jacob, 1977). These proverbs reveal a lot about African religious beliefs, since they are mostly formulated from human experiences and reflections that fit into particular situations of life throughout the ages. It is no gainsaying that among Africans, proverbs are cultivated as an art form and cherished as an index of good oratory. For example, among the Yoruba, proverbs are regarded as "horses for retrieving missing words" that are used for conveying deeper meaning. From some of these proverbs one can learn the various attributes of God as creator, omnipresent, holy, merciful and upright, etc. Thus, we find many proverbs referring to God as an object of religious beliefs, such as the Akan proverb "If you want to tell God anything, tell it to the wind"; "God drives away flies for the cow with no tail" (Yoruba); "God has both the yam and the knife, only those whom he cuts a piece can eat" (Igbo). The importance of proverbs to Africans cannot be overemphasized, and this is clearly expressed in the Igbo adage, "A child who knows how to use proverbs has justified the dowry paid on his mother's head."

Names of People

Names are given immediately upon birth and considered to be very much a part of the personality of the person. In most African countries, the name of the Supreme Being is often made part of the child's name (Mbiti, 1969). This shows that they recognize the Supreme Being. Such names are used as practical demonstration of people's religious feelings, an expression of worship, and the events prevailing at the time of birth. This practically demonstrates how much the people associate the Supreme Being with the continuation of life and the birth of children. There are many names which signify a particular attribute of the Supreme Being. This would mostly depend on the circumstances surrounding the child's birth. Among the Yoruba, we have such names as Oluwatobi (God is great), Oluwaseun (God is victorious). The Burundi name their children Bizimana, meaning "God knows everything." A careful study of various names by researchers of African Traditional Religion could give a deeper insight into the people's religious beliefs, especially their belief in the Supreme Being.

Prayers

Prayers are an essential part of religion. They constitute the act of communicating with the Supreme Being, which is the essence of religion. Like other world religions, prayers are an integral part of African Traditional Religion. Africans pray to the Supreme Being for guidance, blessings in matters of daily life, good health, protection from danger, etc. These prayers are directed to Him, the deities, and the ancestors requesting for one favor or another. The prayers may be made privately by an individual or communally at public meetings and for public needs. When Africans pray, their prayers are always short and straight to the point. They do not "beat about the bush." There are different modes by which the people pray to the supernatural beings. There is the direct form of prayer, where people communicate with the Supreme Being without the help of intermediaries. However, the indirect form of prayer is when people pray on behalf of others. These include priests (both men and women), rainmakers, chiefs, kings, and sometimes medicine men (Mbiti, 1975). Africans pray because they believe the Supreme Being listens to them and accepts and answers their prayers. He is believed to be everywhere simultaneously. Here are a few examples of prayers in African Traditional Religion as illustrations.

For example, in the morning, the Yoruba have prayers like, "God, let us be successful today." Before worshipping, the Yoruba also pray, "Father, accept our offering and supplication to you."

When there is drought, Africans pray, "God, give us rain"; "Help us, O God"; "God, pity us." In times of sickness, African prayers implore the Supreme Being: "God, heal our sickness, let the sick be well again"; "Take this sickness away from our house, our town, our tribe." When a journey or other forms of a project are to be embarked on, Africans pray for God's protection and successful completion of the project. Prayers such as, "May God go with you"; "May God help you," etc., are offered. There are also general prayers of blessings, such as "God preserve you and keep you." Prayers are also offered for long life, such as "May God spare you to see your children's children."

It must be stressed that in all situations, the Africans pray to show their belief in and dependence on the Supreme Being. The prayers also provide information on the African concepts about the Supreme Being. These concepts form the center of the African Traditional Religion.

Non-Oral Sources

Apart from the oral sources, through which valuable information on African traditional religion is secured, there are some non-oral devices which provide valuable information on the beliefs and practices of Africans where their religion is concerned. These non-oral sources are identifiable in three forms: (i) artifacts; (ii) wooden masks; and (iii) the sacred institutions (Abioye, 2001). These three non-oral traditions are essentially artistic expressions that in concrete terms "showcase" the African traditional religion in all its ramifications. Here is a brief discussion of each of them.

Artifacts

All African societies are very rich in artifacts. These artifacts have become concrete reflections of African belief and devotion to the Supreme Being, the divinities, and the ancestors. The artifacts associated with the African Religion are in two categories. There are objects that are products of archeological findings. Artifacts in the second category are made up of the works of contemporary artists. Archeological excavations have, in some cases, led to more information and better understanding of certain African beliefs and practices. An example of this is the discovery of the temples and altars of Onyame, the Ashanti Supreme Deity, by R. S. Rattray. This singular discovery has gone a long way to show the inadequacy of the foreigners' usual claim that Africans had no organized worship of the Supreme Being because they did not have the idea of God. Indeed, the discovery has led to the search and successful discovery of many other different forms of organized worship among various African tribes. In addition, contemporary artifacts comprising of dance staffs, apparatuses for divination, musical instruments, votive figures, and many other forms of ritual objects provide information on African religious beliefs and practices. Many of these objects are found in shrines, while others are part of the general stocks of artistic works of many African artists attempting to recapture the rich African cultures in different forms.

Wooden Masks

These are concrete forms of covering the face in the attempt to hide the identity of the persons putting on the masks. The practice of putting on masks covers the whole of Africa and is regarded as a part of basic rituals, particularly having to do with the ancestral worship and the cult's expressions of the African people. In the first form, people who are regarded as incarnations of the spirits of the ancestors put on masks to conceal the earthly personality behind the mask and give cogency to the belief that the person wearing the mask is an ancestral spirit. In the second form, members of secret societies in Africa put on masks. Examples of mask usage are found among the Ogboni in Yoruba land and the Poro among the Mende of Sierra Leone.

In addition to the masks, there have been stools found in shrines. They are regarded as having religious implications in their artistic expression. The stools become objects of religious expression by the fact that they are not only found in shrines, but also in some other places. For example, among the Akan of Ghana, the stools have become altars upon which the head of the Akan lineage offers food and drink to their ancestors on appropriate occasions, thereby praying for the protection of the lineage. He also prays for good health and long life with an abundance of harvests.

Sacred Institutions

Beliefs of Africans in the Supreme Being and all other aspects of their religion are reflected in the several traditional institutions all over Africa. Traditionally, these institutions are regarded as sacred. An example of such institution is the traditional ruling institution. Among Africans, the traditional rulers are not mere political heads. They indeed represent the Supreme Being. Thus, the authority they have is in trust for the Supreme Being. This is why traditional rulers are not seen as ordinary persons. They are sacred. For example, the Yoruba call an *oba Igbakeji Orisa* (deputy of the Supreme Being). Among the Ashanti, the golden ornaments the king wears symbolize the belief that the Supreme Being is personified by the sun. Thus, when the Ashanti king wears the golden ornaments, he signifies the eternal fire of the sun (Abioye, 2001). In addition, among the Yoruba and the Akan, the cult of thunder has become a kind of sacred institution. In both African societies, the ax has assumed the symbol of the Supreme Being's judgment. The Supreme Being is regarded as the ultimate judge, and he can express his wrath against evildoers. The ax is the tool for this wrath. For the Yoruba, the divinity executing Olodumare's wrath is Sango. Consequently, axes are found in his shrines. Indeed, the original thunder divinity among the Yoruba was Jakuta, which literally means "one who throws stones." The stones are also found in the shrines of Sango, the new divinity of thunder. The Akan of Ghana refer to the ax as *nyame akuma* (God's ax), and the ax is found in the shrines of Onyame as a symbol of his wrath.

Review Questions

1. To what extent should African Traditional Religion be regarded as the "window" of African heritage?
2. In your opinion, what features of African Traditional Religion constitute the unique nature of the religion?
3. Examine and explain the context and significance of the words "African" and "Traditional" in constituting the name of the religion.
4. Why has it been so easy for "outsiders" to give misleading nomenclatures to African Traditional Religion?
5. Describe how the "fanatical" veneration of divinities by devotees of African Traditional Religion reflects African sociological values in the traditional society.

6. African traditional religion professes monotheism. Compare this form of monotheism to that found in Christianity and Islam.
7. What challenges and future do you envisage for ATR in the global competition for religious space and relevance?

Bibliography and Further Reading

Abioye, S. O. 2001. "African Traditional Religion: An Introduction," in G. Aderibigbe and D. Aiyegboyin, eds. *Religion: Study & Practice*. Ibadan: Olu-Akin Press.

Abraham, W. E. 1982. *The Mind of Africa*. London: Weidenfeld & Nicolson.

Aderibigbe, G. 1995. "African Religious Beliefs," in A. O. K. Noah, ed. *Fundamentals of General Studies*. Ibadan: Rex Charles Publications.

Adewale, S. A. 1988. *The Religion of the Yoruba: A Phenomenological Analysis*. Ibadan: Daystar Press.

Awolalu, J. Omosade. 1979. *Yoruba Beliefs and Sacrificial Rites*. England: Longman.

Awolalu, J. O. and P. A. Dopamu. 1979. *West African Traditional Religion*. Ibadan: Onibonoje Press.

Bascom, William. 1969. *Ifa Divination: Communication Between Gods and Men in West Africa*. Bloomington: University of Indiana.

Courtlander, H. 1973. *Tales of Yoruba Gods and Heroes*. New York: Crown Publishers.

Ekpunobi, E. and S. Ezeaku, eds. 1990. *Socio-Philosophical Perspective of African Traditional Religion*. Enugu: New Age Publishers.

Ellis, A. B. 1894. *The Yoruba-Speaking People of the Slave Coast of West Africa*. London: Chapman & Hall.

Idowu, E. B. 1973. *African Traditional Religion: A Definition*. London: SMC Press.

_____. 1962. *Olodumare: God in Yoruba Belief*. London: SMC Press.

Jacobs, A. B. 1977. *A Textbook on African Traditional Religion*. Ibadan: Aromolaran Press.

Kayode, J. O. 1979. *Understanding African Traditional Religion*. Ile-Ife: University of Ife Press.

Kierman, Jim. 1995b. "African Traditional Religion in South Africa." In Martin Prozesky and John de Gruchy, eds. *Living Faiths in South Africa*. Cape Town: David Philip.

_____. 1993c. "The Impact of White Settlement on African Traditional Religions." In Martin Prozesky and John de Gruchy, eds. *Living Faiths in South Africa*. Cape Town: David Philip.

King, M. O. 1970. *Religions of Africa*. New York: Harper & Row Publishers.

Lucas, J. O. 1948. *Religions in West Africa and Ancient Egypt*. Lagos: CMS Books.

Mazrui, Ali A. 1986. *The Africans: A Triple Heritage*. London: BBC Publications.

MacVeigh, Malcolm J. 1974. *God in Africa: Conception of God in African Traditional Religion and Christianity*. Cape Coast: Claude Stark.

Mbiti, J. S. 1991. Introduction to African Religion, 2nd ed. Oxford: Heinemann.

_____. 1982. *African Religion and Philosophy*. London: Heinemann Educational Press.

_____. 1970. *African Concept of God*. London: SMC Press.

Merriam, A. P. 1974. *An African World*. Indiana University Press.

Reading 2.2

Africans in the Americas

Anthony B. Pinn

In This [Reading]

With a definition of African American religion in place, this [reading] discusses the slave trade and the establishment of the African presence in North America. It does so through a general presentation of what is commonly called the "Middle Passage," or the mass transportation by force of enslaved Africans into the Americas. It also presents information concerning the early formation of African American communities in the North American colonies and in the subsequent United States. Attention is given, as well, to the religious sensibilities brought by enslaved Africans to the Americas as a consequence of this forced movement. The [reading] also addresses the ways these sensibilities were brought into contact with practices already present in North America.

Main Topics Covered

- The context and reasons for the African slave trade
- The way the slave trade was conducted and the locations for it in the Americas
- The religious practices and beliefs Africans brought with them to the Americas

Anthony B. Pinn, "Africans in the Americas," *Introducing African American Religion*, pp. 15-29. Copyright © 2013 by Taylor & Francis Group. Reprinted with permission.

Why and How the African Slave Trade Began

There is some debate over when Africans made contact with the "New World" of the Americas—by "Americas" we mean North America, Central America, South America, and the Caribbean. Some scholars argue that long before Columbus (1492) and the development of the slave trade during the sixteenth century (and lasting for roughly 350 years), Africans had already made themselves known in the Americas—with evidence for this coming from artifacts like sculptures available in locations such as Mexico. While findings to support this claim are noteworthy, most agree that the largest movement of Africans into the Americas is the result of the slave trade that forced upward of 10 million Africans into locations such as North America, Brazil and the Caribbean to serve as labor for Europeans seeking wealth through agriculture and natural resources. Although there are written records that note the presence of "black" slaves in Europe, as early as the 1300s, it is in 1444 that we find Africans transported by a Portuguese sea captain for the purpose of servitude to Portugal. Spain allowed the transporting of small numbers of enslaved Africans to colonies in the 1500s. Initially the movement of enslaved Africans during this early modern period was small. This would change as European countries recognized the great wealth that could be secured in the "New World." One thing was clear: they needed laborers to work the land and aid in the production of items such as cotton, sugar and the mining of gold in the Americas. Some attention was given to the use of Native Americans as slaves and indentured European workers who labored for a set number of years in exchange for land. Early in the development of the colonies, it was actually less expensive to use indentured servants than to purchase slaves. However, neither of these two sources of labor—Native Americans and Europeans—proved sufficient. For instance, Native Americans knew the land well and controlling them and keeping them on plantations was difficult. Furthermore, periodic wars between colonists and Native Americans only added to the difficulties. There was also a growing interest in religious work amongst them and those interested in saving their souls questioned use of them as slaves. (Africans in North America would come to have a complex relationship with Native Americans in that they at times provided aid, but it was not uncommon for Native Americans to also own slaves.) Indentured Europeans servants couldn't be physically distinguished from landowners, and this could make maintaining them as servants difficult. In addition, and more importantly, European servants did not come to the colonies in sufficient numbers to meet the labor need, and they only worked for a fixed (and often legally arranged) period of time. However, as the number of Africans brought to the Americas increased, the cost of securing them became more easily absorbed. Africans seemed a plentiful source of laborers—ones who had agricultural skills and could easily adapt to the environmental conditions found in South America, North America and the Caribbean. Nonetheless, it is important to note that not all of the first small groupings of Africans brought to North America were slaves for life. This arrangement changed as the need for and benefits associated with their labor became increasingly apparent. They were made slaves for life.

Religion provided an important rationale for this development. Readers should keep in mind that many Europeans who came to the colonies left their homes in search of religious freedom, believing that God has something special for them in the "New World." In this way, religious language and commitment provided a rationale for leaving their homeland, and for assuming the geography of the Americas was theirs to do with as they pleased. Religion, however, performed another task in that it also provided a rationale for their treatment of Native Americans and Africans. Europeans made selective use of the Bible and theological ideas about the nature of humanity to provide religious grounding for the socio-political and economic need for free labor. That is to say, religious ideas about original sin, the curse of Ham's son, and so on, provided talking points for justifying the enslavement of Africans.

The largest numbers of enslaved Africans were brought to places like Brazil and the Caribbean, but North America also received many shipments from West Africa. According to many historians, the first Africans brought to North America arrived in Virginia in roughly 1619. And although most of the enslaved Africans brought to North America worked on plantations in the Southern colonies, growing rice and tobacco, the Northern colonies in New England also received so many slaves that, by 1775, they accounted for something like 10 percent of the total population in the region. However, on most plantations the number of Africans remained relatively small, but the total number of enslaved Africans brought to North America would with time reach roughly 500,000. Those who did not secure enslaved Africans directly from slave traders tried to increase their labor force through the birth of babies by slaves.

BOX 2.2.1

Enslaved Africans

- Enslaved Africans from West Africa were brought to the Americas as early as the 1500s.
- The first Africans brought to the North America colonies arrived around 1619.
- The total number of enslaved Africans brought to North America during the period of slavery was roughly 500,000.
- The slave trade lasted in the Americas for roughly 350 years.

There was a great deal of money to be made in the capture and transportation of enslaved Africans to labor markets in the Americas. It was a dangerous journey, but the financial rewards for those willing to undertake this travel were substantial. The trip involved equipped ships leaving Europe. Those Africans brought to the Americas were at times sold to slave traders as prisoners of tribal wars but traders, who moved into West Africa, stole the vast majority of Africans forced into the slave trade. These traders worked their way inland as far as they could and used their firepower to subdue and control Africans who were then made to travel by foot from where they were to the coast of countries like the Gold Coast. Those that did not die along the way were placed in dungeons in coastal fortresses until they could be loaded onto ships. There could be a substantial amount of time before a ship arrived, and so due to poor conditions, some Africans who survived the walk to the dungeons would die while awaiting transport. The men, women, and children who survived this ordeal were loaded onto ships and taken away. They resisted as best they could, and some jumped out of the smaller boats that took them to the ships.

BOX 2.2.2

When our slaves were come to the seaside, our canoes were ready to carry them off to the longboat ... if the sea permitted, and she convey'd them aboard ship, where the men were all put in irons, two and two shackled together, to prevent their mutiny or swimming ashore. The negroes are so willful and loth to leave their own country, that they have often leap'd out of canoes, boat and ship, into the sea, and kept underwater till they were drowned, to avoid being taken up ...

(Captain Thomas Phillips as quoted in Hugh Thomas, *The Slave Trade: The History of the Atlantic Slave Trade, 1440–1870*. New York: Simon & Schuster, 1997, 404)

Still others struggled in different ways once loaded on the ships and once the ships were away from land, but subduing their captors was difficult at best.

Abroad these vessels one typically found a captain in charge of the journey; a doctor to care for the crew and the enslaved Africans; a small group of people responsible for the business records; a crew to work the ship as well as weapons to protect the boat from attack. Ship crews experienced harsh conditions and physical challenges, but this is nothing in comparison to what Africans on the ships encountered. While we do not have direct records from enslaved Africans concerning the journey, we do have historical documents from Europeans that give us some sense of what was involved. The boats were neither designed nor arranged for the comfort of enslaved Africans in that the captain's financial profit was based on the number of slaves transported. The more loaded on each ship, the greater the chance for a big payday. Male slaves were loaded below deck and typically secured to prevent them from harming the crew, or destroying the ship in order to secure their freedom. Males were positioned head to foot in order to get as many on board as possible. Women and children posed less of a threat and so they had a greater range of motion. It was assumed women and children could be overpowered should they attempt anything, and they could be controlled using whips and other tools of punishment.

The air below deck quickly became hot and the floors became littered as Africans experienced seasickness, and developed other illnesses. Their clothes would be taken away to help lessen sickness and to make cleaning them easier. Periodically, men were brought above deck for exercise in order to make certain the captain could make good money through the arrival of somewhat healthy slaves. Those who did not voluntarily dance and move around when above deck would be beaten to get them "dancing," as the crew labeled it. And those who refused to eat were forced to eat in order to maintain their strength, size, and financial potential. This forced feeding was not without damage in that the devices used to hold open their mouths could easily break teeth and

Figure 2.2.1 Africans on the deck of the slave bark Wildfire, brought into Key West on April 30, 1860. Courtesy of the Library of Congress, Prints and Photographs Division [LC-USZ62-41678].

cause other problems. The crew kept a careful eye on the slaves to make certain healthy slaves did not jump overboard or throw their small children overboard in order to end their pain and free them from the pain and terror of the "Middle Passage." Those who became ill without perceived possibility of improvement or those who died on the ship would be thrown off the ship.

The journey could take a good deal of time. But, the enslaved Africans who survived the voyage were oiled down, dressed and prepared for the slave market where they would be sold to the highest bidder and transported to plantations to begin their slave labor. On plantations and other locations of slave labor, treatment varied. However, what remained consistent was the fact that enslaved Africans were not free like European colonists. The labor they provided was too important to have slaves questioning the justification of their enslavement, and planters certainly couldn't afford to have slaves seeking freedom. One way to avoid this was to deny them the Christian faith that might spark disruptions to the colonists' way of life.

BOX 2.2.3

Selling Slaves

The slaves are put in stalls like the pens used for cattle—a man and his wife with a child on each arm. And there's curtain, sometimes just a sheet over the front of the stall, so the bidders can't see the "stock" too soon ... Then, they pulls up the curtain, and the bidders is crowdin' around. Them in back can't see, so the overseer drives the slaves out to the platform ...

(Quoted in James Mellon, ed. *Bullwhip Days: The Slaves Remember*, New York: Weifenfeld & Nicholson, 1988, 291)

During these early years, the vast majority of colonists had limited access to religious communities; however, this was extended to enslaved Africans in that supporters of slavery assumed they did not have the intellectual ability—and perhaps not a soul—necessary to appreciate and accept the gospel message. It was recognized that part of what God wanted accomplished in the "New World" was the conversion of sinners to the Christian faith, but they weren't convinced this included their African slaves. Embedded in this thinking was a fear that efforts to convert Africans once they were in North America might also cause slaves to question their status and seek freedom.

Figure 2.2.2 Slave sale in Charleston, South Carolina. From a sketch by Eyre Crowe c.1856. Courtesy of the Library of Congress, Prints and Photographs Division [LC-USZ62-49867].

Attention to the Souls of Africans

While some Africans in North America were free because they had either escaped slavery, purchased their freedom, or had been granted their freedom, the vast majority of Africans in North America were enslaved. Regarding those enslaved, there is a tension in the argument concerning religion: if enslaved Africans were actually meant for slavery based on the scriptures, how could efforts to address their spiritual needs alter this status? Other colonists believed that Africans might be inferior, but this did not rule out their ability to understand and embrace the Christian faith. In fact, they reasoned, colonists had an obligation to bring enslaved Africans into the Christian community. This work, however, had to take place based on an agreement that spiritual salvation did not alter the physical condition of enslaved Africans. They were to remain slaves. It was even hoped embrace of the Christian faith would make enslaved Africans better slaves because they would understand their servitude as part of God's will for their lives and the lives of their descendants.

Christians concerned with the spiritual health of enslaved Africans were not simply Protestants, but Roman Catholics as well. In fact, Roman Catholicism had a presence in the Americas as early as the 1500s, and this included Southern portions of North America where Catholic missionaries worked. More to the point, the first reported African Catholic in North America was Esteban in 1536.

The willingness of slaveholding Catholics to baptize slaves made their involvement in the Catholic Church more feasible, and this was particularly true in Florida. Even though this did not affect their legal status in most cases and did not involve complete involvement in the church, there is evidence of an African presence in Roman Catholicism. For example, before 1800 there was a reported 100 African Catholics in Pensacola, Florida, alone. The Catholic Church was also present in the middle colonies, in locations such as Maryland. However, travel was difficult and a limited number of priests to conduct missionary work made mass conversion of whites and Africans unthinkable. This, one might imagine, was not a situation only affecting the Catholic Church.

Although ministers were in short supply, some Protestant Christian churches put resources into the development of organizations with the purpose of taking the gospel to slaves—while mindful of the restrictions imposed by slave owners. Beginning with limited conversions in the 1660s, some effort was made to take Christianity to slaves throughout the colonies with enslaved Africans being told that a redeemed soul was worth the price of perpetual servitude. There, however, were limitations to the success of early efforts. For example, in the Northern colonies the emphasis on the Bible and reading the Bible made attention to slaves difficult in that slaves, by law, couldn't be taught to read or write. But Protestantism in those colonies assumed access to the written word. Generally speaking, the results of missionary efforts were only minimally successful because the need to safeguard slavery hampered the work of ministers.

Questions arose: how do preachers avoid harming the slave-based economy and still bring the gospel of salvation to slaves? Did the first concern contradict the second concern? In the South, efforts were also made on a limited scale to convert enslaved Africans, but these activities took place under the watchful eye of plantation owners and their staff who made certain the preachers and missionaries didn't say anything that might result in rebellion on the part of slaves. The intimate relationship between Christian churches and the system of slavery was often portrayed in graphic ways through the presence of Christian ministers who were also slaveholders. Some slave owners were willing to open their plantations to missionaries as long as their activities did not challenge their authority and the religious instruction did not involve teaching slaves to read or write. And all efforts to Christianize the slaves had to take place on the only day they weren't in the fields—Sunday. However, the fact that Sunday was their only day to take care of their own needs often made religious services that simply celebrated their enslavement less than appealing to the enslaved.

Efforts to convert slaves simply limped along without much success until there was a general change in the attitude of colonists toward their own spiritual needs. This came in the 1730s when services highlighted fiery preaching and energetically expressed concern for the saving of souls. This period, called the Great Awakening, brought people back to a strong sense of the need for personal salvation. Through the preaching of ministers such as George Whitefield (1714–1770) there was expressed an equal excitement for converting whites and Africans, and the churches felt that God could make use of anyone in this ministry who was willing to serve God. As a consequence, Baptist and Methodist churches allowed enslaved Africans (and free Africans) to preach, and on some occasions they preached to mixed audiences of whites and Africans. Sermons were passionate and straightforward in their message as black and white preachers told audiences that salvation was answer to all human problems. Whitefield and those like him captured the imagination of huge crowds—preaching the importance of salvation and the joy it provided. This was matched by warnings to those rejecting the Christian faith that they would experience the pain of hell. The passion and energy of these preachers, typically called evangelists because of their effort to convert people to Christ through energetic preaching about personal salvation, was matched by an emotional response from their listeners. The numbers of Africans in Christian churches was once small, but it exploded during the Great Awakening, with tens of thousands joining Methodist and Baptist churches. While slavery continued, within these churches there was shared worship.

The success of the Great Awakening sparked a second Great Awakening in the early 1800s, in the middle of the country, marked by large revival services. These services, led by preachers such as Charles G. Finney (1792–1875), took place over the course of days and drew those seeking salvation. The second awakening had the same energy, the same demand for surrender to God, and access to pulpits for enslaved Africans who felt called to preach. This only served to further increase the number of enslaved and free Africans involved in Christian ministry as well as the number who made their home the churches offering these services. The Great Awakenings brought enslaved Africans and free Africans (those who were not slaves) into churches but conversion did not mean social or political equality. Africans remained subject to abuse and discrimination in that they remained a necessary source of free labor.

BOX 2.2.5

Converting Enslaved Africans

- The First Great Awakening, beginning in the 1730s, brought large numbers of enslaved Africans into the Methodist and Baptist churches.
- The Second Great Awakening was also composed of revivals and energetic camp meetings that brought colonists and Africans to the Christian faith, but this one in the 1800s took place further south.

These two Great Awakenings worked so well because the camp meetings and revivals allowed missionaries and evangelists to travel with fewer restrictions than pastors would have. It is also believed by many scholars that Methodist and Baptist practices appealed to enslaved Africans because they served as a reminder of practices going back to Africa. For example, many African religious practices involved the importance of water and water spirits. And baptism within Baptist and Methodist churches placed a similar importance on water and spiritual change resulting from being in the water. In addition, being filled with the Holy Spirit within these churches may have reminded some Africans of spirit possession they had encountered in Africa. These are just two of the reasons for the appeal of Baptist and Methodist forms of Christianity in particular. However, this argument also points to the presence of other religious traditions within the newly forming African communities in the North American colonies and later within the growing United States. It is reasonable to believe some Africans, rather than embrace practices and a religious faith offered by colonists, simply continued to practice their original religious traditions as best they could under the conditions of life in North America. Put another way, to the extent Christianity helped Africans in North America make sense of their new world, and develop meaningful life that provided answers to the major questions of life, they embraced the tradition. But this was not the case for all, and those Africans for whom Christianity did not address their concerns embraced other practices and beliefs.

What Africans Brought With Them

By the time Africans embraced Christianity in significant numbers during the first Great Awakening, they had been in North America for almost 100 years. We should not believe that Africans were simply waiting around for their captors to provide them with religious rituals and beliefs. These were people who had come from areas with rich and longstanding religious systems and practices, and they did not forget all they knew of these systems just because they were no longer in Africa. Memory and even limited opportunities to practice based on these memories kept traditions beyond Christianity alive.

The Middle Passage was harsh, and no real attention was given to making certain that Africans from particular cultural groups were kept together, and the ability to maintain their religious practices developed in Africa was hard. However, there is no reason to believe that the trauma of being transported to a new land, where the language is unknown and the social arrangements are foreign, was enough to wipe out *all* practices and beliefs associated with their homes in Africa. Certain things were maintained—words from their languages, artistic practices, social norms, and some elements of their religious traditions. Some religious practices and beliefs were maintained during the period of slavery because they continued to be useful and the elements necessary to keep them in place were available around plantations. For instance, in the French Quarter of New Orleans in what was known as Congo Square, Africans both free and enslaved were allowed to gather, dance, and sing. During these gatherings it was not uncommon for voodoo practices to take place as the centerpiece of the community activities, with whites present. Drumming and songs spoke to the presence of African gods. In the bayous and swamps even more of these activities took place, organized rituals conducted by voodoo priestess and priests. A creative blending of their African religious heritage and the Catholicism encountered in the colonies allowed for the growth of a rich and complex religious landscape composed of a growing African Christian presence as well as the continuation of African traditional practices from West Africa. In addition to ceremonies, small bags of dirt from the cemetery called gris-gris were believed to have particular powers for protection and good luck, and would be carried by Africans for such purposes. These bags and other charms are signs of the existence in North America of West African religious practices. Furthermore, the practice of voodoo in the United States—as attested to by these bags and ceremonies—only intensified when the revolution in Haiti freeing the island from French rule brought slaveholders and their slaves to the United States. Of course, they brought with them their religious practices and blended with those already in place.

BOX 2.2.6

By means of song, news of the meeting of a voodoo society would be carried from one end of the city [New Orleans] to another and upon the appointed night Negro men and women would slip from their beds before midnight and would assemble for their ceremonies.

(Quoted in Robert Tallant. *Voodoo In New Orleans*, New York: Collier Books, 1946; Macmillan, 1971, 35)

Even efforts to end the practice of voodoo served only to force Africans to hide their practices, but attention to voodoo gods and spirits continued. In addition, with time, some of the particular elements of voodoo were lost, but specialists with recognized abilities would still be sought out by Africans in North America to provide rituals or powerful items that could be used to change their circumstances or secure something they really wanted—such as avoidance of harm by slave holders or the overseers who controlled the plantations on a day-to-day basis.

Outside Louisiana in other Southern locations such as North and South Carolina and Georgia, Africans maintained traditional practices in a somewhat looser manner through systems of magic and conjure that we often call hoodoo, root work, or simply conjure. The signs of these practices could be detected in conversation, and were also represented in items found in the possession of Africans. At times, however, practices could be maintained without a great deal of interference. In particular, the islands off the coast of the Carolinas were the home to slaves but there was a limited white presence that made them ideal locations for the preservation of African practices. Africans were able to conduct themselves in accordance with the beliefs and rituals that had marked life in Africa and they could do this without interference from whites that might find these African retentions a threat to the slave system and the dominance of white slave owners.

BOX 2.2.7

Signs of More Than Just Christianity

- Similar rituals involving water and possession by God were similar to activities in Africa and this made Methodist and Baptist churches somewhat appealing, but this also pointed to the continued presence of African religious practices despite efforts to destroy them.
- Practices similar to Vodou in West Africa are present in North America in the form of voodoo, hoodoo, conjure and root work
- Roman Catholicism's attention to saints provided a way for Africans to maintain traditions brought from Africa without slaveholders being fully aware of what they were doing.

The African gods survived the Middle Passage and found new homes in the Americas, including North America, where Africans continued their devotion, rituals, and requests to the cosmic forces they knew in Africa. But in addition to this, some enslaved and free Africans maintained another tradition brought with them from Africa. Islam had been an important religious tradition on the continent of Africa, moving from East Africa to West Africa long before the slave trade began. By the time ships loaded Africans to take them to the Americas, Islam was firmly established and it was the tradition of many on those ships. While not all of these African Muslims would have landed in North America, there is evidence that some of them did and they maintained as best they could the elements of their faith. The evidence of their presence isn't as readily available as it is for Christianity within African communities in North America, but there are signs nonetheless. For example, there were advertisements for the capture of runaway slaves that described them using Islamic names. Muslims we do know about, such as Umar Ibn Said (1770–1864) from North Carolina provided a sense of the religious practices maintained in North America.

BOX 2.2.8

When I came to the Christian country, my religion was the religion of Mohammed, the Apostle of God—may God have mercy upon him and give him peace.

Quoted from Umar Ibn Said's autobiography

There are five fundamental elements of Islam, referred to as the five pillars of Islam—(1) affirmation that there is only one God, Allah; (2) prayer five times each day; (3) giving of alms; (4) fasting during Ramadan; (5) pilgrimage to Mecca. Clearly, some of these could not be done because of the restrictions of slavery, but others including prayer, feast days associated with the religion, and dietary restrictions were observed.

Other Africans found all forms of theism—Christianity, Islam and African traditions—problematic. For them only attention to their own humanity without reliance on God or gods would work. Evidence for this type of thinking is found in the cultural production of the early period of slavery in things such as work songs, folktales, and the blues that critique reliance on the supernatural and instead celebrate human creativity and ingenuity. This approach to life represents the early signs of what we have come to call African American humanism.

BOX 2.2.9

I prayed for twenty years but received no answer until I prayed with my legs.

Frederick Douglass, abolitionist, political leader, and writer

---

The Religious Landscape

Prior to the nineteenth century, Africans both free and enslaved developed a rich and complex religious life. It was composed of humanism, Christianity, Islam, and a host of African-based traditions all meant to provide life meaning within a troubled and troubling world. Africans brought many of these traditions with them to North America and they were exposed to others once enslaved. In both cases, they made these traditions work for them; they made these practices their own and blended them in ways meant to meet their particular needs and address their concerns. It was easier for African-born slaves, who did not know English but communicated in indigenous African languages, to maintain African practices and pass elements of these traditions to their children. However, North American-born slaves, who spoke English and were familiar with the North American context, were further removed from African practices. When they maintained them, they did so in ways that reflected their new location. In all cases, however, they thought about religion in light of their needs and tried to shape practices and beliefs so as to fit their circumstances. Some of this involved holding onto what they could remember and maintain of their African home, but it also involved a creative manipulation of what they discovered in their new land. We see some of this developing during the 1600s and 1700s, but it is within the 1800s—the nineteenth century—that the practice of these traditions really grows amongst Africans and takes on unique and creative aspects and dimensions. Efforts to control how, where, and when Africans practiced their various faiths failed. And they failed in large part as Africans shaped their own versions of religion and used it as an increasingly visible tool for struggle against oppression. [...]

Key Points You Need to Know

- Both Catholics and Protestants participated in efforts to Christianize enslaved Africans.
- Successful Christianizing of Africans takes place in large part because of two religious Great Awakenings.
- African gods were brought to the Americas, and there are reports concerning voodoo in North America that date back to the 1700s.
- Africans brought Islam to North America, and there are clear indicators of its presence.
- Religious conversion did not affect the status of Africans because they remained slaves.
- Some Africans rejected theism altogether and instead relied on an approach to life centered on human creativity and ingenuity.
- Diversity defines the religious landscape of African life prior to the nineteenth century.

Discussion Questions

1. Why did some slaveholders oppose efforts to convert Africans to Christianity?
2. What were the reasons provided by those who were interested in missionary work amongst enslaved Africans?
3. Why did Methodist and Baptist churches appeal to Africans?
4. What are some of the signs of Islam's presence in North America?
5. What were some of the early practices in North America related to African gods?

Further Reading

Allen, Norm Jr. *African American Humanism: An Anthology.* Buffalo, NY: Prometheus Books, 1991.

Austin, Allan D. *African Muslims in Antebellum America: Transatlantic Stories and Spiritual Struggles.* New York: Routledge, 1997.

Balmer, Randall and Lauren Winner. *Protestantism in America.* New York: Columbia University Press, 2002.

Davis, Cyprian. *The History of Black Catholics in the United States.* New York: Crossroads, 1991.

Holloway, Joseph E., ed. *Africanisms in American Culture.* Bloomington, IN: Indiana University Press, 1990.

Pitts, Walter F. *Old Ship of Zion: The Afro-Baptist Ritual in the African Diaspora.* New York: Oxford University Press, 1993.

Tallant, Robert. *Voodoo in New Orleans.* New York: Collier Books, 1946; Macmillan, 1971.

Turner, Richard. *Islam in the African-American Experience.* Bloomington, IN: Indiana University Press, 1997.

CRITICAL REFLECTIONS

- Prior to reading this unit, what were your initial perceptions of African religions and/or belief systems? Did you have any preconceived notions? Please share.
- After reading the unit, have your perceptions changed?

Unit III

Black Sociology and Psychology

Introduction to Unit III

A typical depiction of African American Studies is that it is a discipline created, formulated, and articulated from a race-first position. "Race-first", within this context, alludes to the construct (race) serving as the primary basis of inquiry and analysis. However, this assumption is false because it (African-American studies) is interdisciplinary, utilizing numerous variables within its investigations of phenomena impacting the continental and diasporic African. The discipline specifically incorporates cultural, historical, social, and spiritual variables (along with race) within its investigations and critiques.

Psychology and sociology respectively examine the individual and the group, analyzing and critiquing the effects of numerous variables upon each one. However, once you ascribe the adjective "Black" to the disciplines, they assume additional responsibilities and bear extra burdens. The disciplines (psychology and sociology) are required to adhere to the traditional tenets of academia. Yet, assigning the term "Black" requires said practitioners to assume an interdisciplinary approach to inquiry. Given the multifaceted nature of the Black experience, Black psychologists and sociologists must follow established conventions (unfortunately, to "justify" the validity of their work) to accentuate the differences between the traditional psychology or sociology and Black psychology or sociology within investigations of nuances associated with the Black experience.

The reason for this extra effort is found in this reading. Steven M. Buechler's *"The Social Construction of Race"* breaks down the impact and influence of race nationally and internationally. Given the fact that the American economy was built using a racist system (slavery) and that American society still wrestles with eradicating racial segregation, it is important for us to examine how this construct became so powerful and how it has disproportionately affected Black people and people of color. Within this reading, the reader will be informed about the construction, implementation, and articulation of race and why the lie of race is so powerful.

Reading 3.1

The Social Construction of Race

Steven M. Buechler

T HE ANALYSIS OF SOCIAL CLASS HAS been part of sociology from the beginning. Race is different. Although scholars like W. E. B. Du Bois (1903) had crucial insights into race relations more than a hundred years ago, sociology was slow to see race as an important subject in its own right.

This gradually changed after Gunnar Myrdal's *An American Dilemma* (1944) placed racial prejudice at the forefront of public consciousness. Along with other work, it helped establish race and ethnic relations as a major subfield within sociology. Group dynamics, racial conflict, prejudice, and discrimination attracted increasing sociological attention.

What really invigorated the study of race were not academic developments but social conflict. As the civil rights movement overturned the most explicit forms of racial segregation and discrimination in the 1950s and 1960s, race became even more central in public awareness and academic study. As the movement evolved from liberal integration to black power to cultural nationalism, different understandings of race emerged. These movement-inspired analyses revealed how race was embedded in social structure.

Current sociological understandings of race thus have a dual legacy. The slowly developing academic study of race has been infused with critical insights from race-based social movements. [...], much the same can be said for the impact of the feminist movement in jump-starting sociology's understanding of gender issues.

What is Race?

Few things seem more obvious than someone's race. As we interact with others, we unthinkingly place them within familiar racial categories. On rare occasions, someone doesn't easily fit the categories. We might regard them as odd or unusual, but we rarely use such cases to question the categories themselves.

When we "see" race like this, we are also likely to assume race is rooted in biology. The physical differences between races (skin color, facial features, eye shape, hair texture) seem so self-evident as to be beyond question. Everyday consciousness assumes these features reflect well-established biological, physiological, and genetic differences that distinguish races. Well-meaning people might struggle to avoid prejudices and stereotypes, but they are likely to see race as a biologically self-evident reality.

This is a good time to recall Peter Berger's (1963) sociological insight that things are not always what they seem. Beneath the seemingly self-evident biology of race, there are complex social, political, and cultural forces that sustain that appearance. Put differently, race is not biologically determined but rather socially constructed. This implies two seemingly contradictory things. First, racial categories are arbitrary. They have little scientific or biological foundation. They are not "real." Second, these categories nevertheless *become real* through social definitions. As W. I. Thomas noted long ago, if a situation is defined as real, it will be real in its consequences. When the definition is embedded in centuries of institutions and interactions, then race becomes as real as any social phenomenon can be. Race is an illusory biological fiction but a powerful social fact.

There are several reasons to question the biological basis of race. Human beings share almost 99 percent of our genetic composition with higher primates. Put differently, homo sapiens are only 1 to 2 percent genetically different from chimpanzees. If the genetic margin separating two species is so small, the likelihood that there will be consistent genetic differences *within* the category of homo sapiens that sort humans into genetically distinct races is highly implausible.

A second reason to doubt the biological basis of race involves the logic of categories and classification. Such logic makes sense when things fall into mutually exclusive categories based on many relevant traits. It makes less sense if there is a lot of overlap between things in supposedly separate categories. The logic is weakest when there is more individual variation within categories than the average variation between categories. And yet it is this weakest version that applies to race. On any number of physical traits, individual variations within races far exceed average differences between them. When categories persist in such situations, it is because they are based on social definitions rather than on logically compelling reasons or scientifically verifiable data.

A third reason to doubt the biological basis of race involves the history of racial typologies. Systems of racial classification have been proposed for centuries, with none of the logical consistency, cumulative advances, or increasing specificity that define scientific progress. Throughout this history, there has been major disagreement over things as basic as how many races exist. After centuries of work, the only real lesson here is that the very idea of distinguishing races in biological terms is not scientifically feasible.

A fourth reason to question the biological basis of race involves social and legal definitions. When Southern legislators defined people as "Negro" if one thirty-second of their ancestry was African, this was a social definition and not a biological fact. When Native American tribes use similar measures to determine who is a legitimate tribal member, this is also a social definition and not a biological fact. Because racial definitions vary by place, you can change your race by flying to Brazil where an unusually complex set of racial distinctions will define your race differently from the place you just left (Henslin 2005, 327). Racial definitions also change over time; consider "how the Irish became white" (Ignatiev 1995) in nineteenth-century US history.

One final example: People sometimes defend a biological conception of race based on medical conditions. In the United States, sickle-cell anemia is considered a "black disease." In reality, a predisposition to sickle-cell anemia derives from geography and evolution and not race. In places where malaria was a big threat to human health, a few people had a natural immunity. Through natural selection, they reproduced in greater numbers. However, the same factors creating the immunity also made them susceptible to sickle-cell anemia. Thus, some but not all Africans are susceptible, and some non-Africans from Mediterranean regions and South Asia are susceptible. It is difficult to see how this qualifies as a "racial" disease (Adelman 2003).

It is not physical but social facts that make races "real." This social construction of race is a historical process. People have always noted human differences, but a new discourse of race emerged during European exploration, conquest, and colonization typically dated from the "discovery" of the "New World" in 1492. Thus, Columbus's diaries refer to the "savages" he encountered. With each subsequent encounter between European colonizers and indigenous groups, the discourse of race grew to describe these "others" in racial terms (Winant 2004).

This discourse rested on two premises. The first was that races were biological realities. The second was that races existed in a hierarchy of superiority and inferiority. In these hierarchies, whites, Europeans, or some subgroup of Europeans were inevitably located at the top of the hierarchy. Despite many variations, some races (the people doing the classifying) were always superior to others (the people being classified). The very concept of race is *racist*, because beliefs about superiority and inferiority have always been part of the concept.

The reasons are not a big mystery. European colonization was often brutal and inhumane. It contradicted many social norms, religious principles, and moral imperatives of the colonizers. It required some type of legitimation of the contradiction between humane values and inhumane behavior. Thus the invention of race/racism.

Colonialism only poses a moral dilemma if people are seen as equals. The social construction of race/racism defines the colonized group as inferior or subhuman. The more their humanity is denied, the more brutality becomes acceptable. Consider that few people have qualms about the slaughter and consumption of animals because they are seen as a different species. It hardly occurs to us that this requires a justification. Some versions of racism also suggest that "others" are a different species, so the moral code of the dominant group does not apply. The same logic operates in warfare; it is easier to kill people who are seen as less than human. It is no accident that the most extreme versions of racial thinking culminate in genocide, where others are not only seen as subhuman but as a threat that must be eliminated.

The social construction of race links biology, inferiority, and racism in fateful ways. Like race, racism has many variations. It can provide justifications for enslavement and genocide. It can seek to convert others who have not yet had the benefits of "civilization." It can portray "others" as innocent children requiring protection and guidance. In every version, however, a presumption of racial inferiority is central.

The social construction of race and racism was vital in legitimizing European colonization and conquest. The United States followed suit in the exploitation of African slaves, the conquest of Native peoples, and racist relations with Latino/a and Asian populations. The timing and groups were different, but the history of US race relations mirrors the European model quite closely.

Although race is a biological fiction, there is a social logic to why this fiction arose and how it shapes contemporary society. The challenge of seeing race as a social construction is to balance the seeming contradiction that something arbitrary has been socially constructed into something as "real" as any social fact can be.

Race vs. Ethnicity

The social construction of race also becomes evident by contrasting "races" and "ethnic groups." Common sense equates race with biology and ethnicity with culture. Although the link between race and biology is problematic, the equation of ethnicity and culture is sound.

Ethnic groups are distinguished by cultural differences in language, customs, norms, values, and religious beliefs. Although their members might be geographically dispersed, ethnic groups often trace their roots to a distinctive place. Although it is culturally learned, ethnicity "feels" natural to people. Ethnocentrism is a common expression of the "naturalness" or superiority of one's group and way of doing things.

As socially constructed categories, "races" lump together many ethnic groups in the same racial category. Each of the major races typically recognized in the United States (African Americans, European Americans, Latino/a Americans, Native Americans, and

Asian Americans) includes multiple ethnicities. The most obvious expression of racism is the blatant division between the dominant racial group of European Americans and all other subordinate racial groups.

A subtler expression of racism is that ethnic variations within the dominant racial group are often recognized, whereas variations within subordinate racial groups are not. Thus, in both popular consciousness and much sociological work, ethnicity really means cultural variations among European Americans (Polish, Swedish, Italian, German, etc.) whereas race lumps others into broad racial categories (blacks, Hispanics, Native Americans, etc.). This practice obscures the fact that "white" is also a socially constructed race and that other races have internal ethnic differences.

A long history of unequal treatment has made these arbitrary distinctions into powerful realities. Consider the following contrasts. Members of white ethnic groups typically entered the United States voluntarily, could sometimes conceal their ethnicity, were seen as variations on a common theme of being white, were eventually pressured to assimilate, and had at least some opportunities for integration and upward mobility. Members of racial minorities, by contrast, became part of the United States involuntarily, could rarely conceal their race, were seen as fundamentally different, were subject to strict segregation, and had few opportunities for integration and upward mobility until quite recently. Such differences suggest different models of ethnic and race relations.

For white ethnic groups, the main story is assimilation. However, the melting pot image of assimilation is misleading by implying that all groups change equally as they are "melted" into something new. In reality, there has always been a hierarchy among white ethnic groups. WASPs, or white Anglo-Saxon Protestants, have been at the top, followed by other Northern Europeans, and then Central and Southern Europeans. Assimilation has not meant blending but rather change by subordinate white ethnic groups. Consider that the United States did not create a new language through assimilation. Assimilating groups gave up native languages and adopted English. Assimilation involved a trade-off in which subordinate white ethnic groups sacrificed ethnic distinctiveness in exchange for admission into mainstream society.

Assimilation involves several stages that begin with cultural assimilation (Gordon 1964). This occurs when a newly arriving white ethnic group learns and adopts the culture of the dominant group. This is the only stage the subordinate group can control. Indeed, they might initially resist this stage, in which case assimilation will not occur. If and when they do initiate the process, control passes to the dominant group.

This is evident in the second stage of structural assimilation. This means acceptance of the subordinate group by the dominant group. Such acceptance initially occurs in secondary groups like the workplace and other public settings. It then involves accepting people as neighbors or in churches and voluntary organizations. It culminates with acceptance into primary groups like friendship networks. At each stage, the subordinate group can initiate contact, but the dominant group retains the power to accept or reject it.

Assimilation then proceeds through other stages that reflect still greater acceptance. Marital assimilation occurs when members of different groups intermarry with increasing frequency and decreasing disapproval. Identificational assimilation occurs when members of the assimilating group switch identities from their original ethnicity to their new nation. This could take generations. Immigrants might retain their Italian identity, while the next generation identifies as Italian American, and subsequent generations identify as American.

Subsequent stages include attitudinal assimilation, indicated by a reduction in prejudicial attitudes about the subordinate group. This often corresponds with behavioral assimilation, evidenced by a reduction in discrimination against members of the group. The process culminates with civic assimilation, signified by the elimination of ethnic conflict.

Although the story of assimilation seems to offer a happy ending, it is shaped by unequal power throughout. The dominant group provides the standard for what assimilation means (becoming like them), and it controls the pace. They retain their dominance because their culture becomes normative for all. The subordinate group pays the cost by relinquishing their ethnic heritage. When the costs seem worth the benefits, groups seek assimilation. Although abstract models oversimplify complex histories, this model accurately describes the assimilation of a number of white ethnic groups in the United States.

Given their different treatment, it is not surprising that the assimilationist model doesn't fit racial groups in the United States. Some insist that with enough time, racial minorities will also assimilate, but this is a dubious claim. The histories of these groups are different, the scope of discrimination is wider, and resistance to assimilation has been substantial. Moreover, the persistence of distinctive racial cultures suggests that many people in these groups would not seek assimilation even if it were possible.

Such differences drew many scholars to the model of internal colonialism to analyze racial dynamics (Omi and Winant 1994, 44–46). This model rests on an analogy between race relations within a single country and colonial relations between countries. In the analogy, the white power structure in a single country is like the colonial power, and racial minorities in that country are like colonies.

Several parallels lend credence to the analogy. Both relationships begin with forced contact, because colonial powers and white power structures use coercion to establish the relationship in the first place. Coercion might be resisted, but the power imbalance has allowed colonial powers and white power structures to retain dominance for centuries.

A second parallel involves cultural domination. The beliefs and practices of the colonized group or the racial minority are denigrated as primitive or uncivilized. Sometimes there are efforts to convert the subordinate group to the culture of the dominant group, but in all cases the dominant group attempts to undermine the culture of the subordinate group.

Political control is a third parallel. In the colonial situation, extensive staffs of governors and administrators were sent to the colony to run its political affairs on behalf of the colonizing power. With internal colonialism, the dominant group uses both formal and informal political mechanisms to ensure a similar degree of control by the white power structure. The underrepresentation of racial minorities in positions of political power is the tip of the iceberg of political control by the dominant group.

Perhaps the most important parallel involves economic exploitation. This is the driving motive of colonial relations, whether the resources involve cheap labor, raw materials, or commodity markets. With internal colonialism, the role of racial minorities as a secondary labor force with lower pay, fewer benefits, and higher unemployment is merely one indicator of the economic exploitation that is central to this relationship.

Both traditional and internal colonialism create institutional discrimination, as social organizations and practices are built on discriminatory principles. This creates racial inequalities and racially coded practices not just in the economy and polity, but also in housing, education, health care, and criminal justice.

A final parallel is racist legitimation. Systematic beliefs about the inferiority of the subordinate group accompany both forms of colonialism. These beliefs seek to legitimate unequal treatment. At their most powerful, such racist legitimations make colonial domination seem logical, natural, and even beneficial for subordinate groups.

No analogy is perfect, but the history of US race relations more closely approximates internal colonialism than assimilationist integration. What the colonial model underscores is that race relations are rooted in conflicting interests between dominant and subordinate groups. Dominant groups who benefit have a vested interest in maintaining such relations; subordinate groups who pay the price of these relations can be expected to change them if possible.

The question of group interests requires a closer look. The dominant group is really a white power structure of elites who make economic, political, and cultural decisions with far-reaching consequences. This group most clearly benefits from exploitative race relations. The subordinate group refers to racial minorities disproportionately located toward the bottom of class and other hierarchies of inequality. This group most clearly pays the price of racial oppression.

What is less clear are the interests of "ordinary whites." They belong to the dominant racial group but are not in positions of institutional power and do not receive the same material benefits from institutional racism that dominant whites do. This status inconsistency between race and class could lead this group to define its interests in rather different ways.

On one hand, ordinary whites may primarily identify with their race. This links them to dominant whites of the same race but of a different class and distances them from racial minorities with whom they might share similar class positions. Historically, this identification allowed even poor whites to claim status on the basis of race; no matter how economically deprived they were, they were still white in a society where that meant a great deal. Ordinary whites can thus derive a social-psychological benefit from their racial identity regardless of material circumstances. But the benefits are more than psychological. Ordinary whites might also derive material benefits from discrimination against minorities if it expands their opportunities at the expense of minorities. By this logic, ordinary whites might see their interests in alignment with powerful whites despite their class differences.

On the other hand, ordinary whites might primarily identify with their class position, which would distance them from powerful whites and align them more closely with racial minorities. This suggests a class alliance across racial lines in which the material similarities of working-class whites and minorities trump racial differences. Such an alliance could challenge racial discrimination, and there is a logic for doing so. Where racial discrimination is high, it allows employers to use a divide-and-conquer strategy that ultimately undermines living standards for both whites and racial minorities (Reich 1981). Racial discrimination thus hurts minorities directly and ordinary whites indirectly. In this scenario, the collective self-interest of ordinary whites is to align with racial minorities and oppose racial discrimination.

The colonial model remains an imperfect analogy, but it frames important questions about the future of race relations. Even without clear answers, it sensitizes us to how group interests shape the social construction of race.

Forms of Discrimination

The colonial model offers a big picture of race relations that rests on many small episodes of discrimination. It is these practices, enacted on a daily basis, that sustain the social construction of race.

Discrimination ranges across many institutions and social arenas. It obviously includes the economy, employment, and political representation. It also includes differences in health, mortality, and life expectancy as a result of differential access to physical and mental health services. It includes deeply rooted patterns of residential segregation that create other problems like unequal access to education. It includes very different probabilities of becoming caught up in the criminal justice system. The effects of discrimination are cumulative, as initial disadvantages become larger inequities over time. Acts of discrimination are the building blocks of racial inequality.

The traditional view of discrimination is that prejudicial attitudes cause discriminatory behavior (Feagin and Feagin 1978). The term *prejudice* means to "prejudge" people on the basis of their group identity. Such judgments often involve negative stereotypes about an entire category of people that are attributed to all its members.

The discrimination that results from prejudice can be explicit, as when people engage in name-calling, racist behavior, or hate crimes. But it can also be subtle or covert. If someone is advertising a job or an apartment and the "wrong" applicant appears, that applicant might be told that the job has been filled or the apartment rented. When the "right" applicant comes along, the apartment or job suddenly becomes available again. In this case, intentional harm is done to someone who might not be aware that they have been the victim of discrimination. Explicit discrimination grabs headlines, but subtle, covert forms are more common and often go undetected. Indeed, it is impossible to know the full extent of discrimination, because much of it is hidden in this fashion. The common thread is a prejudicial attitude. In the traditional model, discrimination occurs when "evil motives" are translated into action.

This model implies that reducing prejudice reduces discrimination. This was part of the logic behind social policies and court decisions favoring integration. It was thought that, with more social contact between groups, people would rethink their prejudices and treat others as individuals and not stereotypes. If prejudice melted away, discrimination would, too. Although the logic seems plausible, there's a problem. By many measures, prejudice in the United States has declined, but racial discrimination has not shown a corresponding reduction.

This prompted a closer look at the traditional view. It became clear that prejudice alone might not lead to discrimination. Prejudiced people need the power to act on prejudice if it is to become discrimination. It also became more evident that discrimination can occur without prejudice. Thus, an employer might have no prejudice against certain people but still refuse to hire them out of a belief that it would drive customers away.

More generally, discrimination limits opportunities for "others" and increases them for discriminators. In such cases, discrimination simply flows from group interest without prejudice. Such discrimination without an "evil motive" can also be an unintentional by-product of institutional policies. As the limits of the traditional model became more evident, sociologists developed another way of thinking about what causes discrimination.

The result was the institutional model in which organizational practices replace prejudice as the major cause of discrimination (Feagin and Feagin 1978). The idea is that social institutions routinely discriminate against many people. In contrast to the traditional model, the institutional model sees discrimination as a normal, routine, chronic outcome rather than a sporadic one. It recognizes that most discrimination is subtle or covert, although overt institutional discrimination still happens, too. It sees discrimination as something that affects thousands if not millions of people, because it is embedded in major social institutions like the criminal justice system or the labor market. Finally, institutional discrimination can be either intentional or unintentional.

Intentional institutional discrimination occurs when there is a conscious goal of unequal treatment. It might be rooted in prejudice, racism, group interest, or some other motive. As with the traditional model, there is an "evil motive" behind such action. Unlike the traditional model, it is not individuals but large organizations that enact these behaviors. In systems of apartheid or legalized segregation, discriminatory purposes are officially proclaimed.

When segregation becomes illegal, intentions to discriminate might no longer be publicly stated but can continue to shape institutional functioning. The redlining of certain neighborhoods as poor credit risks is one example. The use of racial profiling in police practices is another example. The purging of voter registration lists is a third example of intentional, institutional discrimination (Moore 2001). While rarer hate crimes grab headlines, more routine institutional discrimination affects many more people on a daily basis.

Institutional discrimination can also be unintentional. This is indicated by effects rather than motives. Here, we must work backward from discriminatory outcomes to identify the practice or policy that produced them. An example is "side-effect" discrimination that occurs as an unintended by-product of some other practice. Imagine a university that uses an entrance exam to screen applicants. Assume the exam contains no subtle racial biases. Nonetheless, if applicants have been unequally prepared by previous schooling to perform well on this exam, it will produce discriminatory outcomes despite the best of intentions.

A related example is "past-in-present" discrimination where a current practice unwittingly perpetuates prior discrimination. Consider a layoff policy based on seniority. This is not discriminatory in itself. But to whatever extent racial minorities or women have shorter or more episodic work histories as a result of past discrimination, implementing layoffs by seniority will benefit white males and harm minorities and women despite good intentions.

Unintentional discrimination harms many but remains elusive, because it cannot be traced back to a specific person or group with evil motives. In a final twist, it is also possible for "sophisticated racists" who *do* have evil motives to use practices that do not *appear* to intentionally discriminate, knowing that such practices are difficult to identify (Feagin and Feagin 1978).

According to the traditional model, reducing discrimination requires reducing prejudice. According to the institutional model, reducing discrimination requires changing institutions. Whereas the traditional model is "optimistic" that increased social contact will reduce prejudice and discrimination, the institutional model is "pessimistic" that institutions will not simply evolve into less discriminatory behavior. Indeed, the institutional model suggests that if nothing is done, discrimination will continue indefinitely, because institutions are self-perpetuating and because some groups benefit from discriminatory practices.

This is the logic behind affirmative action. It assumes that discrimination will continue unless affirmative action is taken to change the practices that produce it. As a policy, most affirmative action programs involve voluntary efforts to increase the diversity of a pool of qualified applicants. Such policies target informal practices whereby people tend to recruit, hire, or admit people like themselves. By creating policies that require looking beyond familiar social circles when recruiting applicants, affirmative action programs have made modest contributions to reducing discriminatory outcomes.

The persistence of racial inequality in the United States has also prompted a rethinking of the traditional focus on individual prejudice. New research has led one analyst to conclude that in the post–civil rights era, we have entered a time of "racism without racists" (Bonilla-Silva 2003). This argument downplays prejudicial attitudes by suggesting that racism rests on a material foundation of group interests and white privilege. Racism persists because whites derive substantial material benefits from it. Thus, even when whites do not have stereotypical views of minorities, they often perpetuate racism in ways that obscure its victims and beneficiaries.

Where traditional prejudice often assumed biological differences, "color-blind racism" is a more complex racial ideology emphasizing cultural differences. Four distinct frames express color-blind racism (Bonilla-Silva 2003). "Abstract liberalism" uses familiar political discourse about individual rights and equal opportunity to subtly deny structural barriers and implicitly blame victims. "Naturalism" suggests that segregation reflects freely chosen preferences of people to associate with others like them. "Cultural racism" identifies supposedly defective values, beliefs, and practices within minority cultures that are responsible for their lack of progress. Finally, "minimizing racism" acknowledges lingering problems of discrimination while emphasizing how much progress has been made. The implication is that such problems no longer require systemic solutions.

None of these frames sound overtly racist. Indeed, they sound quite reasonable by comparison. They still function, however, as an ideology legitimizing racial inequality. Color-blind racism denies or minimizes institutional barriers and uses the rhetoric of individual opportunity and cultural differences to blame minorities and excuse whites for racial inequality. The emergence of "racism without racists" illustrates how racial meanings and definitions change over time. To analyze such changes, we need to revisit the idea that race is socially constructed.

Racial Formation

The theory of racial formation sees the social construction of race as a contested process of ongoing conflict (Omi and Winant 1994; Winant 1994, 2004). "[R]ace can be defined as a *concept that signifies and symbolizes socio-political conflicts and interests in reference to different types of human bodies*" (Winant 2004, 155; italics in original). The theory of racial formation also insists on the "reality" of race despite its origins as a social construction.

The challenge is to understand the simultaneous "arbitrariness" and "reality" of race. It arises once race is decoupled from biology. This has often led social scientists to reduce race to some other kind of group and transpose their experiences onto races. This problematic response implies that if race is not about biology, then it is not about anything real. The theory of racial formation maintains that race is not about biology, but it *is* still about something very real. That reality, moreover, needs to be understood on its own terms and not reduced to something else.

One way mainstream perspectives have denied the reality of race is by equating it with ethnicity and using the ethnicity paradigm to analyze race relations. This inevitably turns the discussion back to assimilation. Despite the different histories of racial minorities and white ethnics in the United States, some maintain that racial minorities will eventually undergo the same assimilation as white ethnic groups in earlier decades and centuries. Rather than analyzing race on its own terms, this substitutes the history of ethnic assimilation as a goal for race relations.

This reduction of race to ethnicity is problematic, because it denies the unique features of racial formation (Omi and Winant 1994). It falsely transposes white experience onto nonwhites. It denies ethnic variations within racial groups by equating broad racial categories ("African American") with specific white ethnicities ("Italian"). The ethnicity paradigm also advocates individualistic solutions like upward mobility. The reduction of race to ethnicity thus obscures the distinctiveness of racial oppression and proposes unachievable or undesirable solutions to racial conflict.

An alternative is the class paradigm. This approach reduces race to class or sees the real meaning of race through a class lens. The class paradigm underscores how members of racial minorities are disproportionately located in the working class or lower socio-economic levels. The logic is that their fates are determined more by their class position than by their racial identity. Moreover, race has been used to reinforce class exploitation when employers designate racial minorities as a secondary labor force, divide workers along racial lines, and play one group off the other to the detriment of both. In this paradigm, race is important for its role in a more fundamental set of class dynamics.

Although it illuminates intersections of race and class, this paradigm is not sufficient for understanding racial formation on its own terms. It simply assumes class is fundamental and race is secondary. Moreover, the equation of racial minorities with only one class oversimplifies race and implies that middle- or upper-class minorities face no racial barriers. "It would be more accurate to say that race and class are competing modalities by which social actors may be organized" (Omi and Winant 1994, 32). If so, the class model with its reduction of race to class is insufficient.

A third alternative is the nation paradigm or the internal colonialism model discussed earlier. As we saw, this model emphasizes differences between the assimilationist history of white ethnic groups and the quasi-colonial status of racial minorities. The metaphor of colonial relations has much to tell us about the history of race relations within the United States. As a viable model of contemporary racial formation, however, it has serious limitations.

In a postcolonial world of global mobility, equating races with geographically bounded nations is an increasingly implausible way to think about race relations. There is substantially more interracial contact in contemporary, racially diverse societies than in classic colonial relations. The nation paradigm also obscures increasingly important class differences among minorities by reducing them to a homogeneous, cultural nationality. Although more instructive than the ethnicity and class paradigms, this one also falls short as a way to understand racial formation.

The problem is that each paradigm—ethnicity, class, and nation—reduces race to something else. Each fails to see race on its own terms. The solution is to move beyond these paradigms to a model that sees race as an independently constructed social reality.

This means seeing racial formation as a process in which social, economic, and political forces determine the meaning of racial categories in a given historical context. To emphasize the importance of process, the term *racialization* is coined (Omi and Winant 1994) to refer to the extension of racial meanings to relationships that were previously not classified in such terms.

Consider slavery. Although US planters used African Americans as slave labor for centuries, the practice did not originate for racial reasons. It derived from the economic realities of plantation agriculture. In order to be profitable, such agriculture requires the cheapest possible labor. Planters first used white indentured servants from Europe and then captured Native Americans (Geschwender 1978). Neither group worked out well in the long run. Importing African slave labor gradually emerged as a later alternative in the search for cheap labor. Once the practice was institutionalized, slavery was racialized through racist beliefs and legitimations to justify the use of black slave labor by white, "God-fearing" Christians. Slavery became racialized over time. In other words, "we know that racism did not create slavery, but that slavery created racism" (Winant 2004, 84).

Institutions, practices, and beliefs become "raced" when they are shaped and understood through racial categories. Consider how many urban social problems have become "raced," as popular consciousness and media representations link race with poverty, welfare, gangs, drugs, and crime. These issues involve many more whites than nonwhites, but their racialized nature becomes a self-fulfilling prophecy. Thus, people act on racialized beliefs about crime and who commits it, leading to highly disproportionate numbers of racial minorities being suspected, arrested, convicted, and incarcerated for "raced" definitions of crime. The differential penalties for crack cocaine used by minorities and powder cocaine favored by whites is one of the more blatant examples of such racialization.

The most important raced institution is the state. In a racially divided society, the state racializes many social dynamics. "For most of U.S. history, the state's main objective in its racial policy was repression and exclusion" (Omi and Winant 1994, 81). It commenced with the Naturalization Act of 1790 that limited citizenship to free, white immigrants. The pattern continued throughout the nineteenth century as racialized policies of repression and exclusion regulated race relations. A more recent example of state power is the creation of the category "Hispanic" in 1980, racializing a new group of people and embedding the category in state policies, practices, and institutions. States and racial formation are thus closely intertwined.

Racial formation is not just about top-down power. When a collective identity is constructed and used to dominate people, that same identity will eventually become a rallying point for resistance. Whether the identity involves race, ethnicity, gender, nationality, or sexuality, domination provokes resistance. Thus, racial formation is a contested process. People fight back, and even powerful elites cannot completely control racial formation for long. It is more accurate to see racial formation—and the social construction of race more generally—as an ongoing struggle over what race means. Authorities use race to subordinate groups, and racially defined groups use it to resist subordination.

The contested quality of racial formation is evident in recent racial politics. On the eve of the civil rights movement of the 1950s and 1960s, racial formation took the form of domination. White power was the norm, backed up by coercion, segregation, exclusion, and violence. In this period, racial formation was a top-down affair, because of the overwhelming power of whites. Collective resistance appeared futile.

Social changes nevertheless created opportunities to contest racial formation. The disruptions of World War II, the partial integration of the armed forces, the mechanization of Southern agriculture, and migration from the rural South to the urban North all undermined racial domination. When the civil rights movement appeared in the 1950s, it echoed the ethnicity paradigm with themes of individualism, opportunity, and integration. That such a modest agenda provoked such a ferocious backlash is revealing. Simply asking for what whites took for granted amounted to an almost revolutionary challenge to racial domination.

The movement soon transcended the ethnicity paradigm, in part because of the resistance it encountered to its integrationist goals. But the shift was also sparked by "the rearticulation of black collective subjectivity" (Omi and Winant 1994, 98). In other words, black activists made the redefinition of racial identity a central goal. The movement *made* racial formation a two-way street by challenging static notions of race and racial hierarchy. In effect, activists reclaimed the meaning of race from a white power structure and made it their own.

These events transformed the civil rights movement. Activists adopted multiple racial paradigms and diverse political strategies. "Entrists" argued that strategic participation in elections and mainstream institutions could transform the state. Socialists tried to build class alliances across racial lines and link struggles against racism and capitalism. Nationalists encouraged a separatist response of institution building and cultural pride within minority communities. None met with complete success. The entrist, socialist, and nationalist strategies had the same shortcomings as the ethnicity, class, and nation paradigms on which they were based. Each reduced race to something else and missed the complexity of racial formation. This activism nevertheless shattered older understandings of race and put racial formation center stage (Omi and Winant 1994).

As the movement became more complex, so did the response of the raced state. In some instances, it brutally repressed militant leaders and groups that challenged its authority. More broadly, the state shifted from racial domination to racial hegemony. This meant incorporating oppositional challenges in ways that defused their transformative potential. "Under hegemonic conditions, opposition and difference are not repressed, excluded, or silenced (at least not primarily). Rather, they are inserted, often after suitable modification, within a 'modern' (or perhaps 'postmodern') social order" (Winant 1994, 29). Although hegemony might be less violent than outright domination, it amounts to a more complex system of racial control.

Racial hegemony has sparked competing racial projects on both sides. On the reactionary side, the far right still equates race with biology and advocates violence to prevent all forms of "race mixing." The new right translates old-fashioned racism into code words that are not explicitly racist but nonetheless trigger racist attitudes and actions among those who know the code. The neoconservative right uses egalitarian language to advocate individualism and reject group-oriented solutions. They use the rhetoric of a color-blind society while ignoring the historical legacy of being a color-conscious society. This is the most sophisticated defense of the white power structure. It uses familiar, liberal ideas to argue for illiberal ends. It exemplifies "racism without racists" advocating "color-blind racism" (Bonilla-Silva 2003).

On the progressive side, pragmatic liberalism appeals to group identities to mobilize political support for racially progressive policies, including affirmative action. It advocates pluralism and tolerance and attempts a difficult balancing act between advancing minority rights and maintaining social peace. Finally, radical democrats seek full acceptance of racial difference and identities in the name of autonomy. They seek democratization of the state and redistributive policies to foster racial equality (Winant 1994).

Racial formation is thus a dynamic, contested set of social and political meanings. The current diversity of racial politics—consisting of at least five distinct and competing racial projects—testifies to the fluidity of racial formation and the social construction of race.

The Construction of Whiteness

It is intriguing that whites attribute "race" to "people of color" but don't see "white" as a "color." It's as if race applies to people who differ from the norm but not the group that is the norm. Given this, it is important to turn the microscope back on the dominant group and its construction of whiteness.

Like other socially constructed racial categories, whiteness emerged historically. Consider how "the Irish became white" over decades of conflict and eventual assimilation in the United States. More pointedly, this is the story of "how the Catholic Irish, an oppressed race in Ireland, became part of an oppressing race in America" (Ignatiev 1995, 1). When Irish immigrants first arrived in the United States, they were perceived as an inferior race by Anglo-Saxon powers on both sides of the Atlantic. However, rather than joining with other subordinate races, the Irish distanced themselves from minorities and aligned with whites. They pursued the classic assimilationist trade-off: "In becoming white the Irish ceased to be Green" (Ignatiev 1995, 3). This suggests that assimilation means moving toward the dominant group and away from minorities, because the dominant group is defined precisely by its distance from racial minorities. Until a group made both moves, assimilation was unlikely.

The Irish example fits a broader template of how whiteness was created through an amalgamation of initially diverse ethnicities. This history falls into three periods (Jacobson 1998, 13–14). From the founding of the country into the mid-nineteenth century, citizenship was confined to "free white" immigrants, implicitly meaning Anglo-Saxon and sometimes other Northern European peoples. From the mid-nineteenth century to the early twentieth century, immigration from Southern, Central, and Eastern Europe challenged the equation of whiteness and Northern European descent. During this period, a complex racial politics initially defined these immigrants as inferior races at the same time that they sought a broadening of the definition of "white" to include them. It has only been since the 1920s that ethnic differences were downplayed and a more generic white identity was forged. This period "redrew the dominant racial configuration along the strict, binary line of white and black, creating Caucasians where before had been so many Celts, Hebrews, Teutons, Mediterraneans, and Slavs" (Jacobson 1998, 14).

By the mid-twentieth century, whiteness became the dominant racial norm. This proved short-lived, as "it is no longer possible to assume a 'normalized' whiteness, whose invisibility and relatively monolithic character signify immunity from political or cultural challenge" (Winant 2004, 50). As race-based social movements recast their own racial subjectivity, white identity also became more self-conscious.

As white dominance was challenged, it triggered "grievances of the privileged." Some whites claimed they were under attack "simply for their race." Others decried a world in which minorities seemed to get advantages withheld from whites through "reverse discrimination." Still other whites lamented the lack of a distinct and vivid white culture they could identify with just as other races identified with theirs. Such defensive responses imply that although whites are still dominant, such dominance can no longer be taken for granted.

These responses also belie the ongoing privileges of the dominant group. White privilege means that despite recent challenges to the racial order, it continues to be organized in ways that benefit the dominant group. Such privilege is often invisible to those who benefit, while being highly visible to those who pay the price.

This is nicely captured in Peggy McIntosh's (2005) efforts to teach about male privilege in women's studies courses. Her female students quickly grasped the concept and readily supplied examples. Her male students conceded that women faced certain disadvantages but denied their male privilege. To understand this denial, McIntosh examined her own dual status as a white woman. As a woman, she could readily see male privilege. As a white, she had difficulty seeing her racial privilege, just as men had difficulty seeing male privilege. The broader pattern is that privileged groups rarely recognize their own privileges and perceive any challenge to them as victimization. Such complaints are not simply disingenuous; they reflect a real inability to see how whiteness and maleness continue conferring privileges even in a social order undergoing challenge and reformulation.

These privileges come in two categories. "Unearned advantages" are "positive" privileges that should not be abolished but made available to all. The privilege of not being a crime suspect simply on the basis of one's race is an unearned advantage for whites that should ideally be an unearned entitlement for all. "Conferred dominance" involves "negative" privileges that need to be abolished to create racial equality. Discrimination that benefits dominant groups at the expense of subordinate ones fits this type; it should be abolished in any society seeking racial equality (McIntosh 2005).

These are now the goals of a "new abolitionist racial project." Proponents of this movement identify white privilege as the lynchpin of white supremacy and see rejection of privilege by whites as essential to creating a just racial order. Advocates put a positive spin on the epithet "race traitor" by countering that "treason to whiteness is loyalty to humanity" (Winant 2004, 63). As this racial project unfolds alongside others described earlier, it is difficult to deny that we are in a period of highly contested racial formation.

Understanding race requires looking beyond taken-for-granted appearances. It also requires a multilayered analysis of domination. Critical sociology is tailor-made for both tasks. It illuminates both the social construction of race and the challenges seeking to deconstruct racial hierarchies in the name of a more egalitarian society.

References

Adelman, Larry. 2003. *Race: The Power of an Illusion.* Videodisc, California Newsreel.

Berger, Peter. 1963. *Invitation to Sociology.* New York: Doubleday.

Bonilla-Silva, Eduardo. 2003. *Racism without Racists.* Lanham, MD: Rowman & Littlefield.

Du Bois, W. E. B. 1903/1989. *The Souls of Black Folk.* New York: Bantam Books.

Feagin, Joe, and Clairece Booher Feagin. 1978. *Discrimination American Style.* Englewood Cliffs, NJ: Prentice Hall.

Geschwender, James. 1978. *Racial Stratification in America.* Dubuque, IA: Wm. C. Brown.

Gordon, Milton. 1964. *Assimilation in American Life.* New York: Oxford University Press.

Henslin, James. 2005. *Sociology.* 7th ed. Boston: Allyn and Bacon.

Ignatiev, Noel. 1995. *How the Irish Became White.* New York: Routledge.

Jacobson, Matthew. 1998. *Whiteness of a Different Color.* Cambridge, MA: Harvard University Press.

McIntosh, Peggy. 2005. "White Privilege and Male Privilege." In *Great Divides,* ed. Thomas Shapiro, 300–307. New York: McGraw-Hill.

Moore, Michael. 2001. *Stupid White Men.* New York: Regan.

Myrdal, Gunnar. 1944. *An American Dilemma.* New York: Harper and Row.

Omi, Michael, and Howard Winant. 1994. *Racial Formation in the United States.* 2nd ed. New York: Routledge.

Reich, Michael. 1981. *Racial Inequality.* Princeton, NJ: Princeton University Press.

Winant, Howard. 1994. *Racial Conditions.* Minneapolis: University of Minnesota Press.

———. 2004. *The New Politics of Race.* Minneapolis: University of Minnesota Press.

- Within his thesis, the author lists five reasons for us to question the "biological conception of race." Do you find one (or more) of his reasons far-fetched? Please explain.

Unit IV

Black Economics

Introduction to Unit IV

Prior to the Great Migration, Black economic power primarily resided in Black communities, Black neighborhoods, and Black enclaves across the nation. The Black dollar—a moniker ascribed to African American spending and economic power—freely circulated within these pockets of Black assemblage. These mom-and-pop establishments and small business thrived for two reasons: their proximity to patrons and the danger associated with "going into town" to purchase goods from white businesses. The impetus for the latter resulted from the influence of systemic racism (and subsequent segregation) within the areas of physical proximity, civics, and economics.

However, the Black dollar would change hands in the years following World War II. Most Blacks lived in rural areas due to their enslavement or the enslavement of their ancestors. The geographical (and inherently political) arrangement did not afford them many opportunities to actively participate within the local or national economy. With promises of better jobs (and the promises of the ability of providing a better way of life for themselves and their families), many poor Blacks left the rural South for the more urban North. The change in location proved lucrative for most. Increased wages afforded them new levels of comfort and provided them more disposable income. However, as a result of the exodus, those small Black businesses that survived and thrived on community support had to close their doors because most of their consumer base left for "greener pastures."

Conversely, white businesses capitalized on the influx of new consumers. Through research, shrewd business practices (in some cases), and some self-destructive tendencies (on the new consumer's part), white business owners gained control of the Black dollar. Robert Weems's "African American Consumers Since World War II" chronicles the migration of Black spending power and white businesses' approach to attracting and retaining the Black dollar.

Reading 4.1

African American Consumers since World War II

Robert E. Weems, Jr.

I N THE DECADES FOLLOWING WORLD WAR II, African Americans, as consumers, helped to change the social and economic landscape of the United States. The strategic use of black spending power represented the cornerstone of the celebrated civil rights movement. Also, as the collective spending power of African Americans increased, corporate marketers in a variety of commercial sectors accelerated their efforts to reach this important segment of the consuming public. To provide an illuminating cross-section of this economic phenomenon, this [reading] will include, among other things, a discussion of campaigns instituted by Major League Baseball, the radio industry, Hollywood, mainstream financial-services firms, and the purveyors of alcoholic beverages and tobacco products that aimed to generate enhanced African American consumer support. These and other post–World War II advertising campaigns directed at African Americans generally featured imagery that counteracted past stereotypical depictions of blacks. Yet while increased African American consumerism has had some positive consequences for blacks, the evidence also suggests that in recent decades, African American spending *power* might be better characterized as spending *weakness*. It appears ironic that the last decades of the twentieth century witnessed a simultaneous increase in African American spending power and the decline of both historic black businesses and urban black America's infrastructure. This disturbing trend is further complicated by the emergence of the hip-hop-inspired "bling-bling" phenomenon, with its emphasis on conspicuous consumption. Unless contemporary African Americans are merely content to enhance the profit margins of corporate America, a revisitation of self-determined, proactive, consumer activism appears appropriate.

It is impossible to discuss the growing importance of the postwar African American consumer market without linking it to the dramatic urbanization of African Americans during the same period. Once dismissed as poor, rural southerners with limited disposable income, African Americans became, after World War II, an increasingly urban and geographically dispersed group with enhanced employment options.

Between 1940 and 1960, the proportion of African Americans who lived in cities grew from 48.6 to 73.2 percent. Significantly, by 1960, for the first time in U.S. history, the percentage of blacks who lived in cities exceeded that of whites. A decade later, as the 1970 census revealed, 81 percent of the national African American community resided in urban areas, compared to 72 percent of whites.[1]

The massive mid-twentieth-century migration of African Americans to cities across the country resulted not only in a change of address for the migrants, but also in a distinct improvement in their occupational status. For instance, between 1940 and 1960, the percentage of African Americans in relatively low-paying southern agricultural work declined dramatically. Conversely, in the same period, more African American men and women moved into more prestigious and better-paying occupations.[2] These significant demographic developments contributed mightily toward increasing the perceived importance of the black consumer market.

Major League Baseball was one of several industries that viewed post–World War II African Americans as a consumer market worth pursuing. By the mid-1940s, the national per capita income of African Americans stood at $779, compared to $1,140 for whites. Moreover, the per capita income of blacks residing in cities with Major League Baseball teams compared very favorably with national white per capita earnings. In fact, in some cities, blacks possessed a higher per capita income than the national white average.[3] These demographic realities, coupled with the fact that African Americans were avid baseball fans (who had sustained their own Negro Leagues), motivated Branch Rickey of the Brooklyn Dodgers to conduct what one author has called "baseball's great experiment" when he hired Jackie Robinson.[4] Rickey's coordination of Robinson's historic 1947 entry into Major League Baseball reflected Rickey's business acumen. He reportedly

1   Daniel M. Johnson and Rex R. Campbell, *Black Migration in America* (Durham, NC: Duke University Press, 1981), 132, 152; U.S. Bureau of the Census, *The Social and Economic Status of the Black Population in the United States: An Historical View, 1790–1978* (Washington, DC: GPO, 1979), 14.

2   Daniel O. Price, *Changing Characteristics of the Negro Population: A 1960 Census Monograph* (Washington, DC: U.S. Bureau of the Census, 1969), 119; Marian Hayes, "A Century of Change: Negroes in the U.S. Economy, 1860–1960," *Monthly Labor Review*, December 1962, 1364.

3   "Negro Incomes and How They Are Spent," *Sales Management* 54 (June 15, 1945): 106.

4   Jules Tygiel, *Baseball's Great Experiment: Jackie Robinson and His Legacy* (New York: Vintage Books, 1984).

told his family that "the greatest untapped reservoir of raw material in the history of the game is the black race! The Negroes will make us winners for years to come. ... And for that I will happily bear being called a bleeding heart and a do-gooder and all that humanitarian rot."[5]

If Branch Rickey viewed black players as an "untapped reservoir," it appears plausible to assume that he viewed black consumers similarly. Since Major League Baseball profits, in the days before huge television contracts, were closely linked to attendance at games, Rickey clearly hoped that African American fans, coming out to see African American players, would make him a winner both on the field and in the box office. In fact, as Ken Burns's 1994 documentary *Baseball* revealed, on April 15, 1947—the date of Jackie Robinson's official entry into the major leagues—blacks made up more than half of Ebbets Field's capacity crowd.[6] Similarly, Robinson's presence dramatically enhanced attendance at Brooklyn Dodger road games.[7]

As other teams followed the example of the Brooklyn Dodgers, one of the consequences of the simultaneous desegregation of major-league rosters and the "courting" of black consumer support was the subsequent decline and disappearance of black-owned baseball teams. Moreover, racial desegregation's negative impact on the Negro Leagues would subsequently be reenacted in other economic venues.[8]

While Major League Baseball used African American interest in baseball to make inroads in this consumer market, other industries began using African American interest in music to make their own inroads among black shoppers. The dramatic growth of "Negro-appeal" radio stations in postwar America exemplified this trend.

As late as 1949, *Sponsor*, the advertising trade journal of the broadcasting industry, referred to black consumers as "the forgotten 15,000,000."[9] Nevertheless, data from the 1950 census removed any lingering doubt about the efficacy of actively seeking black customers. Between 1940 and 1950, the number of African American city dwellers increased from 6,253,588 to 9,120,000, a 46 percent increase.[10] Consequently, by the early 1950s, the national African American community represented a significant segment of America's largest (urban) markets. Moreover, this dramatic demographic development would have far-reaching economic consequences, especially for the radio industry.

---

5   Ibid., 52.

6   *Baseball: A Film by Ken Burns; Inning Six: The National Pastime* (New York: Baseball Film Project, 1994).

7   Tygiel, *Baseball's Great Experiment*, 189.

8   Neil Lanctot's *The Negro Leagues: The Rise and Ruin of a Black Institution* (Philadelphia: University of Pennsylvania Press, 2004) provides an illuminating discussion of the impact of racial desegregation on the Negro Leagues and other historic black institutions.

9   "The Forgotten 15,000,000," pts. 1 and 2, *Sponsor* 3 (October 10, 1949): 24ff.; *Sponsor* 3 (October 24, 1949): 30ff.

10   "The Negro Market: $15,000,000,000 to Spend," *Sponsor* 6 (July 28, 1952): 31.

In 1952 *Sponsor*, in a follow-up to its 1949 article, featured an extensive section titled "The Forgotten 15,000,000 ... Three Years Later." First and foremost, it seemed clear that black consumers were far less forgotten (or ignored). Whereas only a handful of U.S. radio stations carried "Negro-appeal" programming in 1949, by 1952 there were more than two hundred stations that featured this format on a full- or part-time basis. Moreover, these stations were attracting an increasing amount of corporate advertising.[11]

As a service to its readers, *Sponsor* provided not only demographic information about the increasingly important "Negro market," but also tips on how to use radio advertising to most effectively reach black consumers. For instance, the July 28, 1952, issue featured two articles on this topic: "The Negro Market: $15,000,000,000 to Spend" and "Negro Radio: 200-Plus Specialist Stations—More Coming," which used a question-and-answer format to give white businesses a "crash course" on marketing to blacks.

Ironically, *Sponsor*'s 1952 "primers" related to black consumers gave scant attention to the role of black disk jockeys in marketing to blacks. Yet by the mid-1950s, corporate marketers were increasingly told that the success of their radio campaigns (aimed at African Americans) depended almost solely upon the showmanship and salesmanship of these black community icons. By 1955, the amount of "Negro-appeal" radio stations had grown to six hundred, nearly triple the amount of three years earlier. A major reason for this proliferation was the growing stature of black disk jockeys.[12] These individuals, referred to as "personality deejays," were noted for their ability to flawlessly meld regular programming with advertisements. One example was New Orleans's "Okey Dokey," described by radio station WBOK's promotional material as "a frantic race showman that sells and sells."[13]

Besides relying upon *Sponsor* and other advertising trade journals, white businesses seeking insights about the "Negro market" and how to reach it also consulted with the Commerce Department's Division of Negro Affairs in the postwar period. This unit, which existed from 1927 to 1953, conducted numerous studies related to the economic life of black America and came to be viewed as a clearinghouse for such information.[14]

For instance, in May 1943 Emmer Lancaster, who headed the Division of Negro Affairs from 1941 to 1953, sent a memorandum to Assistant Secretary of Commerce Norman W. Baxter seeking support for a proposed survey of African American income and purchasing power. After citing requests for such a study from such disparate sources as the Atlanta Regional Office of the Bureau of Foreign and Domestic Commerce, the North Carolina Mutual Life Insurance Company, the National Association for the Advancement of

---

11   "The Forgotten 15,000,000 ... Three Years Later," *Sponsor* 6 (July 28, 1952): 29.

12   "Highlights of 1955 Negro Radio," *Sponsor* 9 (September 19, 1955): 107.

13   Radio station WBOK advertisement, *Sponsor* 7 (August 24, 1953): 94.

14   See Robert E. Weems, Jr., and Lewis A. Randolph, "The Right Man: James A. Jackson and the Origins of U.S. Government Interest in Black Business Development," *Enterprise & Society*, June 2005, 254–77.

Colored People (NAACP), and the Pepsi-Cola company, Lancaster declared that "this office will attempt to comply with these requests by conducting a survey of incomes of Negro professionals including lawyers, clergymen, teachers, college professors, and physicians in 36 cities wherein the Negro population is 25,000 or more."[15]

In the years following World War II, the Commerce Department's Division of Negro Affairs, because of its research and its reputation, received an ever-growing number of requests for such items as the convention dates of prominent African American organizations; the names and addresses of black firms with at least one hundred employees; the types of supplies and products used by black beauticians and beauty-shop operators; information that could be incorporated into business courses aimed at African American students; and a listing of black disk jockeys in America.[16] Even the venerable W. E. B. Du Bois, then working on a project examining African American business development and property accumulation, contacted this office for assistance in October 1947.[17]

By the early 1950s, the vast majority of information requests received by the Division of Negro Affairs were related to the increasingly important "Negro market." Moreover, a brief article entitled "Negroes Offer a Big Growing Consumer Market," which appeared in the May 9, 1953, issue of the *Kiplinger Washington Letter*, explicitly cited this office as a source of information about black consumers. Not surprisingly, after this exposure, the number of such inquiries to the Division of Negro Affairs increased dramatically.

Significantly, Emmer Lancaster, an African American who had once served as president of the Akron, Ohio, chapter of the NAACP,[18] wanted to ensure that the increased interest in the "Negro market" would have some tangible benefits for blacks. For instance, his responses to the more than five hundred inquiries resulting from the *Kiplinger Washington Letter* article[19] included recommendations that promoted black newspapers

15   Memo, Emmer M. Lancaster to Norman W. Baxter, May 12, 1943, box 8, folder L, RG 40, Records of the Advisor on Negro Affairs, National Archives.

16   I. J. Chisolm (Director of Promotion and Publicity for the Southern Field Division of the National Urban League) to U.S. Department of Commerce, July 28, 1948, box 1, folder C; Don Brown (an advertising representative for Johnson Publishing Company) to Emmer M. Lancaster, November 5, 1952, box 3, folder M; Ann Crawford (publisher of *Modern Tresses* magazine) to U.S. Department of Commerce, October 7, 1952, box 1, folder C; Robert S. Browne (an instructor at Dillard University who would go on to become a prominent black economist and, among other things, the founding editor of *The Review of Black Political Economy*) to Emmer M. Lancaster, January 15, 1949, box 3, folder M; Thelma Dale (assistant campaign manager of the Progressive Party) to Emmer M. Lancaster, June 6, 1952, box 1, folder D, all in RG 40, Records of the Advisor on Negro Affairs.

17   Hugh H. Smythe (for Dr. Du Bois) to Office of Advisor on Negro Affairs, October 27, 1947, box 1, folder D, RG 40, Records of the Advisor on Negro Affairs.

18   G. James Fleming and Christian E. Burckel, *Who's Who in Colored America*, 7th ed. (Yonkers-on-Hudson, NY: Christian E. Burckel and Associates, 1950), 330.

19   Memo, Emmer M. Lancaster to John C. Worthy, Assistant Secretary of Commerce for Administration, June 24, 1953, box 245, Negroes folder, RG 40, Records of the Assistant Secretary of Commerce for Administration, National Archives.

and salesmen. The following excerpt is representative of how Lancaster replied to businesses seeking advice on how to secure more African American customers:

> I think the best methods of reaching Negro residents in your area would be to advertise in the local Negro newspaper and to employ competent Negro sales personnel to market your products with the Negro community. For your general information there are approximately 200 Negro sales representatives now employed by 30 national merchandising firms; these include IBM, Remington Rand, BBDO and all the tobacco companies.[20]

After the Eisenhower administration terminated the Commerce Department's Division of Negro Affairs in 1953,[21] publications such as *Sponsor* and *Sales Management* accelerated their provision of information about the "Negro market" (and gained additional readers in the process). Also, as more companies began to take the "Negro market" more seriously in the postwar period, blacks increasingly realized they could use this economic reality to stimulate positive social change. In fact, African Americans' proactive use of their spending power represented a cornerstone of the celebrated civil rights movement.

Although African American consumer power reached a high point of effectiveness and visibility through such events as the Montgomery Bus Boycott of 1955–56 and the "sit-in" movement of the early 1960s, these represented the continuation of a long tradition of organized black consumer action. For example, in the early twentieth century, African Americans in twenty-five southern cities boycotted streetcars segregated by Jim Crow laws.[22] A June 9, 1906, editorial in the black-owned *Lynchburg* (Virginia) *News* summed up the goal of this movement when it stated, "Let us touch to the quick the white man's pocket. Tis there his conscience often lies."[23] Nearly sixty years later, the activist

---

20   Emmer M. Lancaster to Miss K. Hancock, June 2, 1953, box 20, Miscellaneous Folder 2, RG 40, Records of the Advisor on Negro Affairs. Hancock was the secretary-treasurer of Brodie's Home Appliances, based in San Francisco; she had written to Lancaster on May 11, 1953, seeking information and advice concerning the "Negro market" (ibid.).

21   The cause of the Commerce Department's sudden termination of the Division of Negro Affairs in late 1953 remains unclear. Jonathan J. Bean's *BIG GOVERNMENT and Affirmative Action: The SCANDALOUS History of the Small Business Administration* (Lexington: University Press of Kentucky, 2001), 7–8, suggests that the termination of the division was part of a perfunctory reassessment of the federal bureaucracy. However, Kenneth O'Reilly, in *Nixon's Piano: Presidents and Racial Politics from Washington to Clinton* (New York: Free Press, 1995), 165–69, insinuates that Eisenhower's racism contributed to the termination of the division and of Emmer Lancaster.

22   August Meier and Elliott Rudwick, "The Boycott Movement against Jim Crow Streetcars in the South, 1900–1906," *Journal of American History* 55 (March 1969): 758.

23   Ibid., 761.

politician Adam Clayton Powell, Jr., echoed this sentiment (more colorfully) when he asserted that blacks were ready to "withhold the dollar to make the white man holler."[24]

Given increased African American urbanization and consumer activism in post–World War II America, the evidence suggests that the celebrated Civil Rights Act of 1964, which provided for blacks' unfettered access to public accommodations, represented more an acknowledgment of growing African American economic power than a morally based acknowledgment of African Americans' intrinsic civil and human rights. For instance, as the June 20, 1964, issue of *Business Week* noted, white businessmen, on the basis of self-interest, played an important role in ensuring that Congress passed this monumental legislation.[25] In fact, one can characterize the relationship between white businesses and black consumers since 1964 in the context of how European American–owned businesses profited from both the civil rights movement and increasing African American urbanization. A classic case of this phenomenon was Hollywood's promotion of the "blaxploitation" movie genre during the early 1970s.

By 1970, eight out of every ten African Americans lived in urban areas. Conversely, "white flight" to suburban areas, which accelerated during the 1950s and 1960s, contributed to the creation of what the popular black musical group Parliament referred to in 1975 as "chocolate cities and their vanilla suburbs."[26] At the same time that America's cities were becoming increasingly black, Hollywood producers were desperate for ways to resuscitate an ailing motion-picture industry. Television's birth and growth had contributed to a dramatic decline in U.S. movie attendance. Between 1946 and 1970, the average weekly attendance at U.S. theaters dropped from 90 to 17.7 million moviegoers. Moreover, "white flight" to the suburbs included the abandonment of large downtown movie theaters. Consequently, in what one contemporary observer called "one of the greatest ironies of our time," Hollywood turned to urban black consumers to help it avert financial ruin.[27]

The huge financial success of Melvin Van Peebles's 1971 independent film *Sweet Sweetback's Baadasssss Song* clearly demonstrated the potential profits associated with appealing to black moviegoers. Shot in nineteen days with a budget of $500,000, *Sweet Sweetback*, which chronicled the radicalization of a black stud, grossed more than $10 million within a couple of months. This feat appeared all the more remarkable because no major distributor would touch this film. Because of *Sweet Sweetback*'s overt sexual

24   John Britton, "Negroes Ready to Go for Broke," *Jet*, October 17, 1963, 49.

25   "Smoothing a Way for Rights Law," *Business Week*, June 20, 1964, 32.

26   U.S. Bureau of the Census, *The Social and Economic Status of the Black Population*, 14; Johnson and Campbell, *Black Migration in America*, 152; Parliament, *Chocolate City*, LP record, Casablanca Records, NBLP 7014-B, 1975.

27   Corbett S. Steinberg, *Film Facts* (New York: Facts on File, 1980), 46; James P. Murray, "The Subject Is Money," *Black Creation* 4 (Winter 1973): 26.

content, Van Peebles, an African American filmmaker, had to rely upon Cinemation Industries, a small distribution house that handled only pornographic films, to distribute *Sweetback*. Although the film debuted in only two theaters, one in Detroit and one in Atlanta, it quickly broke box-office records in both locales. Moreover, through word of mouth, *Sweet Sweetback* soon became a nationwide box-office smash.[28]

After the success of *Sweet Sweetback*, Metro-Goldwyn-Mayer made its own explicit appeal to black moviegoers, with its 1971 release of *Shaft*. This film, described as a black James Bond movie, proved to be an economic godsend to MGM, which had posted losses of $43 million for the previous two years. Costing only $1.8 million to produce, *Shaft* reportedly grossed more than $17 million within a year.[29] Predictably, MGM's success with *Shaft* reverberated throughout major Hollywood studios. In fact, by late 1972, nearly 25 percent of Hollywood's total planned films were black-oriented. By contrast, only 3 percent of Hollywood's 1970 releases were films intended primarily for African American audiences.[30]

Although by 1972 Hollywood had committed itself to actively woo the African American filmgoing public, the emphasis appeared to be on quantity, not quality. In fact, the overwhelming commercial success of the low-budget *Sweet Sweetback* and *Shaft* apparently convinced Hollywood producers that movies made for African American consumers did not need large budgets to be successful. Moreover, in the majority of the black-oriented movies of the 1970s, African American audiences were given extra-heavy doses of Hollywood's unholy trinity of sex, violence, and crime. The term "blaxploitation" thus arose to convey the film industry's exploitation of black consumers during this period.[31]

Contemporary black critics of blaxploitation movies decried not only the dubious screen images presented in these films, but also how another set of white business owners—namely, proprietors of movie theaters—were generating huge profits from black moviegoing. During this period, out of the approximately fourteen thousand motion-picture theaters in the United States, fewer than twenty were owned and operated by African Americans.[32]

A study of movie theaters in downtown Chicago in 1974 revealed just how profitable it was to show films that appealed to black consumers. The eight theaters in downtown Chicago featured black-oriented films (by themselves) fifty-five times in that year. These engagements of a week or longer generated box-office receipts of $7,716,534, or

28   Donald Bogle, *Toms, Coons, Mulattoes, Mammies, & Bucks: An Interpretive History of Blacks in American Films* (New York: Continuum, 1989), 238; Fred Beauford, "Black Movies Create Box-Office Magic," *Black Enterprise* 4 (September 1972): 53.

29   Steinberg, *Film Facts*, 86–87; "Hollywood's New Public," *The Economist*, May 19, 1973, 53.

30   Murray, "The Subject Is Money," 26.

31   Ibid.; "Hollywood's New Public," 53.

32   James P. Murray, *To Find an Image: Black Films from Uncle Tom to Superfly* (Indianapolis, IN: Bobbs-Merrill, 1973), 168.

an average of $140,300 per engagement. By contrast, these eight Loop theaters fea-tured white-oriented films (by themselves) ninety-four times. These movies generated box-office receipts of $8,667,900, or an average of $92,212 per engagement. The same downtown Chicago movie houses featured Asian martial-arts films (by themselves) thirty-one times. This genre, which was also very popular among urban black moviego-ers, generated box-office receipts of $2,778,329, or an average of $89,624 per engagement. Combined, black-oriented and Asian martial-arts movies clearly generated the majority of box-office receipts for downtown Chicago theater owners. This pattern was repeated across America.[33]

While whites apparently received the bulk of the profits associated with the black-oriented movies of the 1970s, some African Americans did materially benefit from this phenomenon. Besides Melvin Van Peebles's stunning success with *Sweet Sweetback's Baadasssss Song*, two African American musician-songwriters, Isaac Hayes and Curtis Mayfield, achieved far-reaching success during this period.

Part of the formula associated with attracting black consumers to blaxploitation movies was the utilization of popular African American recording artists to develop film scores. Isaac Hayes's soundtrack album to the 1971 film *Shaft* earned him an Academy Award and also generated several million dollars in sales. Likewise, Curtis Mayfield's 1972 soundtrack album for the movie *Superfly* went to platinum, with more than a million sold.[34] Other notable blaxploitation soundtracks that successfully encouraged African Americans to make two purchases (movie ticket and album) included Marvin Gaye's *Trouble Man* (1972), Willie Hutch's *The Mack* (1973), Roy Ayers's *Coffy* (1973), and James Brown's *Black Caesar* (1973).

Besides witnessing the emergence of the blaxploitation genre, the 1970s saw a dra-matic increase in collective African American spending power. In 1969, D. Parke Gibson, a noted African American marketing consultant to white corporations, wrote a book called *The $30 Billion Negro*, whose title reflected collective black spending power at the end of the 1960s. Nine years later, Gibson wrote a sequel, *$70 Billion in the Black: America's Black Consumers*.[35] Ironically, while white-controlled companies profited mightily from this increase in collective African American spending power, black-owned enterprises, such as insurance companies, were unable to do likewise.

---

33   Renee Ward, "Black Films, White Profits," *Black Scholar* 7 (May 1976): 19–22; Murray, *To Find an Image*, 168; "The Black Film Boom," *Newsweek*, September 6, 1971, 66.

34   Roland F. Jefferson, "The Black Film Boom: Decerebrate, Dangerous, and Declining," *Journal of the National Medical Association* 67 (January 1975): 12; Ed Guerrero, *Framing Blackness: The African-American Image in Film* (Philadelphia: Temple University Press, 1993), 97.

35   D. Parke Gibson, *The $30 Billion Negro* (New York: Macmillan, 1969); *$70 Billion in the Black: America's Black Consumers* (New York: Macmillan, 1978).

During the first decades of the twentieth century, white-owned insurance companies either ignored or discriminated against the black consumer market. Given this economic manifestation of Jim Crow, black-owned insurance companies were established to provide these needed services to the African American community.[36] Like other white businesses, mainstream insurance companies, beginning in the 1950s, became increasingly cognizant of the economic ramifications of accelerated African American urbanization and the evolving civil rights movement. Consequently, companies such as Prudential and Metropolitan Life rescinded their discriminatory stance toward black consumers and aggressively pursued potential black policyholders. One technique widely used by white-owned insurance companies to make inroads among black consumers was to recruit top agents from black insurance companies by offering them higher pay.[37]

In a subsequently futile attempt to compete in a desegregated marketplace, black insurance companies put considerable effort into securing potential white clients. For instance, the black-owned Chicago Metropolitan Assurance Company, during the early to mid-1960s, aggressively sought to recruit white agents. Yet while some black agents with black companies eagerly defected to white-owned companies, white insurance agents were not similarly attracted to employment with black firms. Thus, by the end of the 1960s, Chicago Metropolitan and other black insurers had all but abandoned hopes of desegregating their labor force and client base.[38]

By the 1970s, black-owned insurance companies, facing increased competition from white companies (for black clients), found themselves having to adjust to a new socioeconomic reality. The Black Power movement of the late 1960s, with its emphasis on "buying black," had provided black insurers a temporary respite from increased white competition. Nevertheless, many black consumers seemingly welcomed the wider range of buying choices associated with racial desegregation. As a contemporary analysis of the black insurance industry noted, "There is another side to the 'buy black' coin. It is 'buy white.' Many blacks evidently feel that whites and white companies give superior products and superior services. There exists, moreover, among blacks the feeling that dealing with white companies constitutes a status symbol, a badge of 'arrival' for upwardly mobile blacks."[39]

African American insurance companies' heavy reliance on "industrial" insurance further hindered their efforts to impress black consumers. Industrial insurance, a form of coverage characterized by the weekly collection of premiums in policyholders' homes

---

36   Robert E. Weems, Jr., *Black Business in the Black Metropolis: The Chicago Metropolitan Assurance Company, 1925–1985* (Bloomington: Indiana University Press, 1996), 39–41.

37   Ibid., 103.

38   Ibid., 103–4.

39   Jacob M. Duker and Charles E. Hughes, "The Black-Owned Life Insurance Company: Issues and Recommendations," *Journal of Risk and Insurance* 40 (June 1973): 223.

and by low policy face values, had long been de-emphasized by mainstream companies. By 1970, only 2.9 percent of all U.S. companies provided industrial coverage. On the other hand, industrial insurance represented 43.9 percent of black companies' total insurance in force.[40]

Despite the disadvantages of industrial insurance, which included high administrative costs that were passed on to consumers, some African American insurance company executives reminded their critics that this form of coverage represented the cornerstone of the historic personal relationship between black insurers and their policyholders. Still, as the 1970s unfolded, it seemed increasingly clear that African American consumers were becoming less interested in nostalgia and more concerned about saving money in the present.[41]

As previously stated, there existed a linkage between white companies' interest in reaching black consumers and the perceived ramifications of the mid-twentieth-century civil rights movement and accelerated African American urbanization. Yet by the 1980s, it was crystal clear that while African Americans were a solidly urban people, not all blacks were benefiting equally from the desegregation of America. The introduction of the terms *buppie* (to describe black urban professionals) and *underclass* into the national vocabulary represented one manifestation of growing class distinctions in the black community. Moreover, corporate marketers, in response to this demographic reality, developed class-specific advertising aimed at African Americans.

Before the 1980s, when many corporate marketers approached black consumers with a one-size-fits-all mentality, advertisements aimed at African Americans regularly featured black "street" dialect to allegedly help black consumers better identify with a particular product. While the use of "slanguage" did indeed appeal to some elements of the African American consuming public, an important contemporary marketing study warned that such advertisements ran "the risk of turning off another segment of black consumers, particularly middle class blacks."[42]

Using this information, financial-services companies made considerable inroads among well-to-do blacks during the 1980s. Instead of using overtly "ethnic" marketing campaigns to attract more black clients, banks, white-owned insurance companies, and investment-brokerage firms employed general-market advertising campaigns that included a requisite number of African Americans in desegregated professional settings.[43]

---

40   Ibid., 225.

41   Ibid., 226.

42   Jerome D. Williams and William J. Qualls, "Middle-Class Black Consumers and Intensity of Ethnic Identification," *Psychology & Marketing* 6 (Winter 1989): 270, 272.

43   James C. Lawson, "Financial Services Target Segment within a Segment," *Advertising Age*, August 25, 1986, S-1, S-2.

Although financial-services companies tended not to employ special advertising to reach black clients, they used other techniques to "invite" African Americans to use their products. One especially innovative strategy was a joint venture between *Black Enterprise* magazine and the investment brokerage Dean Witter Reynolds. In 1986, *Black Enterprise*, a premier gateway to the black middle class, and Dean Witter Reynolds teamed up to cosponsor four-hour seminars for African American professionals in several major U.S. cities. The large crowds that attended these meetings heard Dean Witter professionals talk about personal finance and career planning. This project proved so successful that *Black Enterprise* and Dean Witter held similar seminars in additional cities in 1987. Other financial-services companies quickly sought their own partnerships with *Black Enterprise*.[44]

Sadly, while black middle-class consumers in the 1980s increasingly attracted the attention of financial-services companies and other upscale industries, blacks who had not materially benefited from the civil rights movement increasingly attracted the attention of liquor and cigarette manufacturers. One glaring example of this was the proliferation of outdoor billboards marketing these products in urban black enclaves across America.

During the 1980s, the number of eight-sheet billboards (three hundred square feet or less) that extolled the social "benefits" of drinking alcohol or smoking cigarettes proliferated at an alarming rate in African American neighborhoods. For example, the Los Angeles metropolitan area, with a population of nearly eight million people, contained 1,373 eight-sheet billboards in 1986. Of these, 663, or 48 percent, were placed in predominantly black neighborhoods. This was especially significant considering that the 1.2 million African Americans in the Los Angeles area represented just 15 percent of the total population. Similar data for St. Louis appeared even more striking. Although African Americans represented only 28 percent of that city's population, 95 percent of the eight-sheet billboards in that city were located in the black community.[45]

To put the above data in clearer context, it should be noted that the consumption of alcohol and cigarettes has historically been viewed (by some) as effective short-term escapes from the sometimes harsh realities of everyday living. For a significant number of urban blacks during the Reagan administration, "reality" consisted of protracted, demoralizing unemployment. In this context, the accelerated marketing of alcoholic beverages and cigarettes in the 1980s in urban African American enclaves can be construed as an attempt to profit from human misery.

The 1980s witnessed not only corporate marketers' class-targeted attempts to reach black consumers, but the spread of hip-hop culture, which would ultimately be

44   Ibid., S-2.
45   George A. Hacker, Ronald Collins, and Michael Jacobson, *Marketing Booze to Blacks* (Washington, DC: Center for Science in the Public Interest, 1987), 22–23.

transformed into another marketing bonanza for corporate America. Ironically, considering hip-hop's future seizure by corporate interests, one of the first ways this musical genre endeared itself to its primarily urban African American audience was by providing a "platform" to speak out against the obvious inequities associated with being black and poor in late-twentieth-century America.

Arguably, the most noteworthy early hip-hop group to engage in explicit social commentary was Grandmaster Flash and the Furious Five. Their 1982 classic "The Message" was described in a *Los Angeles Times* review as "a revolutionary seven-minute record" that was "a brilliantly compact chronicle of the tension and despair of ghetto life that rips at the innocence of the American Dream." Another reviewer, in *Newsweek*, asserted that "The Message" was "a Reagan record. ... It has to do with the perception that all pretenses toward equity have been abandoned."[46]

Another aspect of early hip-hop, which would open the door for corporate exploitation, was the vigorous competition among emcees (rappers) to determine who was the best at their craft. A classic example of this phenomenon was Kool Moe Dee's 1987 album *How Ya Like Me Now*. Besides featuring a "rapper report card," where Kool Moe Dee received the highest grade among current emcees, *How Ya Like Me Now* featured the artist on the cover with a customized Jeep and flashing various pieces of diamond and gold jewelry in an urban vacant lot. In the context of later expressions of hip-hop artists' success, which featured rappers in mansions, on yachts, and driving Bentleys, Kool Moe Dee's braggadocio appears almost comical. Still, *How Ya Like Me Now* represents an important precursor to the bling-bling phenomenon, with its focus on conspicuous consumption, that came to dominate hip-hop and influence its fans.[47]

By the 1990s, although such hip-hop artists as Public Enemy, KRS-One, and Dead Prez continued the tradition of Grandmaster Flash and the Furious Five in using hip-hop as a means to engage in relevant social commentary, it increasingly appeared that other hip-hop artists had "sold out" to "get paid." As one of the contributors to *The Vibe History of Hip Hop* noted, "Ironically, the hip hop nation, once so proudly self-sufficient, became obsessed with the finer things in life: designer clothing, imported champagne, Cuban cigars, luxury automobiles, and fine jewelry—all the things that prove how successful you are by American Dream standards."[48]

Perhaps the most troubling aspect of hip-hop's evolution toward conspicuous consumption was that the promoters of bling-bling and their fans (who sought to emulate the buying patterns of their hip-hop heroes) were being overtly exploited by corporate

---

46   Liner notes, *Grandmaster Flash and the Furious Five: Greatest Messages*, LP record, Sugarhill Records, SH 9121, 1984.

47   Kool Moe Dee, *How Ya Like Me Now*, LP record, Zomba Productions, J1-1079, 1987.

48   Emil Wilbekin, "Great Aspirations: Hip Hop and Fashion Dress for Excess and Success," in *The Vibe History of Hip Hop*, ed. Alan Light (New York: Three Rivers Press, 1999), 288.

America. Since the 1930s, corporate marketers have known that African Americans, because they were the only group to have been enslaved in this country, occupy a precarious place in the nation's consumer culture. Thus, large U.S. companies know that some blacks, in an attempt to distance themselves from their slave and Jim Crow past, developed buying patterns designed to enhance their respect and dignity.[49]

Although many young African American urban consumers in the 1990s were apparently captivated by the actions and lifestyles of hip-hop's foot soldiers for corporate America, there were important voices of dissent. George Curry, former editor in chief of *Emerge* magazine, used this publication to provide thoughtful analyses of hip-hop-stimulated conspicuous consumption. For instance, in an editor's note titled "Walking Billboards," Curry asserted:

> After conducting successful campaigns to remove certain billboards from our neighborhoods, perhaps, it's time to launch a campaign against another kind of billboard in our community—our youth (and some adults) who are walking advertisements for Nike, Polo, Tommy Hilfiger, Nautica, and too many other labels to list in this space. ... There is an obsession with having someone else's name plastered on our baseball caps, shirts, bags, and the back of our jeans. In addition to spurring some of our youth to commit crimes against African Americans in order to sport these expensive brand name items, we're lining pockets of designers who show contempt for us, but not for our $400 billion per year spending power.[50]

To buttress his statements, Curry cited a quotation from the popular designer Tommy Hilfiger in *Forbes* magazine: Hilfiger told *Forbes* that "many of these people [blacks] would rather have a Rolex than a home."[51]

While not all hip-hop artists of the late twentieth and early twenty-first centuries are ambassadors of bling-bling, there are enough proponents of African American conspicuous consumption to generate increasing concern about the future of black America. Given that hip-hop's primary audience is young people under the age of twenty-five, hip-hop artists, because of their wide media exposure, are shaping the worldview of a future generation. When contemporary ten-year-olds are fed a steady stream of messages glorifying individualistic conspicuous consumption, how will this manifest itself when these children become adults?

---

49   Robert E. Weems, Jr., *Desegregating the Dollar: African American Consumerism in the Twentieth Century* (New York: New York University Press, 1998), 27.

50   George E. Curry, "Walking Billboards," *Emerge* 9 (December 1997–January 1998): 8.

51   Ibid.; Hilfiger quoted in *Forbes*, April 21, 1997, 144.

While it is impossible to answer this question with precision, the evidence suggests that the conditioning of young African Americans to secure as many flashy trinkets as possible (jewelry, big cars, fancy clothes, gold-plated teeth) may have dire consequences for the African American community. The focus of bling-bling on *individual* accumulation seemingly diminishes and trivializes any notions of *collective* social, political, and economic activity. This is especially disturbing considering that historically, African American survival and progress has repeatedly been linked to proactive, communal struggle.

Another way in which corporate America has used hip-hop to manipulate African American consumers has been through paying artists to write and perform songs about particular products. Songs such as Run-DMC's "My Adidas" and Busta Rhymes's "Pass the Courvoisier" are examples of this genre.[52] In 2005 Maven Strategies, a Maryland-based entertainment-marketing firm (whose stable of hip-hop artists included Kanye West, Twista, the Franchise Boys, and Petey Pablo), developed a marketing plan that would enable its corporate clients to maximize their profits with little or no financial risk by getting hip-hop artists to write and perform songs about their products. This arrangement provided further proof that many hip-hop artists, despite their brashness and bravado, are little more than obedient intermediaries between corporate marketers and African American consumers.

In a March 23, 2005, *Advertising Age* article entitled "McDonald's Buying Way into Hip-Hop Lyrics," Tony Rome, president and CEO of Maven Strategies, outlined the economic parameters of McDonald's proposed relationship with Maven's hip-hop "posse." The following excerpts from this article are extremely illuminating:

> For the deal involving the Big Mac, McDonald's receives first approval of the lyrics, but it will ultimately allow artists to decide how the sandwich is integrated into songs. ... Maven's already started receiving several songs for consideration. Maven receives a consulting fee for its services. *Music acts, however, will not receive payment up-front. Instead they will earn anywhere from $1 to $5 every time their song is played on the radio.* (emphasis added)

> That payment strategy not only limits the risk for McDonald's or any other brand partner looking to partner up with music acts, but also encourages artists to produce a hit song. *"At the end of the day, this has to work for the brands, and we want to deliver quantitative results,"* Mr. Rome said. *"The risk*

---

52 Dipannita Basu, "A Critical Examination of the Political Economy of the Hip Hop Industry," in *African Americans in the U.S. Economy*, ed. Cecilia A. Conrad et al. (Lanham, MD: Rowman and Littlefield, 2005), 261, 268.

involved for upfront payment is all eliminated. If an artist isn't able to deliver [a hit], there's no out-of-pocket cost to the client." (emphasis added)[53]

The following day (March 24, 2005), the Campaign for a Commercial-Free Childhood (CCFC) issued a press release denouncing the proposed collaboration between Maven Strategies and McDonald's. It featured the following statement from noted African American psychiatrist Dr. Alvin F. Poussaint: "This campaign undermines McDonald's claim that they are serious about combating childhood obesity. Even as McDonald's is drawing praise for pushing salads and apples, they are finding new ways to market high calorie standbys like the Big Mac to children." This press release, with the catchy title "Children's Coalition Raps McDonald's Supersized Hypocrisy," also provided some chilling information: "Obesity rates have soared among children in recent years and are highest among African Americans, who comprise a disproportionate share of the hip-hop audience. A report in last week's *New England Journal of Medicine* found that due to obesity-related illnesses, the current generation of children may have shorter life expectancies than their parents."[54]

Another especially illuminating response to the proposed collaboration between Maven Strategies and McDonald's appeared in the online publication *Stay Free! Daily*. A brief commentary with the appropriate title "McDonald's Pimps Hip-Hop" included this pertinent analysis: "If a group's Big Mac plugging cut fails to become a hit, McDonald's doesn't have to pay them anything. But if the song does get lots of airplay, a suit from Maven [Tony Rome] points out that 'there's a strong likelihood it will be played in clubs, be downloaded, be turned into a ringtone and sell more CDS.' In other words, hits will reap a lot of free exposure for McDonald's since it only has to pay artists for radio play."[55]

This proposed manipulation of African American consumers and artists by McDonald's and Maven Strategies represents just the latest instance of white corporate hostility and insincerity as it relates to blacks. During the late nineteenth and early twentieth centuries, when African Americans were perceived to be a group with very limited spending power, many companies employed the derogatory term "nigger" in naming products. By the mid-twentieth century, when the growing African American consumer market could not be ignored, white companies, which had previously practiced employment

---

53   Marc Greer, "McDonald's Buying Way into Hip-Hop Lyrics," http://www.commercialfreechildhood.org/news/articles/mcdonaldsrap.htm.

54   Campaign for a Commercial-Free Childhood, "Children's Coalition Raps McDonald's Supersized Hypocrisy: Hip-Hop Songs to Feature Big Macs," press release, March 24, 2005, http://www.commercialfreechildhood.org/pressreleases/mcdonaldsrap.htm. For detailed information about the alarming rise of obesity in the African American community, see B. Denise Hawkins, "Weighing in on African American Obesity," *Black Issues in Education* 21 (January 27, 2005): 24–31.

55   Carrie McLaren, "McDonald's Pimps Hip Hop," *Stay Free! Daily*, March 28, 2005, http://blog.stayfreemagazine.org/2005/03/mcdonalds_pimps.html.

discrimination, began hiring blacks to serve as "Negro market" specialists and consultants. Today, these firms extract huge profits from African American consumers, while paying relative "chump change" to a few black hucksters pushing their products.[56]

Given the power and effectiveness of corporate America's ongoing strategies to reach black consumers, it is not hyperbole to assert that in recent decades, African American spending *power* might be better characterized as spending *weakness*.[57] As table 4.1.1 indicates, collective African American spending power grew from $367 to $679 billion between 1996 and 2004. Yet if one were to take a stroll (or drive) through most urban black enclaves in America, one would be hard-pressed to see where increased African American spending has improved the infrastructure and the ambiance of these neighborhoods. Black consumers, who now spend the vast majority of their money in shiny downtown and suburban shopping malls, enhance the economic bases of these outside areas, to the detriment of their own enclaves. One of the most visually stunning verifications of this unfortunate reality appeared in Lizabeth Cohen's 2003 book *A Consumers' Republic: The Politics of Mass Consumption in Postwar America*. Her use of photographs taken thirty years apart of a prominent inner-city Newark intersection shows how a once vibrant commercial district has become an urban "wasteland."[58]

Table 4.1.1 African American Buying Power, 1996–2004

Year	Total disposable income of African Americans
1996	$367,000,000,000
1997	391,000,000,000
1998	441,000,000,000
1999	491,000,000,000
2000	543,000,000,000
2001	601,000,000,000
2002	631,000,000,000
2003	656,000,000,000
2004	679,000,000,000

Source: Target Market News, "The Buying Power of Black America," http://targetmarketnews.com/Buying-Power05.htm; http://targetmarketnews.com/buyingpowerstats.htm.

---

56   Weems, *Desegregating the Dollar*, 8, 49–54.

57   The apparent originator of the notion of contemporary African American "spending weakness" is James Clingman, in his work *Blackonomics: The Way To Psychological and Economic Freedom for African Americans* (Los Angeles: Milligan Books, 2001), 103–5.

58   Lizabeth Cohen, *A Consumers' Republic: The Politics of Mass Consumption in Postwar America* (New York: Knopf, 2003), 379.

Perhaps ironically, the ongoing decline of urban black America's infrastructure appears linked to the ongoing decline of black-owned insurance companies. On the surface, as stated earlier, it appears that contemporary African Americans are being better served by large white insurers than by historic black insurers. Just as supermarkets can offer more economical prices than mom-and-pop grocers, large mainstream insurers can offer cost-conscious African American consumers more economical coverage than can much smaller black-owned insurance companies. Yet, notwithstanding the dynamics of economy of scale, the contemporary abandonment of black insurance companies by black consumers has seemingly helped accelerate the disintegration of black urban enclaves across the country.

The history of the African American insurance industry reveals these firms' longtime commitment to reinvesting a significant proportion of their premium income back into the black community, primarily in the form of mortgage loans.[59] As these companies have declined (and disappeared) in recent years, there has been a simultaneous decline in the amount of money they have designated for community reinvestment. Thus, the seeming simultaneous deterioration of African American insurance companies and urban black America's infrastructure appears far from coincidental. Significantly, while white-owned insurers readily take African Americans' premium payments, they appear far less enthusiastic about investing in African American enclaves.

The clearly observable decline of urban black America's infrastructure in recent decades seemingly validates the central message of William K. Bell's controversial 1958 book *15 Million Negroes and 15 Billion Dollars*. Unlike other contemporary works related to black consumers, which sought to assist white corporations in their quest for more black customers and clients, Bell's book urged African Americans to use their increasing spending power for their own benefit.

> Why should not 15 MILLION NEGROES become more conscious of their condition by developing their own market for the advancement of their own lives? There is no record in history to show that any race on the face of this earth has ever become great that did not develop itself economically. ... 15 MILLION NEGROES cannot be kept from gaining economic power if they determine to keep within the race a certain portion of that 15 BILLION DOLLARS that is running daily through their fingers, as water does over a dam. ... There is GREAT POWER IN 15 BILLION DOLLARS.[60]

---

59   See Walter B. Weare, *Black Business in the New South: A Social History of the North Carolina Mutual Life Insurance Company* (1973; Durham, NC: Duke University Press, 1993); Alexa B. Henderson, *Atlanta Life Insurance Company: Guardian of Black Economic Dignity* (Tuscaloosa: University of Alabama Press, 1990); and Weems, *Black Business in the Black Metropolis*.

60   William K. Bell, *15 Million Negroes and 15 Billion Dollars* (New York: William K. Bell, 1958), x–xi.

As a new century unfolds, the history of African American consumerism since World War II clearly suggests that African Americans, since the civil rights movement, have not effectively leveraged their power as consumers. Although aggregate African American spending figures are approaching *$1 trillion dollars*, this money has enhanced the profit margins of major corporations, rather than promoted urban black community development. Future research related to African American consumer history, especially in the realm of television's impact on the consumption patterns of blacks in the postwar period, should provide even more details concerning how corporate America profited from increased black urbanization and the civil rights movement.

CRITICAL REFLECTIONS

- After reading the article, do you agree with the tactics the sports, entertainment, and insurance industries used to gain the Black dollar?
- What are your thoughts on the "bling-bling" culture described by the author?
- In your opinion, should the Black dollar circulate more within the Black community or remain as is?

Unit V

Black Creative Production

Introduction to Unit V

Unit V concerns a topic that is as complex and nuanced as the Black experience. The term "Black creative production" can be defined as the creation, appropriation, and dissemination of Black cultural expression. The readings selected illustrate the importance of Black cultural expression within the American narrative. They also highlight complexities within the cultural narrative of Africans within the diaspora. While often discounted, the experiences of Africans in America are integral within a proper retelling of American history.

While not the only vehicles of the Black experience, music, literature, and cinema are three mediums predominantly used to articulate the history, culture, spirit, ethos, and motif of Africans in America. Waldo F. Martin, Jr.'s "The Sounds of Blackness: African-American Music," is a critical analysis of popular genres within Black music. Specifically, the author discusses the origins and nuances of Black Gospel Music, the Blues, and Jazz. Gerald Early's "Black Voices: Themes in African-American Literature" concerns prominent themes within African-American literature. He examines notions of identity and motivations for expression. Additionally, he analyzes the "Black Literary Aesthetic," literature within the Black community, and the future of the genre. Lastly, Jacqueline Najuma Stewart's "We Were Never Immigrants: Oscar Micheaux and the Reconstruction of Black American Identity" deals with the legendary African-American movie director Oscar Micheaux's expression of the Black experience in film and how his take served as what he himself describes as "an instructive voice and an empowering interpreter of Black life for the community."

Reading 5.1

The Sounds of Blackness
African-American Music

Waldo F. Martin Jr.

M USIC HAS DEEPLY INFLUENCED AND INFORMED the culture of Africans in the Americas from the initial days of New World African enslavement. Throughout the African sojourn in the Americas, enslaved Africans continued to practice music as they had in their various African societies. Music operated in a unified intellectual and emotional world where mind and body were inseparable, where the sacred and the secular were understood as a whole. The enduring power of New World African music can be traced to this belief and the ability of music to integrate function and meaning.

Notwithstanding similarities of form and content, significant differences emerged between native African and diasporan African music. These dynamic processes of cross-cultural influence can be seen across the changing cultures of the interacting peoples of African, European, and indigenous New World descent. And indeed a critical element of the fashioning of New World African cultures was the ongoing tradition of cross-cultural sharing among Africans themselves, which yielded mixed African-American cultures unlike their parent cultures in crucial ways. Music has played a key role in this complicated process of the creation and elaboration of a sense of identity at once American and African-American. Attracted by the beauty of the American ideal while at the same time repelled by the racism of the American reality, Africans have sought to realize the former by ceaselessly struggling to undermine the latter. African-American music vividly captures the powerful dialectic at the center of this continuing struggle.

The African influence in the United States can be illustrated in part by looking at the Americanization of Africans in the New World. This same influence can also be viewed by looking at the Africanization of the Americas. African-American music illuminates, on the one hand, the cultural interpenetration of Africa, Europe, and the New World. On the other hand, and even more crucial for our purposes here, the social history of African-American music sheds much-needed light on African agency and the powerful African impact on the cultural mapping of the Americas. The argument here is that American culture possesses an intrinsic Africanness within its creole complexity. This Africanness is a principal defining quality of American culture as well as African-American culture.

When contrasted with its African roots, African music in the North American colonies and subsequently the United States reveals significant continuities and shifts that can be traced primarily to the critical changes indigenous African music withstood in the New World. First, as slaves coming from different African societies, African Americans created music that resulted in part from the melding of diverse African influences. Notwithstanding the dominance of certain African musical cultures in specific areas, like the Bakongo among the Gullah in coastal South Carolina, African-American music reflected various African traditions. An important consequence of this merging of African musics was the pushing forward of similarities as well as the resolution of differences in the development of African-American music. Second, African-American music developed under the influence of the various types of European music it encountered. Third, Africans also encountered Native-American music in certain areas, and scholars have traced these influences in vocal and instrumental musical traditions. Not surprisingly, however, the evidence of cross-cultural musical influence among Native Americans and Africans is rare compared to that found among European Americans and African Americans.

Despite these influences, several developments gave emerging African-American music unusual resiliency and power. First, where similarities existed among the different traditions—as in certain vocalizing and drum techniques, and the key role of music and dance in rituals and ceremonies—African musical traditions found reinforcement, even enrichment. Second, the traditional African musical openness to outside influences and emphasis on innovation enabled African Americans to incorporate into their own musical practices innumerable outside ones. In effect, they reinterpreted these practices—like the playing of the violin, or the singing of hymns—within their own musical style and repertoire, making these practices their own. Finally, the ubiquitous presence of music within African-American cultures enhanced the music's significance.

The African Roots of African-American Music

These emphases—upon improvisation, inclusiveness, innovation, and flexibility—were vital to the enduring vitality and impact of African-American music. At the center of this pan-African musical consciousness is rhythmic complexity and a corresponding hypnotic feel. This complicated musical heartbeat—encompassing polyrhythms and cross rhythms—propels and unifies the various elements. Other defining elements include the call-and-response, or antiphony (back-and-forth exchanges between groups/individuals within the music-making event); a social, or collective, setting; an intimate tie to dance and bodily movement, a crucial part of its performance feature; and an emotive, even ecstatic, temper.

In varying combinations, these characteristics make African-American music distinctive and must be understood to originate in the West African and west-central African cultures from which the bulk of the slaves came. The sites of capture and transfer to the slave ships for the forced passage to the New World witnessed terrible scenes of loss, separation, grief, and mourning. The shrieks, groans, moans, and songs were in part strategies of survival and adjustment. These plaintive stirrings often found the captives seeking solace from their traditional gods and ancestors and pleading with, cursing, and condemning their captives and disclosed inter- and intragroup communication among the captured. Various descriptions of these haunting vocal messages noted their musicality as well as their insight into the captives' thoughts and feelings. Furthermore, the musical sounds accompanying the horror of capture and enslavement laid the basis for a cultural memory rooted in resistance, struggle, and hope amid "unspeakable" oppression. That memory found musical remembrance in many ways, perhaps most tellingly in the nineteenth-century crucible of the spirituals and the turn-of-the-century crucible of the blues.

BOX 5.1.1

Mungo Park Describes African Music in the Eighteenth Century

Of their music and dances, some account has incidentally been given in different parts of my journal. On the first of these heads, I have now to add a list of their musical instruments, the principal of which are,—the *koonting,* a sort of guitar with three strings;—the *korro,* a large harp with eighteen strings;—the *balafou,* an instrument composed of twenty pieces of hard wood of different lengths, with the shells of gourds hung underneath to increase the sound;—the *tangtang,* a drum open at the lower end;—and lastly, the *tabalu,* a large drum, commonly used to spread an alarm through the country. Besides these, they make use of small flutes, bow-strings, elephants' teeth, and bells; and at all their dances and concerts, *clapping of hands* appears to constitute a necessary part of the chorus.

With the love of music is naturally connected a taste for poetry, and fortunately for the poets of Africa, they are in a great measure exempted from that neglect and

(Continued)

BOX 5.1.1 (*Continued*)

indigence, which in more polished countries commonly attend the votaries of the Muses. They consist of two classes; the most numerous are the *singing men,* called *Jillikea* mentioned in a former part of my narrative; one or more of these, may be found in every town; they sing extempore songs in honour of their chief men, or any other persons who are willing to give "solid pudding for empty praise." But a nobler part of their office is, to recite the historical events of their country; hence, in war, they accompany the soldiers to the field, in order, by reciting the great actions of their ancestors, to awaken in them a spirit of glorious emulation. The other class are devotees of the Mahomedan faith, who travel about the country, singing devout hymns, and performing religious ceremonies, to conciliate the favour of the Almighty, either in averting calamity, or in insuring success to any enterprize. Both descriptions of these itinerant bards are much employed and respected by the people, and very liberal contributions are made for them.

Source: *Travels in the Interior Districts of Africa, Performed Under the Direction and Patronage of the African Association in the Years of 1795, 1796, and 1797,* by Mungo Park, Surgeon (New York, 1800).

During the dreaded Middle Passage (the hellish slave voyage to the Americas), the practice aboard slave ships of forced merrymaking among the enslaved offers similar evidence of an early site of African-American music making. Serving as entertainment for the slavers (who often got in the act) as well as exercise/recreation for the slaves, "dancing the Negroes" also allowed for the initial reworking of African music and dance, often in concert with European influence. In the course of the slave trade, on the African coast, on the slave ships, and in the Americas, spoken communication and musical wails often employed pidgin languages that combined African and European elements. Nevertheless, this creolized music remained fundamentally African, reinforcing the growth of a pan-African sense of identity among the enslaved.

Once in the Americas, music remained a revealing expression of a distinctive African-American culture. During the eighteenth century, when the bulk of the African slaves were imported, the constant infusion of African cultural influences continually revitalized the music's Africanness. In the nineteenth century, with the abolition of the transatlantic slave trade and the subsequent expansion of the domestic slave trade, memory, tradition, and the continuing practices of music making sustained the Africanness of this most vital African-American cultural framework. In rural and urban settings, North and South, African-American music during slavery revealed an increasingly singular sense of pan-African consciousness, in spite of the differences among African Americans, that reflected common critical elements derived from the African source. These elements included a sacred understanding of the cosmos, a cyclical sense of time, and a reliance on the oral transmission of culture.

These fundamental emphases found expression in African-American musical aesthetics, notably rhythm. Where melody formed the basis of European music, African music was anchored in rhythm. Consequently, rhythm, particularly expressed through drumming, provided a common syntax and grammar. The intense rapid rhythmic pulse of the drum enabled African Americans to evoke and thus to communicate with the ancestral spirits, to delineate musical time, to punctuate cultural events, to provide a foundation for song and dance, and to communicate as with words. Indeed the notion of "talking drums," or "drum language," signified the wide-ranging communicative abilities of skillful players and listeners, permitting multiple uses and complex statements.

The power of the drum and its percussive corollaries united and sustained African Americans politically as well as culturally and references to its role in slave social life and unrest can be found throughout the colonies. The drum served to draw together African Americans in ways that promoted instances of individual resistance, such as absconding to freedom, and collective resistance, such as uprisings. Increasingly aware of the drum's subversive capacity, especially in the eighteenth century, European Americans throughout the colonies officially banned African-style drumming. (Interestingly, African Americans, slave and free, played drums along with trumpets and fifes in militia bands. The approved style was European, simple and straightforward.) While the ban on African drumming appeared effective, in fact it pushed the practice underground. The rhythmic engine of the music resurfaced in the increased use of other percussion instruments, of nonpercussion instruments played percussively, and of the voice and the body itself used as percussion instruments.

If the drum was in many ways the most powerful of the African instruments to come to North America, the banjo was among the most popular. Accounts of fine banjo playing by African Americans are not hard to find. Similarly, clear evidence exists of African Americans playing a variety of other African instruments, including horns, small flutes, thumb pianos, bells, rattles, and pipes. African Americans also became exceedingly proficient on a variety of European instruments, including flutes, horns, and violins. When playing these instruments, African Americans evinced what observers often characterized as unique techniques or approaches: a distinctive African-derived style.

Music in the Slave's World

Both African Americans, free and slave, and European Americans, especially slave masters, appreciated African-American musical virtuosity. Within the black and white communities considerable status and prestige resulted from the demonstration of musical talent. These musicians often had special privileges, such as extra provisions and greater mobility for slaves and more pay for free blacks. Many musicians performed in social gatherings, formal and informal, among both whites and blacks. Whereas African Americans themselves preferred those African-American musicians skilled in African-style music, European Americans favored those skilled in European-style techniques. The experience of music making in both African and European styles enhanced the cross-fertilization of both styles and expanded the musicians' repertoires.

African-American stylistic distinctiveness was evident in vocal as well as instrumental music. The song style of African Americans was highly expressive: more percussive than lyrical. Ample reference is made to the resounding singing of African Americans among themselves, as well as the overpowering vocal might of African Americans drowning out European Americans when both groups sang together in religious as well as secular settings. In addition to great volume and emotional intensity, African-American song style blended vocal gestures—including shouts, falsetto, trills, and slurs—and physical movements like foot stomping, hand clapping, body weaving, and head bobbing. While reinforcing a fundamental rhythmic thrust, this song style also reflected the intimate tie of the music to bodily motion and dance, of music making to performance.

Indeed, African-derived sensibilities and movements have dominated the history of American dance. Like the music of which it is an integral part, dance was a vital social practice binding the group together and projecting a collective sense of identity. Also like the music, dance reflected fundamental cultural ideals: rhythm, flexibility, innovation, spontaneity. The movements themselves reflected a physicality, an earthiness, a comfortableness with the body. Specific features included dragging and gliding steps, pelvic movement, impersonations (notably of animals), little contact between dancers, and numerous gestures—subtle, vigorous, and smooth. Broadly speaking, European dances tended toward the more formal and rigid, African dances toward the more open and expressive. Despite the cross-fertilization between traditions, in the development of both African-American dance and music African styles and movements prevailed.

The significance of the dance-music nexus was evident in sacred as well as secular contexts, playing a central aspect in ritual celebrations and ceremonies ranging from funerals to corn shucking. The Christmas-New Year term was an important season for parties and celebrations showcasing music and dance. Likewise, regional antebellum celebrations such as Election Day and Pinkster Day in New England, the John Canoe festival in eastern North Carolina, and Sunday celebrations in New Orleans's Place Congo were structured around the dance-music dynamic. Throughout those areas with a more pronounced African presence, such as the South Carolina-Georgia Sea Islands, music, dance, and especially ritualized celebrations vividly preserved that influence. Funerals often included libations, grave decorations, and animal sacrifices, evidencing the traditional African emphasis on veneration of the ancestors and a holistic world-view uniting the spirit and physical worlds, while the music and the dance ranged from the somber and reverential to the joyful and ecstatic. Similarly, secular events like corn shucking parties found African Americans singing and dancing, often quite vigorously, as an expression of sociality as well as conviviality. Even with whites present and under the sobering influence of Christianity, African modes of celebration persisted in highly expressive social events both binding the community together and reflecting a collective sensibility.

At least since the nineteenth century, the history of African-American dance—secular and religious—has emphasized the influence of the ring shout and its various permutations. Both informal and formal religious worship services, as well as sacred ceremonies like funerals, might feature variations of this kind of holy dancing. In this African-derived movement, participants sway in a counterclockwise circle propelled by the spirit, going from a slow-motion shuffle to a more rapid rhythmic series of steps, while powerful interlocking singing helped to drive the ritual momentum. Indeed the ring shout has been a vital crucible for countless reworkings of religious tunes. In these intensely charged ritual moments of ecstatic dancing and singing, elements of various religious songs and messages were transformed into African-American sacred music, most notably the spiritual.

Emblematic of the sacred worldview of the slave, the spirituals clearly represent a creole form with deep African roots. Building upon African Americans' religious understandings, the texts of the spirituals—including Biblical stories, psalms, and hymns—emphasize sorrow and optimism, affirmation and deliverance. An intensely moving body of music, the spirituals speak to the life-and-death issues dealt with in sacred music generally. The profundity of the spirituals derives in significant measure from the dialectic between African Americans' search for secular freedom and their deep-seated religious faith. Indeed, this dialectic between liberation struggle and religious commitment shows their interconnectedness; historically, they have informed one another. They have also buttressed a sense of peoplehood, community, or nationality among African Americans.

An important aspect of the world of the spirituals was the personalization of the ties between biblical figures and the African-American community. Religious figures are addressed possessively as "My God," "King Jesus," "Sweet Jesus," "Sister Mary," or "Brother Daniel." Similarly, in the spirituals African Americans likened themselves to the Chosen People, the Jews of Israel, whose destiny it was to overcome persecution and deracination. God had brought the Jews out of bondage and he would do the same for African Americans. Secular as well as spiritual freedom, then, was understood to be a consequence of Christian faith and "Steal Away to Jesus" was an urging for untold numbers of slaves to make the break and run to freedom. This extraordinary sacred music—like much of African-American music—has helped African Americans to transcend their earthly oppression, if only momentarily. This psychic relief has contributed to the deep spiritual reservoirs that strategies of endurance and self-affirmation have demanded.

In light of the holistic worldview of antebellum African Americans, especially slaves, it is not surprising that their secular music making was quite similar to their religious music making in style and power. At social occasions and seasonal ceremonies (like those marking the end of planting and harvesting seasons) music was an essential element of the merry-making. Lyrically, this music ranged from the political and the satirical to the ordinary and frivolous. Frederick Douglass provides a striking example of the satirical slave song in his autobiography where the speaker complains, "We raise de wheat, Dey gib us de corn. We bake de bread, Dey gib us de crust." Clearly these more subversive lyrics were most likely to be found in those situations where blacks were less constrained by white surveillance.

Work songs were particularly prominent in the secular music repertoire. Song could be heard during housework, field work, industrial work, and work on the wharves and waterways. Certain public forms of secular musical expression were notable for their effectiveness at combining work with song. Street cries were used by itinerant salespersons to draw attention to their wares. Spirited field hollers were observed throughout the plantation South. Water calls were an effective means of communication on the waterways. Those African Americans laboring on the lakes, rivers, and oceans as well as the ports not only developed engaging tunes depicting their lives but also were a vital conduit for the migration of musical influences as black musical styles traveled up and down the Mississippi River.

BOX 5.1.2

Go Down, Moses

Go down, Moses,
Way down in Egyptland
Tell old Pharaoh
To let my people go.

When Israel was in Egyptland
Let my people go
Oppressed so hard they could not stand
Let my people go.

Go down, Moses,
Way down in Egyptland
Tell old Pharaoh
"Let my people go."

(Continued)

BOX 5.1.2 (*Continued*)

"Thus saith the Lord," bold Moses said,
"Let my people go;
If not I'll smite your first-born dead
Let my people go.

No more shall they in bondage toil,
Let my people go;
Let them come out with Egypt's spoil,
Let my people go."

The Lord told Moses what to do
Let my people go;
To lead the children of Israel through,
Let my people go.

Go down Moses,
Way down in Egyptland, Tell old Pharaoh,
"Let my people go!

Steal Away to Jesus

Steal away, steal away, steal away to Jesus!
Steal away, steal away home,
I ain't got long to stay here.

Steal away, steal away, steal away to Jesus!
Steal away, steal away home,
I ain't got long to stay here.

My Lord, He calls me, He calls me by the thunder,
The trumpet sounds within-a my soul,
I ain't got long to stay here.

Steal away, steal away, steal away to Jesus!
Steal away, steal away home,
I ain't got long to stay here.

(*Continued*)

BOX 5.1.2 (*Continued*)

Steal away, steal away, steal away to Jesus!
Steal away, steal away home,
I ain't got long to stay here.
Green trees a-bending, po' sinner stand a-trembling,
The trumpet sounds within-a my soul,
I ain't got long to stay here,
Oh, Lord, I ain't got long to stay here.

Many Thousand Gone

No more peck o' corn for me
No more, no more
No more peck o' corn for me
Many thousand gone.

No more driver's lash for me,
No more, no more,
No more driver's lash for me
Many thousand gone.

No more pint o' salt for me
No more, no more,
No more pint o' salt for me
Many thousand gone.

No more hundred lash for me,
No more, no more,
No more hundred lash for me,
Many thousand gone.

No more mistress' call for me,
No more, no more,
No more mistress' call for me,
Many thousand gone.

BOX 5.1.3

African-American Music in the Nineteenth Century

[The slaves] would sing, with other words of their own improvising—jargon to others, but full of meaning to themselves. I have sometimes thought, that the mere hearing of these songs would do more to impress truly spiritual-minded men and women with the soul-crushing and death-dealing character of slavery, than the reading of whole volumes of its mere physical cruelties. They speak to the heart and to the soul of the thoughtful. I cannot better express my sense of them now, than ten years ago, when, in sketching my life, I thus spoke of this feature of my plantation experience:

"I did not, when a slave, understand the deep meanings of those rude, and apparently incoherent songs. I was myself within the circle, so that I neither saw nor heard as those without might see and hear. They told a tale which was then altogether beyond my feeble comprehension; they were tones, loud, long and deep, breathing the prayer and complaint of souls boiling over with the bitterest anguish. Every tone was a testimony against slavery, and a prayer to God for deliverance from chains. The hearing of those wild notes always depressed my spirits, and filled my heart with ineffable sadness. The mere recurrence, even now, afflicts my spirit, and while I am writing these lines, my tears are falling. To those songs I trace my first glimmering conceptions of the dehumanizing character of slavery. I can never get rid of that conception. Those songs still follow me, to deepen my hatred of slavery, and quicken my sympathies for my brethren in bonds. If any one wishes to be impressed with a sense of the soul-killing power of slavery, let him go to Col. Lloyd's plantation, and, on allowance day, place himself in the deep, pine woods, and there let him, in silence, thoughtfully analyze the sounds that shall pass through the chambers of his soul, and if he is not thus impressed, it will only be because 'there is no flesh in his obdurate heart.'"

Source: Frederick Douglass, *My Bondage and My Freedom* (Boston, 1855), pp. 193–94.

The Blues

Emancipation altered the historical landscape and led African-American music making in new directions. With freedom came increased opportunities for African Americans to make music openly and publicly in proliferating venues, from the juke joints of the rural South to the elegant theaters of the cities. Despite the institutionalization of Jim Crow and the marginalization of black culture, African-American music flowered and sought to give meaning to life under freedom. The most important developments in twentieth-century African-American music—blues, gospel, jazz, and other types of postwar popular music—continue to illustrate efforts by blacks to define themselves as both a distinctive people and as Americans in their ongoing struggle for empowerment and self-definition. In addition, these hybrid yet fundamentally African musical forms demonstrate the continued cross-fertilization among both themselves and with other musics.

These genres had their immediate origins in the postemancipation period and the desire of free and emancipated blacks to substantiate their apparent gains. For untold numbers of former slaves especially, the ability to move from place to place signified freedom. Over time that commitment to migration in search of freedom would transform the African-American landscape, and, in turn, African-American music. In the late nineteenth century, African Americans were overwhelmingly southern and rural. By 1970 they lived mostly in cities outside the South. Similarly, African-American music has gone from pockets of local, regional, and national notoriety in the late nineteenth century to dominance of the world music market in the late twentieth. While African Americans themselves have not always benefited fully from the commercial success of their music, its staying power resides in the fundamental humanism of African-American music: its ability to speak to basic human goals and desires; its willingness to grapple with the complexity of the human condition.

Nowhere is this clearer than in the blues. The origins of the blues date back to the turn of the century and demonstrate the increasing personalization of musical expression, on one hand, and the increasing emphasis on solo artistry, on the other. This growth of the individual voice personifies the postemancipation quest to arrive at a more satisfactory representation of African-American identity and, ultimately, an insightful African-American perspective on the modern existential condition. The blues has most effectively turned inward and explored the complexities of lived experience. Dedicated to a thoroughgoing examination of the thin line between such dichotomies as joy and pain, love and hate, lust and affection, triumph and failure, the blues scrupulously dissects human psychology and emotions. Issues of pleasure and desire animate the music. Sadness is simply one emotion within the wide-ranging emotional palette of the blues, which is ultimately a celebration of the human spirit.

Like the spirituals, the blues is a music of hope and affirmation building upon diverse African-dominated roots. The secular roots of the blues are traceable to minstrel, vaudeville, and ragtime tunes as well as ballads and work music. Religious roots include the spirituals themselves, hymns, and early gospel music. Often characterized as the "devil's music" by those who objected to its unabashed celebration of the pleasures and desires of the flesh, the blues nonetheless prospered in large part because of this sensual and sexual fixation. At the same time, the blues profited enormously from cross-pollination with sacred music. This intense exploration of not just the profound similarities between the sacred and the secular but also the inherent ties between them has been reinforced in African-American music in the course of the twentieth century, and the blues have become a bedrock genre upon which subsequent African-American music, like gospel and soul, has drawn.

The universal appeal of the blues, however, resides primarily in its ability to render the complicated human condition both meaningful and understandable. The form of the blues is the deceptively simple "three-cornered" stanza, with the second line a repetition of the first. Within this uncomplicated structure, the range of vocal and instrumental variations has been impressive. Vocally, the blues has relied heavily upon its folk roots. A favorite blues approach has been the re-creation of emotion through the use of falling pitches. Voices ranging from the smooth to the rough have employed an impressive number of vocal gestures including cries, bends, moans, dips, grunts, and the use of falsetto and vibrato for effect. Instrumentally, blues musicians often accompanied themselves with guitars, banjos, pianos, and harmonicas. As blues musicians have grown in vocal and instrumental dexterity, so too have blues performances. Indeed the emphasis on skilled musical performance, an ability to "bring the house down," has contributed mightily to the influence of all African-American music.

Roughly speaking, there are three widely recognized blues styles: down-home (country); classic women's blues of the 1920s, '30s (and beyond); and urban blues. Needless to say, these divisions often function better as categorical devices instead of analytic ones. While down-home blues styles incubated throughout the early twentieth-century South, the most influential developed in the Mississippi Delta. The most important of these Delta bluesmen was the elusive Robert Johnson, who died violently in 1938 at the age of 28. His slender recorded output belies his enormous impact. Provocative songs like his "Sweet Home Chicago" and "Hellhound on my Trail" attest to a restless, rootless spirit seeking but never quite discovering fulfillment. In addition to a fundamental grittiness and lyrical bite, his music featured a strong delivery, quick bottleneck runs on the guitar, and finely wrought yet earthy vocals.

Ma Rainey, the Mother of the Blues, and Bessie Smith, the Empress of the Blues, exemplified a dazzling blues tradition, which achieved considerable commercial success in the '20s and '30s. In various forms this tradition has tremendously enlivened the whole of African-American music as well as the music of black women vocalists. The huge 1920 hit recording of Mamie Smith's "Crazy Blues" contributed to a two-pronged craze for the music of blues women and blues music in general. While Ma Rainey's work went in a folk direction, that of Bessie Smith was more influenced by jazz. Nevertheless both singers had powerhouse voices, vigorous deliveries, and commanding performance styles. These blues divas worked in a grand tradition of such earlier pioneers as Victoria Spivey, Sippie Wallace, and Memphis Minnie.

BOX 5.1.4

Blues Music

In its origin, modern blues music is the expression of the emotional life of a race. In the south of long ago, whenever a new man appeared for work in any of the laborers' gangs, he would be asked if he could sing. If he could, he got the job. The singing of these working men set the rhythm for work, the pounding of hammers, the swinging of scythes; and the one who sang most lustily soon became strawboss. One man set the tune, and sang whatever sentiments lay closest to his heart. He would sing about steamboats, fast trains, "contrairy" mules, cruel overseers. If he had no home, he sang about that; if he found a home next day, he sang about needing money or being lonesome for his gal. But whatever he sang was personal, and then the others in the gang took up the melody, each fitting it with personal words of his own. If fifty men worked on the gang, the song had fifty verses, and the singing lasted all day through, easing the work, driving rhythm into it. By word of mouth, the songs of these humble, untrained musicians traveled from place to place, wherever the roving workers went, exactly as folksongs always have traveled, all over the world, as expressions of national soul life.

Source: W. C. Handy, "The Heart of the Blues," Etude Music Magazine (March 1940), p. 152.

The music of black blueswomen has been an important creative outlet for a compelling expression of black women's concerns and perspectives. At its finest, this music has been about the intricacies and insights of "truth talking." In the post-World War II period, this tradition has spilled over with wonderful effect into other genres and been influenced by them in turn. The 1950s rhythm-and-blues explosion witnessed the revitalization of this tradition with the work of such artists as Big Mama Thornton, Ruth Brown, and LaVern Baker. Soul music divas Etta James, Nina Simone, and Aretha Franklin likewise revivified the blueswoman tradition, joining it with gospel roots. More recently, not to be neglected is the work of those like dynamic Chicago blueswoman KoKo Taylor. For several decades now, she has presented authentic urban blues from a black woman's point of view.

Black bluesmen likewise had a profound impact on black popular music. They, too, spoke with authority and insight about life from an experiential perspective. Pushed by southern poverty and Jim Crow and pulled by the lure of better jobs and opportunities, especially during World Wars I and II, the migration of huge numbers of blacks to large northern cities, especially Chicago, deeply affected black popular music. Rural blues adapted to urban rhythms and sensibilities, and the music increasingly spoke to the black urban experience. The music of Mississippi Delta bluesmen Muddy Waters, Howling Wolf, and John Lee Hooker vividly captures the post-World War II urbanization of the country blues. This was perhaps best represented not just in the growth of rhythm-and-blues offshoots but also in the revitalizing urban energy represented by the growing use of amplified instruments among blues musicians. The stunning electric guitar work of 1940s blues legend T-Bone Walker captivated audiences and influenced the likes of B. B. King, who continues to personify the extremely influential tradition of electric guitar-based blues.

If blues can be seen as "secular spirituals," then gospel can be seen as "spiritual blues." A performance-based music like blues, gospel also seeks an incandescent emotional peak. Gospel, however, relies far more heavily upon the traditional group-based ethos so central to the collective and spontaneous African-American music-making style. The antiphonal cross-currents, therefore, are far stronger, as these encompass call-and-response among musicians—singers and instrumentalists—as well as the musicians and the audience. Gospel arose as a turn-of-the-century response to one of freedom's dilemmas, evidence of the decline in group spiritual life, especially since emancipation. To recapture that fervent emotionalism of yesteryear, gospel updated the spirituals and the stock of traditional religious music with an injection of ardent evangelism.

Gospel developed its strongest roots initially in the fundamentalist churches. As southern rural blacks came increasingly to cities, gospel took on an urban gloss. Unwritten texts gave way to written texts; the holy fire had to accommodate over time to the more tempered conventions of Black Baptist and Methodist congregations. Critical to the growing popularity of gospel were the efforts of composers like Charles A. Tindley, who early in this century wrote down many gospel songs. Similarly, in the 1930s, the efforts of Thomas A. Dorsey—clearly a father of modern gospel—along with those of gospel singers like Sallie Martin and the incomparable Mahalia Jackson were crucial to the growing popularity of the music. They traveled the country bringing the gospel music news and made innumerable converts, at times even winning over those who saw in the sacred music too much influence of the blues and jazz.

In fact, the increasingly popular "gospel blues" style of Dorsey and his growing legion of supporters provided potent doses of secular musical styles, particularly rhythms, beats, and song structures. For much of the 1920s Dorsey had been a blues pianist and composer of considerable achievement, having worked with Ma Rainey and Tampa Red. As with other forms of African-American music, this cross-fertilization of gospel with blues influences immeasurably enhanced its power and appeal. Furthermore, this blurring of the sacred/secular music border reveals a persistent tension within African-American music between "traditionalists" favoring a tighter boundary and "progressives" favoring a more permeable one. Especially since the 1960s, African-American secular music styles, like soul, have benefited tremendously from the creative borrowing of rhythm and blues from gospel, while gospel progressives have continually revivified their music through creative borrowings from secular genres, like soul.

The desired effect of a gospel performance remains to work the audience into a charged state as a way to strengthen religious commitment, or better still, to bring souls to religion. This tradition persists and illustrates the dramatic intensity of an incandescent musical/ritual experience. The best groups and soloists compete to outshine the others in their "church wrecking" ability. The idea is to make the performers and audience one in the service of God. The music is a critical element of a multilevel process including preaching, praying, testifying, and a broad range of physical responses from foot stomping and moaning to shouting and speaking in tongues. The vocal and instrumental music build up to a spiritual peak, sustain it, and then gear it up to higher levels until the spirit has been satisfied. The experience can be overpowering.

Singing preachers, notably those who specialize in the "performed" sermon, are especially effective at propelling this ritual forward. Reverend C. L. Franklin, Aretha's father, was a master. The singing itself is often awesome in its intensity. The vocal repertoire is vast: runs across octaves, note bending, playing with notes and words/phrases, effortlessly taking syllables/words over several notes (melisma), shouts, grunts, whispers, moans, cries, lyrical flourishes and full-throated ones. For maximum effect, highly dramatic vignettes, often employing gripping narratives such as the crucifixion and resurrection of Christ, accompany the singing. This spiritual ecstasy has clear analogues in the kind of secular ecstasy to which the best blues performance aspires. Therein lies a crucial element of the transgressive power and universal appeal of African-American music: its creative blurring of the secular/sacred border.

The Birth of Jazz

Jazz owes much of its popular appeal to its fruitful working of this same sacred/secular terrain. A most powerful modern urban musical response to the challenges of freedom, principally in cosmopolitan cities like New Orleans, jazz evolved out of an African-American amalgam of various influences. The roots of this exceedingly hybrid musical form include brass band music, syncopated dance music, dance orchestra music, blues, minstrel/vaudeville tunes, ragtime, and sacred music. The key to jazz is its emphasis on improvisation. In an important sense, this music epitomizes the performance basis of African-American music. Through improvisation, jazz endeavors to re-create itself not merely with each formal/musicological advance of the music but also with each performance as well. This is indeed a most difficult challenge.

The major innovator of early-twentieth-century jazz was trumpeter Louis Armstrong, who emerged from his early days in New Orleans and Chicago to revolutionize American music. Two of his signal contributions were his technical brilliance and his development of a stunningly distinctive style as a soloist, especially in the context of group performance. Armstrong of course had influences, notably trumpeters Buddy Bolden, Bunk

Johnson, and King Oliver. What set Armstrong apart, however, was his astonishing and individualized sound. Particularly striking were his tonal range, his octave-leaping runs, his ability to reinvent a melody, his sure-handed rhythmic sense, his feel for the blues, and his ability to swing. These are all basic to the jazz vocabulary. In addition, Armstrong's assertion of a pathbreaking musical voice—like that of blueswomen Ma Rainey and Bessie Smith—epitomized the "New Negro" of the twenties Harlem Renaissance. Although barely glimpsed at the time, Armstrong's signature voice personified that audacious cultural quest for a new, vibrant, and uniquely African-American artistic identity far more vividly than the vast majority of the literary and visual artists most often associated with the movement. In addition, Armstrong was a first-rate entertainer, and from the 1930s until his death in 1971, he was also a major American celebrity. In his most influential music from the late twenties and early thirties, his melodic and rhythmic innovations heralded a fusion of passion and technique in the service of improvisation. From that point on, jazz has never been the same.

As Armstrong expanded the frontier of solo jazz performance, Edward Kennedy "Duke" Ellington challenged the dimensions of jazz orchestra and jazz composition. Building upon the innovations of contemporaries like pianist-composer Jelly Roll Morton and band leaders Fletcher Henderson and Don Redman, by the early 1930s Ellington had created an exceptional band with a remarkable repertoire. His many achievements included successfully resolving the problems of balancing the often-competing demands of improvisation and composition. Likewise, through a rigorous understanding of his band's group strengths as well as its outstanding solo voices, he fashioned music blending these ensemble and individual talents. The music of Ellington is often lauded for its wide-ranging scope, textures, colors, and beauty. Another aspect of his music's greatness is its successful merger of often quite different forms, notably elite and vernacular styles. An excellent pianist, Ellington was also an extraordinary bandleader and an even more impressive composer, with more than fifteen hundred works to his credit. These include film scores, operas, extended concert works, as well as the popular tunes like "Sophisticated Lady" for which he is so well known.

A music born of innovation, jazz continued to evolve. Armstrong and Ellington pushed the music forward, as did other popularizers like white bandleaders Paul Whiteman and Benny Goodman. In fact, the 1930s swing music craze fed the growth of many first-rate black territory bands, most notably Count Basie's hard-driving group out of Kansas City, which went on to international acclaim. Swing offered Depression America a pleasurable respite amidst the gloom. African-American music since the 1940s has been deeply influenced by the growing political assertiveness of the black liberation insurgency. This expanding commitment to both black self-definition and black consciousness found resonance among exemplars of bebop and free jazz and has continued to influence jazz developments. With the decline of swing and swing bands in the forties, bebop reignited the music with its renewed emphasis on improvisational acuity, harmonic and melodic inventiveness, and the ability to play brilliantly at breakneck speed. While the work of many—including trumpeter "Dizzy" Gillespie, pianist "Bud" Powell, and drummers Kenny Clarke and Max Roach—contributed to the music's evolution, the awe-inspiring work of alto saxophonist Charlie Parker exemplified the challenging world of bebop. Not only did he play music of uncommon mastery and beauty but also Parker lived on the edge. Consequently he influenced countless musicians and artists who admired his risk-taking iconoclasm.

BOX 5.1.5

Drummer Max Roach on the 1940s Scene

When you get down to the music, there was a period when the music moved from uptown to downtown, and they had no name for it. ... Nobody considered the music as "bop" until it moved downtown. So to derogate the music and make it look like it was one of them things, they started hanging labels on the music. For example, don't give me all that 'jazz,' or that's 'bop' talk, this thing or the other. We argue these points because words mean quite a bit to all of us. What we name our things and what we call our contributions should be up to us so that we can control our own destiny.

Source: Quoted in John Birks "Dizzy" Gillespie and A1 Fraser, To Be or Not to Bop (Garden City, N.J.: Doubleday, Inc., 1979), p. 209.

Likewise, the development of free jazz involved innovators of the first order. Of particular note is the highly influential work of saxophonists John Coltrane and Ornette Coleman. Their best work exemplifies the quest for full improvisational freedom within the context of collective music making that is the hallmark of free jazz. Coltrane's mesmerizing and dense aural explorations made him immensely popular, especially among those engaged in issues of black cultural aesthetics. That over time his playing took on probing spiritual qualities, reminiscent of the emotional intensity of gospel music at its peak, only added to his aura. Coleman's pathbreaking work beautifully resolves the problems of playing freely yet coherently outside the received strictures of chord changes, rhythms, and harmony. Like the innovations of Ellington and other great jazz composers operating more squarely within traditional limits, however, Coleman's have inspired those seeking to play jazz seamlessly as solo and ensemble, on the one hand, and composition and innovation, on the other.

Black women in jazz have achieved their greatest acclaim as vocalists. Indeed the tradition of jazz vocals has spawned a stellar array of talents. As within other musical genres, jazz vocalists apply their masterful touch to songs from various genres, including pop and blues. Interpretive ability, emotional depth, and stylistic uniqueness set the best apart. From the gripping poignancy of Billie Holiday to the awe-inspiring technical aplomb of Sarah Vaughn, this music has immeasurably enriched American culture. Equally important, black women vocalists whose work operated within and across various genres—such as Dinah Washington, who could apparently sing anything well—carved out a vital creative niche for others like them. An important consequence of these developments has been the growing demand that jazz and jazz musicians be accorded the respect and accolades at home that they receive abroad. In the 1990s jazz's growing popularity as well as its increasing recognition by major national cultural institutions, like the Smithsonian and America's principal concert halls, appear to augur well for the music's future.

BOX 5.1.6

Jazz in the 1960s

Bebop is roots, now, just as much as blues is. "Classical" music is not. But "classical" music, and I mean now contemporary Euro-American "art" music, might seem to the black man isolated, trying to exist within white culture (arty or whatever), like it should be "milked" for as many *definitions* as possible, i.e., *solutions* to engineering problems the contemporary jazz musician's life is sure to raise. I mean, more simply, Ornette Coleman has had to live with the attitudes responsible for Anton Webern's music whether he knows that music or not. They were handed to him along with the whole history of formal Western music, and the musics that have come to characterize the Negro in the United States came to exist as they do today only through the acculturation of this entire history. And actually knowing that history, and trying to relate to it culturally, or those formal Euro-American musics, only adds to the *indoctrination*. But jazz and blues *are* Western musics; products of all Afro-American culture. But the definitions must be black no matter the geography for the highest meaning to black men. And in this sense European anything is irrelevant.

Source: Imamu Amiri Baraka, Black Music (New York, 1967), p. 70.

Conclusion

In the 1950s, popular black music became known as rhythm and blues, an increasingly urban, rhythmically dense, hybrid blues-driven music. The concurrent development of rock and roll greatly increased the exposure, appreciation, and acceptance of African-American music. Even more important for the growing recognition and popularity of

African-American music was the pervasive impact of the Civil Rights and Black Power movements. The ever-increasing visibility of African Americans and the growing white acceptance of the legitimacy of African-American claims for both full-fledged citizenship and full participation in the American dream spilled over into enhanced appreciation for African-American history and culture. Within this context, '60s soul music—evident in the work of Sam Cooke, Ray Charles, Etta James, Aretha Franklin, and James Brown, to name just a few—married the secular power of the blues to the sacred intensity of a gospel style and found enormous popularity.

In the late twentieth century, two tendencies propel the continuing growth and vitality of African-American music. First, as evident in the work of influential jazz trumpeter Wynton Marsalis, the African-American musical tradition is sufficiently rich and complex to sustain both contemporary revisions as well as repertorial interpretations. Second, the richness and complexity of this diverse tradition reveals a powerful dynamism. More recently, there has been effective borrowing from Brazilian, Caribbean, East Asian, European, and African influences. In effect, the ongoing processes of revision and renewal constitute fertile ground that spawns exciting and significant new forms. The most arresting and influential development of the last two decades has to be rap music, itself a diverse and changing music. As a union of various African-American oral traditions with the latest music-making technology, rap has revitalized earlier black music, especially the soul and funk innovations of artists like James Brown, through its ability to sample virtually unlimited bits and pieces of other work. Similarly, through its emphasis on powerfully spoken/chanted lyrics, it revitalizes black traditions of verbal virtuosity such as boasting, signifying, and storytelling. Also important is its telling commentary on late-twentieth-century America, especially the state of America's black inner cities. The extraordinary popularity of rap music, not only in the black community but among a wide variety of listeners, speaks to the enduring influence of African-American music on mainstream culture.

For Further Reading

Baraka, Imamu Amiri [Leroi Jones]. *Blues People: Negro Music in White America*. New York: William Morrow & Company, 1983.

Barlow, William. *Looking Up at Down: The Emergence of Blues Culture*. Philadelphia: Temple University Press, 1989.

Chernoff, John M. *African Rhythm and African Sensibility*. Chicago: University of Chicago Press, 1981.

Cone, James H. *The Spirituals and the Blues: An Interpretation*. Maryknoll, N.Y.: Orbis Books, 1992.

Epstein, Dena J. *Sinful Tunes and Spirituals: Black Folk Music to the Civil War.* Urbana: University of Illinois Press, 1977.

Ferris, William R. *Blues from the Delta.* New York: Da Capo Press, 1988.

Giddins, Gary. *Visions of Jazz: The First Century.* New York: Oxford University Press, 1998.

Gioia, Ted. *The History of Jazz.* New York: Oxford University Press, 1997.

Guralnick, Peter. *Sweet Soul Music: Rhythm and Blues and the Southern Dream of Freedom.* New York: Harper & Row, 1986.

Hennessey, Thomas J. *From Jazz to Swing: African-American Jazz Musicians and Their Music, 1890–1935.* Detroit, Mich.: Wayne State University Press, 1994.

Hirshey, Gerri. *Nowhere to Run: The Story of Soul Music.* New York: Penguin Books, 1985.

Keil, Charles. *Urban Blues.* Chicago: University of Chicago Press, 1992.

Levine, Lawrence W. *Black Culture and Black Consciousness: Afro-American Folk Thought from Slavery to Freedom.* New York: Oxford University Press, 1978.

Litweiler, John. *The Freedom Principle: Jazz after 1958.* New York: Da Capo Press, 1990.

Murray, Albert. *Stomping the Blues.* New York: Da Capo Press, 1989.

Oliver, Paul. *Blues Fell This Morning: Meaning in the Blues.* New York: Cambridge University Press, 1990.

Palmer, Robert. *Deep Blues.* New York: Viking Press, 1995.

Rose, Tricia. *Black Noise: Rap Music and Black Culture in Contemporary America.* Hanover, N.H.: University Press of New England, 1994.

Schuller, Gunther. *Early Jazz: Its Roots and Musical Development.* New York: Oxford University Press, 1986.

———. *Swing Era: The Development of Jazz, 1930–1945.* New York: Oxford University Press, 1991.

Small, Christopher. *Music of the Common Tongue: Survival and Celebration in Afro-American Music.* New York: Riverrun Press, 1994

Southern, Eileen. *The Music of Black Americans: A History.* 3rd ed. New York: W. W. Norton & Company, 1997.

Spencer, Jon Michael. *Protest and Praise: Sacred Music of Black Religion.* Minneapolis: Fortress Press, 1997.

Stearns, Marshall W. *The Story of Jazz.* New York: Oxford University Press, 1985.

Stuckey, Sterling. *Slave Culture: Nationalist Theory and the Foundations of Black America.* New York: Oxford University Press, 1988.

Ward, Brian. *Just My Soul Responding: Rhythm and Blues, Black Consciousness, and Race Relations.* Berkeley and Los Angeles: University of California Press, 1998.

Reading 5.2

Black Voices
Themes in African-American Literature

Gerald Early

I N ONE OF THE ESSAYS IN his 1957 book, *White Man, Listen!*, Richard Wright claims, "The Negro is America's metaphor." By this he meant not only that blacks were the symbolic embodiment of the history of America, an outcast people trying to find a new identity in the New World, but also that they were, through the circumstances of being forced to live in a country "whose laws, customs, and instruments of force were leveled against them," constant reminders of the anguish of being without an identity, constant reminders of human alienation. According to Ralph Ellison, Wright's good friend back in the 1930s, "The white American has charged the Negro American with being without a past or tradition (something which strikes the white man with a nameless horror), just as he himself has been so charged by European and American critics with a nostalgia for the stability once typical of European cultures."

But Wright saw in the African-American's quest for an identity, in his struggle against human alienation, against being a symbol of the abyss of estrangement, a deep political and philosophical resonance that, in fact, gave America both an aesthetic—blues music—and crucial forms of social engagement that blacks, and the political culture of the United States itself, used as forms of dissent against the idea of human alienation: first, abolition, then, Reconstruction, and, finally, the Civil Rights movement. "Is it not clear to you that the American Negro is the only group in our nation that consistently and passionately raises the question of freedom?" asks Wright. "This is a service to America and to the world. More than this: The voice of the American Negro is rapidly becoming the most representative voice of America and of oppressed people anywhere in the world today." In effect, Wright is suggesting that black Americans, within the framework of their isolation, had managed to create community and common cause with other victimized peoples in the world (particularly the "colored" world). Wright suggests that black Americans were to construct a penetrating view of the general human condition through the prism of their own localized experience.

Because the quests for a usable community and for identity have shaped black experience itself in America, Wright argues his essay, these quests ultimately inform all of African-American literature.

A Question of Identity: From Phillis Wheatley to Richard Wright

When one thinks of poet Phillis Wheatley (1753?–1784), the earliest black writer in America to produce an estimable body of work, this observation certainly seems true, not simply about black people generally but about the black writer especially. Wheatley, born in Senegal and brought to America at the age of eight, had to learn both a new language and a new religion, indeed, an entirely new way of life, the same cultural disruption and brutally imposed cognitive dissonance that other Africans experienced as well, except that in some manner, as a child, the adaptation had to be, paradoxically, both easier and harder. Yet she so completely absorbed aspects of her new culture that she was able to write poetry in the leading literary style of the day by the time she was a teenager. Naturally, because of her age, some of her poetry exhibits facility but lacks depth. But the question of identity, while muted in most of her work, still appears here and there, and one must suppose that she thought a great deal about her precarious fate as a favored slave and about the nature of the black community that she was not fully a part of for a good portion of her life in America and which was powerless to support her as a writer. In any case, she never forgot that she was an African. It was hardly likely that she forgot that passage or the circumstances that brought her over to the New World. She wrote in the poem, "To the Right Honorable William Early of Dartmouth, His Majesty's Principal Secretary of State for North America, Etc.":

> Should you, my lord, while you pursue my song,
> Wonder from whence my love of Freedom sprung,
> Whence flow these wishes for the common good,
> By feeling hearts alone best understood,
> I, young in life, by seeming cruel fate
> Was snatch'd from Afric's fancy'd happy seat:
> What pangs excruciating must molest,
> What sorrows labour in my parent's breast?

Steel'd was the soul and by no misery mov'd
That from a father seiz'd his babe belov'd
Such, such my case. And can I then but pray
Others may never feel tyrannic sway?

In these lines, there is not only a sense of being taken away from the life and culture and from parents who felt concern and cared for their child (concerns seldom attributed to Africans by whites at the time) but also a sense of thwarted justice born from having endured the experience of a disrupted community. Wheatley, who died poverty-stricken, abandoned by both the black and white communities, in some ways both voiced and personified the themes of identity and community that were to be fully developed and elaborated upon by later black writers.

"The radical solitude of human life," wrote José Ortega y Gasset in his 1957 philosophical treatise, *Man and People*, "the being of man, does not, then, consist in there really being nothing except himself. Quite the contrary—there is nothing less than the universe, with all that it contains. There is, then, an infinity of things but—there it is!—amid them Man in his radical reality is alone—alone *with* them." Somehow, this seems to capture Wheatley herself, mastering foreign cultural tools for a self-expression that was never quite her own, a sly and complicated ventriloquism that was both the triumph and the tragedy of her assimilation. By redefining her theft from Africa as a providential plot for placing her in a more transcendent community, she might ultimately find closure for her predicament. Thus, she writes, in "On Being Brought From Africa to America":

Twas mercy brought me from my Pagan land,
Taught my benighted soul to understand
That there's a God, that there's a Saviour too:
Once I redemption neither sought nor knew.
Some view our sable race with scornful eye,
"Their colour is a diabolic die."
Remember, Christians, Negroes, black as Cain,
May be refin'd, and join th' angelic train.

In eighteenth-century New England, with the rise of liberalism, Calvinism was forced to retreat before a more humanitarian worldview, before the view that, despite their condition, babies, "idiots," blacks, and others "naturally perverse in their will toward sin" ought not be consigned to hell. This view obviously affected Wheatley in two ways: first, as a product of the new liberalism where her poetry would be appreciated and encouraged as a sign of God's deliverance of the benighted; and second, as a believer in the new liberalism as a way to explain her fate and the form of cultural assimilation that she was experiencing. More important, the idea that blacks could be or had to be, in one way or another, "refin'd" or uplifted as a cure for their alienation or degradation, has been a constant in African-American thought, from the earliest writings in English to the ideas of nationalists like Marcus Garvey (whose organization was called the Universal Negro *Improvement* Association) and Malcolm X. Perhaps one way in which Richard Wright was truly pathbreaking was in his reluctance to think in those terms.

Struck deeply by the alienation described by Ortega y Gasset, Wright was one of the major African-American writers of the twentieth century, a figure so monumental that the era from the late Depression when Wright began publishing through 1960, the year of his death, is often referred to as his epoch. Wright was heavily influenced by Marxism, a philosophy he learned during his days as a Communist writer and editor in Chicago and New York in the early and mid-'30s, and by existentialism, a philosophy he felt intuitively from his youth when it provided a substitute for the Christianity that he abhorred. Wright read deeply about existentialism after World War II, existentialism's heyday. In his major works before his self-imposed exile from America after the Second World War, it was not that Wright introduced new themes to African-American writing. Instead, he concentrated, as had others before him, on the quests for identity and for usable community. However, partly because Wright was born and reared, for the most part, in Mississippi, the most backward and brutal state in the Union on the matter of race, no black writer before him achieved either Wright's visceral intensity in describing black-white relations or displayed as deep a passion for seeking broad philosophical implications in black American life. And no black writer before him saw black life in such stark, often cosmically lonely terms. Finally, no black writer until Wright had become as famous, as accepted in this country, and particularly abroad, as a genuine man of letters and a writer of unquestioned stature.

The works for which Wright became known—*Uncle Tom's Children* (1937), a collection of novellas set in the South, *Native Son* (1940), his grand urban novel of crime and punishment set in Chicago, and *Black Boy* (1945), his autobiographical exploration of black adolescence in the American South—emphasize a deep sense of estrangement in characters unable to connect with a larger aggregate of humanity, characters trying heroically to establish their identities but confounded by incredible forces that manipulate and annihilate their sense of place and belonging, by forces that transform anxiety into impotent rage and turn fear into inexhaustible dread. The stories in *Uncle Tom's Children,* all about black rebellion against the violent white power structure, move from heroes who are unconscious of any political significance in their acts, largely buffeted by the tides and whimsies of a cruel, indifferent world, trying desperately to extricate themselves from a seemingly inescapable fate, to more politically aware heroes (the heroine of the last story is a Marxist as well as a deep believer in black solidarity) whose revolts are self-consciously motivated. But even in the most restricted circumstances, Wright gives his black characters choices. Wright was never to abandon his Marxist/existentialist belief that man makes his world, makes his circumstances, and makes his fate.

In *Native Son*, considered by most critics Wright's masterpiece, the reader is given the most vehement critique against the idea of welfare-state liberalism ever written by a black to this time. In this ideologically driven novel, Wright presents welfare-state liberalism, which for the rich, white Dalton family of the novel, represents a mere mask for exploitative power and for maintaining the status quo of keeping black families like that of Wright's protagonist, Bigger Thomas, poor and huddled in ghettos. Digger's psychotic attempt at liberation is doomed to failure because he has accepted the terms of blackness that white society has imposed upon him. In other words, he has sought his humanity by becoming the very inhuman thing that white society said he was and, in effect, made him. In *Black Boy*, by looking in an exaggerated and not entirely factual way at his family and rearing in the South, Wright explores exclusively the idea of what black community means. It was in this book that Wright made one of his striking, and, for some, disturbing, statements about the meaning of black community:

> After I had outlived the shocks of childhood, after the habit of reflection had been born in me, I used to mull over the strange absence of real kindness in Negroes, how unstable was our tenderness, how lacking in genuine passion we were, how void of great hope, how timid our joy, how bare our traditions, how hollow our memories, how lacking we were in those intangible sentiments that bind man to man, and how shallow was even our despair. After I had learned other ways of life I used to brood upon the unconscious irony of those who felt that Negroes led so passional an existence! I saw that what had been taken for our emotional strength was our negative confusions, our flights, our fears, our frenzy under pressure.
>
> Whenever I thought of the essential bleakness of black life in America, I knew that Negroes had never been allowed to catch the full spirit of Western civilization, that they lived somehow in it but not of it. And when I brooded upon the cultural barrenness of black life, I wondered if clean, positive tenderness, love, honor, loyalty, and the capacity to remember were native with man. I asked myself if these human qualities were not fostered, won, struggled and suffered for, preserved in ritual from one generation to another.

Wright had two aims in writing this passage: first, despite his own love of sociology, he wanted to lift the level of discourse about the black condition from mere sociology to something philosophical, to something which spoke of the problem of human community. Second, hoping to reverse, harshly and shockingly, a tendency he disliked in earlier black writing, particularly in some of the writing of the Harlem Renaissance, he wanted to de-romanticize and deexoticize black life.

The Foundation of an African-American Literary Tradition

To understand fully how an author like Wright shaped his work, it is necessary to go back to the slave narrative, the earliest form of black American writing that formed a coherent body of work, that expressed a plain ideological task and purpose and set forth the themes of identity and community that were to characterize all the black writing that came after. While poet Phillis Wheatley's work exhibited these themes, almost as a subtext, the antebellum slave narratives sharpened and strengthened these concerns by making the black writer a presence in American life and letters.

One of the antecedents of the antebellum slave narrative was the Indian captivity narrative of the eighteenth century, usually a tale about a white captured and forced to live for some period of time among Indians. Other captivity narratives tell of persons surprisingly impressed in the navy or unfairly or unfortunately seized by the nation's enemy. The earliest black narratives such as *A Narrative of the Uncommon Sufferings and Surprizing Deliverance of Briton Hammon, a Negro Man,* published in 1760, and *A Narrative of the Life of John Marrant of New York, in North America: With An Account of the Conversion of the King of the Cherokees and his Daughter,* published in 1785, were precisely in the captivity narrative mode. Indeed, slavery was scarcely the subject of them in any sort of political way. Built on the captivity narrative model, *The Interesting Narrative of the Life of Olaudah Equiano or Gustavus Vassa, the African* (1791), was the first true slave narrative in that it was a self-conscious and explicit protest against slavery. It was the first self-conscious black or African political literature in English in the Western world.

Although there were important black publications of a political or polemical sort published earlier, works such as *A Narrative of the Black People during the Late Awful Calamity in Philadelphia* (1794) by Richard Allen and Absalom Jones, and *David Walker's Appeal in Four Articles; Together with A Preamble, To the Coloured Citizens of the World, but in Particular, and Very Expressly, To Those of the United States of America* (1829), the full development and enrichment of black literature occurred in the antebellum period of 1830 to 1860. From small tracts and pamphlets to major, polished autobiographies, literally hundreds of slave narratives were published. Sponsored largely by white abolitionist societies in the North, where antislavery had become a major political and social movement in the United States, much of this writing suffered from the same problems as early European-American literature, an imitative or dull style and an overwrought Christian piety. Moreover, because they were unable to appear before the public as guarantors of their own stories, without the aid of a vouching white editor or friend, black authors were at a severe disadvantage. Finally, there was the problem of audience—whom did the slave narrator wish to address and why? Obviously, the slave narrator desired to move white readers to act against slavery. This meant that the literature had to present the black narrator as palatable to whites who were, almost exclusively, committed to white supremacist ideals. But the black narrator, and all black writers since this period, also felt the pressure of being representative of his race and wanted to cast no undue aspersions upon it. That is to say, the slave narratives were meant both to be a protest, crossover literature for whites (to help them understand the true nature of slavery or, one might say, the black American experience) and, in some sense, a "race" literature addressing the needs of black self-esteem and racial community.

The idea or ideal of black community during antebellum America was a difficult one to maintain. First, the black community was a complex set of structures: there were various divisions within slavery, fieldhands versus house servants, artisans versus the unskilled, light-skinned versus dark-skinned, more recent African arrivals versus third-, fourth-, or fifth-generation "detainees." In addition there were the free black communities of both the North and South. Because it was the free blacks who could effectively or at least more visibly agitate for freedom, these free communities, although small, were essential to the much larger slave communities. But the free community was a complex mixture, exhibited many of the same elements that made up the slave communities, and, like the slave communities, was largely at the mercy of the whites who surrounded it. Without a centralized church, any school system worth the name, or any of the normal civic privileges that the average white citizens enjoyed, it was difficult for the free black communities to act as a vanguard for the slave communities.

Second, blacks in antebellum America were experiencing a complex form of cultural syncretism. It must be remembered that a number of ethnically diverse Africans were brought to the New World during the Atlantic slave trade so two simultaneous processes were taking place in the creation of black community. First, the Europeans worked assiduously to remove as many cultural props—language, religion, kinship rituals, rites of passage—that they could to make the Africans a less volatile, less warlike labor presence (which is why, in the end, the African was preferred to the Indian as a slave). Black community was always meant to be, in the eyes of whites, dependent, precarious, impoverished, an area or configuration to be policed and contained. Second, the Africans came to meld or distill the strands of cultural expressions that they were able to maintain to forge a new identity. So, true black community—independent, stabilized, and prosperous—was to become a subversive concept.

The most famous of the slave narratives were Frederick Douglass's 1845 *Narrative of the Life of Frederick Douglass, An American Slave* and his 1855 *My Bondage and My Freedom*, Harriet Jacobs's *Incidents in the Life of a Slave Girl*, published in 1861, *The Narrative of William Wells Brown*, published in 1846, *Running a Thousand Miles for Freedom* by William and Ellen Craft, published in 1860, *The Narrative of Henry Box Brown Who Escaped from*

Slavery in a Box Three Feet Long and Two Feet Wide; Written from a Statement of Facts by Himself, published in 1849, *Life of Josiah Henson, formerly a Slave, Now an Inhabitant of Canada, Narrated by Himself,* published in 1849, and *Twelve Years a Slave: the Narrative of Solomon Northup, a Citizen of New York, Kidnapped in Washington City in 1841, and Rescued in 1853, from a Cotton Plantation Near Red River in Louisiana,* published in 1853. All of these works tried in various ways to create a sense of black community in the narratives by talking not only of the slave narrator's sense of connection to his or her own family (family piety was virtually a cliché in this works) but to the larger community of slaves, who often assisted the narrator in his escape. Moreover, the books tried to create a sense of connection through their texts between blacks in the North and South, slave and free. Of these, the works by Douglass, William Wells Brown, and Jacobs are considered by literary critics and African-American literary experts today to have the most value.

Indeed, Douglass and Brown, both escaped slaves who became veteran speakers on the abolition circuit, were true men of letters. Douglass ran a newspaper for many years, and Brown published several other works including the earliest black novel, *Clotel or the President's Daughter,* published in 1853, and *Three Years in Europe,* the first black travel book, published in 1852. Brown was to publish several more books, including some of the earliest full-scale black histories. Other early black novels published before 1860 were Frank J. Webb's *The Garies and Their Friends,* a novel about free blacks in Philadelphia, published in 1857, Martin R. Delany's *Blake: Or, the Huts of America,* a militant, highly polemical novel about black rebellion and emigration, published in 1859, and Harriet E. Wilson's *Our Nig,* an autobiographical novel about a biracial child's indentured servitude in a cruel white household, published in 1859. Most of these novels received little attention, at least from white audiences. Unquestionably, the most significant piece of racial fiction published during this period was written by a white woman. Harriet Beecher Stowe's epochal antislavery novel, *Uncle Tom's Cabin* was published in 1852 and had an influence that extended far beyond the immediate issue of slavery. The name of the title character was to become a hated epithet among blacks, and the long shelf life of the work as popular theater ensured that a number of troubling stereotypes endured as near myths in the American imagination. Novelist James Baldwin, in declaring his literary independence nearly one hundred years later, was to damn, in particular, the burden of this novel on the work of black writers.

Toward a Black Literary Aesthetic

The slave narratives were, far and away, the most important and most developed black literature in the United States, indeed, in the Western world at that time. They were to establish two major trends in African-American literature: first, a preoccupation with autobiographical and confessional writing that remains to this day; and second, a strong tendency to bind social protest or explicit political consciousness with the aesthetic act of making literature. While the first trend has produced an extraordinarily rich vein of American writing, to Booker T. Washington's *Up From Slavery* to *The Autobiography of Malcolm X*, from Maya Angelou's *I Know Why The Caged Bird Sings* to James Weldon Johnson's *Along This Way*, from Ann Moody's *Coming of Age in Mississippi* to Langston Hughes's *The Big Sea*, the second has been far more problematical.

Black literature has been charged over the years by white critics with being nothing more than social protest, or "mere sociology," or a literature without technique, style, or innovation. It was not until the 1952 publication of Ralph Ellison's *Invisible Man*, nearly one hundred years after the publication of the first African-American novel, that a black fictional work was considered without question to be of superior literary merit, equal to the best white literature. This slow growth of recognition and of true achievement was, in some respects, inevitable. It took nearly two hundred years for white American literature to evolve from sermons and tracts to the works of Whitman, Hawthorne, Melville, and Poe. Black writers who were serious about the craft of making good literature have always been sensitive to the charge from whites of writing second-rate, race-bound works. But they have been equally sensitive to the needs of their black audience and of their group in general, understanding that African Americans would not be interested in a literature that was to given over to "mere aesthetics" or to the idea of art for art's sake, which most would think a frivolous indulgence and not a serious engagement with life and art as they saw those matters. Most black writers saw literature as something that represented their community, that was a force in the ideological and political construction of their community whether or not the literature actually depicted black community as a successfully working enterprise. One aspect of this problem is well captured in James Weldon Johnson's "The Dilemma of the Negro Author," published in the *American Mercury* in 1928 where he raised the issue of different audiences and the inability of the black author to reconcile their expectations, their needs, their perspectives. The reason for the severity of this problem stems in part from the nature of the black community itself and how, historically, it has been forced to function totally for the white community's convenience. The conflict about the purpose of African-American literature—for the question of its content and its craftsmanship comes down to the issue of function—in relation to the formation of community remains of great, even overriding, profundity for black writers and their audience as well as the larger society.

African-American Literature in the Age of Freedom

Since the Civil War, there have been three crucial periods for African-American literature where the conflict about its purpose became explicit: the New Negro or Harlem Renaissance era, the early Civil Rights era of the 1950s, and the Black Arts movement of the late 1960s. Briefly considered, these periods coincide with certain extraordinary developments within the United States itself: Prohibition, urbanization; false prosperity; a new wave of black political consciousness; a rising interest in and concern about communism during the 1920s and 1930s; the cold war; prosperity; a national policy of racial integration; a new assertiveness among blacks; the rise of youth culture in the 1950s; an intense black militancy; a nation deeply divided over the Vietnam War; a rash of political assassinations; a national policy to wipe out poverty; questions about the extent and future of prosperity; and a sharply influential counterculture on the left during the late 1960s. It is important to note two things about these three eras: each occurred during or immediately after a major American war; and in each instance, as has been the case for African Americans in their struggle in the United States since the end of Reconstruction, the major political concerns about citizenship and community are tied, often expressly so, with the meaning and function of African-American art, generally, and African-American literature, in particular.

The era of the Harlem Renaissance, starting with the black migration to the North in 1915 and ending with the rise of Richard Wright—a southern migrant—in the late 1930s, revived the issue of African-American musical theater and African-American vernacular expression, which originated in the 1890s with the famous comedy team of Williams and Walker and the coon song, on the one hand, and the dialect poetry of Paul Laurence Dunbar, on the other. Indeed, James Weldon Johnson, who was such an important presence in both areas in the 1890s, was to be a prime mover and shaker during the Renaissance. African-American musical theater became very big in the 1920s as did experimentation in vernacular poetry leading, in one direction, to the blues lyrics of the young Langston Hughes, and, in another direction, to the sermonic cadences of Johnson's *God's Trombones*.

In each case, old-fashioned, overly sentimentalized, and crudish dialect was eschewed for something more subtle, richer, closer to the actual power and expressive range of black speech. The Renaissance brought together a number of forces: a large nationalist mass movement spearheaded by Marcus Garvey that made Africa and Pan-Africanism thought about in ways that far exceeded the intensity expressed in the 1890s black nationalist movements; the two large black middle-class organizations, the National Association for the Advancement of Colored People and the Urban League; a revolutionary black music called jazz and, in phonograph records, a new technology with which to hear it; an intense historical consciousness that resulted in the formation of the Association for the Study of Negro Life and History and a number of anthologies on black culture including Alain Locke's *The New Negro*, the most storied of the age. It is no surprise, therefore, that this era saw the publication of Jean Toomer's experimental work *Cane* (1923), Claude McKay's *Home to Harlem* (1928), Countee Cullen's *Color* (1925), Langston Hughes's *The Weary Blues* (1926), Nella Larsen's *Passing* (1929), Zora

Neale Hurston's *Their Eyes Were Watching God* (1937), to name only a small number of works by authors who were to become principal names in African-American fiction and poetry. This could only have happened because the black community itself reached a certain level of strength and self-confidence.

Nonetheless, the Renaissance was considered a failure by many black writers and critics, including a number who lived through it. First, it was felt that much of the literature seemed preoccupied with middle-class concerns or with presenting blacks as exotics. This criticism was not entirely deserved, but certainly one of the burning questions of the age was "How Is the Negro to Be Depicted in Literature?" (A version of that question is still a vital concern for African Americans today.) Many white literary types thought this concern to be somewhere between philistine and infantile, but they hardly understood the sensitivity of a group that had been so viciously and persistently maligned by their culture. Second, compared to the incredible experimentation taking place in the best white literature of the day, from Hemingway to Stein, from Joyce to T. S. Eliot, African-American literature seemed tame, indeed, almost old-fashioned in some of its Victorian flavor. Third, the black community was still weak: no major black publishing houses were produced in this era, nor were there any successful black drama companies, despite black popularity on the Broadway musical stage. Indeed, this last point may be the most telling; for unlike white ethnic enclaves like the Jewish or Irish Catholic communities in the United States, the black community was constantly seen by whites as threatening if it were not rigidly controlled and contained. Whites also used the black community as the venue for their own crimes and vices. In short, the larger white community worked very hard to make sure that the black community could never fully function as a community.

Although Wright continued to produce much important work in the 1950s, including political works, a collection of short stories, and three new novels, the 1950s saw the end of the dominance of this artist, whose works largely ended the Harlem Renaissance by reinventing the black novel as a politically self-aware, proletariat mechanism for social criticism and engagement.

In fact, it ended, at least temporally, a black interest in Marxist-oriented art and sheer naturalistic writing. In the early 1950s came such writers as William Demby (*Beetlecreek*), James Baldwin (*Go Tell It On the Mountain, Giovanni's Room*), Ralph Ellison (*Invisible Man*), and Gwendolyn Brooks (*Annie Allen, Maud Martha*) who were to garner great critical recognition and respect from the white literary establishment. None of these novels was a purely naturalistic work and Brooks's poetry was demanding in a way unlike any Harlem Renaissance poet (except possibly the highly experimental Jean Toomer). Just a few years after Jackie Robinson integrated professional baseball, in an era of a more sensitive treatment of blacks in films like "Home of the Brave," "No Way Out," "Cry, The Beloved Country," and "Blackboard Jungle," and right around the time of the Supreme

Court decision to desegregate public schools, there was a considerable willingness on the part of the liberal white intelligentsia to accept blacks into the American mainstream, not realizing that blacks, as Ralph Ellison was to argue so eloquently in his essays, helped to invent the mainstream that had denied them for so long.

Although much of this work still exhibited the despair, hopelessness, and violence that one found in Wright, some, like Baldwin and Ellison quite critically, muted elements of social protest by going off in new directions, writing more textured, densely complex works about the inner psychological life of black people. The end of the decade saw the rise of novelists Paule Marshall and William Melvin Kelly, poet LeRoi Jones, and playwright Lorraine Hansberry. The criticism of the literature of this period was that it was too assimilationist and far too concerned with technique, although these were, in fact, its strengths in moving black literature into the mainstream of American writing. But the movement was not quite as assimilationist as some critics thought. The black writers of the 1950s came to prominence during the liberation movements taking place in Africa and the concerted attacks against European imperialism by the Third World generally. Writers like Baldwin and Hansberry wrote about Africa as black writers have done since the days of Phillis Wheatley. Nearly all continued to attack racism vehemently Several black writers of note found America so difficult to live in that they left the country, opting for Europe instead. The writing of this period certainly reflected not simply what the black bourgeoisie wanted but where the black community as a whole wished to go, not into a white world but away from the restrictions of a black one.

Black Literature and the Black Community

By the late 1960s, LeRoi Jones, having become a much-read poet (*The Dead Lecturer*, *Preface to a Twenty-Volume Suicide Note*), playwright (*Dutchman* and *The Slave*), and essayist (*Home: Social Essays*), changed his name to Imamu Amiri Baraka and launched the Black Arts movement, first in Harlem, then in Newark, New Jersey, in a period lasting roughly from 1965 to 1975. Partly in response to the strong assimilationist tendencies of the Civil Rights movement, partly in response to a growing and more radical black youth movement, partly in response to black nationalism's finally having, in the figure of the recently assassinated Malcolm X, a martyr upon which to hang myths, the Black Arts Movement invented a black nationalist value system called Kawaida. Inspired, in part, by the African socialist philosophy of Julius K. Nyerere, Kawaida spawned the popular black holiday Kwanzaa and insisted that all black art had to be explicitly political, aimed at the destruction of whites or white values, and preoccupied solely with the liberation of black people. Black art had to be aimed at the masses, thus the rise of black theater and an accessible, nearly didactic black poetry. It had to eschew white technique or an overly white, bourgeois concern with the problems of technique or formalistic meaning and process. Much of this work descended into a kind of black agitprop. Yet there was impressive work accomplished at this time including the establishment of several black publishing companies—Broadside in Detroit and Third World Press in Chicago; *Black Fire*, the epochal anthology edited by Baraka and Larry Neal; work by writers like Don L. Lee (Haki Madhubuti), Sonia Sanchez, Nikki Giovanni, Etheridge Knight, and Eldridge Cleaver. It was the time of the black exploitation movies (which spawned the incredible Melvin Van Peebles's film, "Sweet, Sweetback's Badass Song"), the emergence of black radio as a true force in American culture, and the rise of boxer Muhammad Ali (who had changed his name from Cassius Clay) as a black hero of resistance. Self-absorbed with its dramatic self-presentation, the Black Arts movement produced little fiction. The most important novelist of the period, John A. Williams, who wrote the defining work of the age, *The Man Who Cried I Am*, was not associated with the Black Arts movement, nor were Toni Morrison and Alice Walker, who both began their work at this time.

What might be said about all of these creative periods is that the black community evolved or changed in some vital ways or felt itself in a state of crisis. The literature tended not simply to reflect or merely respond to, but actually to be part of the change or crisis itself. How can writing, or literature, continue to serve the black community or help make it continue to function as community in its present condition? In each instance, innovations were produced. But there was also less dependence on the past, less self-conscious creation of tradition than there could have been. Perhaps in the 1920s or even in the 1950s, this was not possible. But in the 1960s, surely, one of the failures of the Black Arts movement to become what the Harlem Renaissance sought to be—a new black cultural-nationalist movement, a political movement for independence through the reinvention of culture—was the inability to formulate a usable black literary past of sufficient strength and diversity to support an atmosphere that would continue to generate innovation and enrichment. This is slowly but surely happening with African-American literature today, with a greater number of recognized writers than at any time in history.

The Future of Black Literature

It has been said that since the end of the Black Arts Movement, women have come to dominate African-American literature. Certainly, with the rise of feminism in the 1970s and a growing self-consciousness about gender on the part of black women, women's issues and concerns in African-American literature have received considerable prominence. Toni Morrison (the first black American to receive the Nobel Prize for literature), Alice Walker, Gloria Naylor, and even more recently, Terry McMillan and Bebe Campbell, have all become best-selling authors. Lesser known but equally well-regarded writers such as June Jordan, Audre Lorde, Octavia Butler, Gayle Jones, and Ntozake Shange have had a considerable impact on the present literary scene. Moreover, as more women—black and white—have become university professors and literary critics, there has been a growing intellectual and scholarly interest in the work of black women. Since the end of the Black Arts Movement, however, there have emerged several black male writers as well: Ernest Gaines, Ishmael Reed, James McPherson, David Bradley, Reginald McKnight, Charles Johnson, and Samuel Delany have all received a great deal of attention.

Moreover, the dominant black figures in public intellectual discourse these days, such as Henry Louis Gates Jr., Stanley Crouch, Houston Baker, Stephen Carter, Shelby Steele, Glenn Loury, and Cornell West, are men. The belief that black women and feminist issues dominate African-American literature today has led to a distinct undercurrent of tension between black men and black women, as the former accuse the latter of unfairly attacking and criticizing them, playing into the hands of the white power structure. This debate has been fueled as well by a concern over the survival of black men in American society, which some think has reached a crisis point.

Once again, these developments point to the burden that black literature, fraught with political and social significance, must bear in constructing the idea of black community and the difficulty it faces in trying to do so. These pressures also point to the problem of audience, as more black writers are currently being recognized and rewarded by the white literary establishment, although there is a more powerful black reading audience than ever. There is, finally, the question of precisely what black literature should be about, how much social protest or sociological weight it should carry, and how black people should be depicted in it. Despite these ongoing concerns, contemporary African-American writing is a richly diverse field and a compelling presence on the American literary scene.

For Further Reading

Angelou, Maya. *I Know Why the Caged Bird Sings.* New York: Bantam Books, 1983.

Asante, Molefi. *The Afrocentric Idea.* Rev. ed. Philadelphia: Temple University Press, 1998.

Baker, Houston A., Jr. *Blues, Ideology and Afro-American Literature: A Vernacular Theory.* Chicago: University of Chicago Press, 1987.

_____. *Long Black Song: Essays in Black Literature and Criticism.* Charlottesville: University of Virginia Press, 1990.

_____. *Singers of Daybreak: Studies in Black American Literature.* Washington, D.C.: Howard University Press, 1983.

Baraka, Imamu Amiri. *Home: Social Essays.* Hopewell, N.J.: The Ecco Press, 1998.

Braxton, Joanne M., and Andree Nicola McLaughlin, eds. *Wild Women in the Whirlwind: AFRA-American Culture and the Contemporary Literary Renaissance.* New Brunswick, N.J.: Rutgers University Press, 1990.

Carby, Hazel. *Reconstructing Womanhood: The Emergence of the Afro-American Woman Novelist.* New York: Oxford University Press, 1990.

Cooke, Michael G. *Afro-American Literature in the Twentieth Century: The Achievement of Intimacy.* New Haven, Conn.: Yale University Press, 1990.

Fischer, Dexter, and Robert Stepto, eds. *Afro-American Literature: A Vernacular Theory.* New York: Modern Language Association, 1979.

Gates, Henry Louis Jr., ed. *The Classic Slave Narratives.* New York: NAL/Dutton, 1987.

————. *The Signifying Monkey: A Theory of African-American Literary Criticism.* New York: Oxford University Press, 1990.

Gates, Henry Louis Jr., and Sunday Ogbonna Anozie, eds. *Black Literature & Literary Theory.* New York: Routledge, 1990.

Huggins, Nathan I. *The Harlem Renaissance.* New York: Oxford University Press, 1973.

Hughes, Langston. *The Langston Hughes Reader.* New York: George Braziller, 1981.

Hurston, Zora Neale. *Their Eyes Were Watching God.* Reissue Ed. New York: Harper Collins, 1999.

Morrison, Toni. *Playing in the Dark: Whiteness and the Literary Imagination.* New York: Vintage, 1993.

Redding, J. Saunders. *A Scholar's Conscience: Selected Writings of J. Saunders Redding, 1942–1977.* Ed. Faith Berry. Lexington: University of Kentucky Press, 1992.

Smith, Valerie. *Self-Discovery and Authority in Afro-American Narrative.* Cambridge: Harvard University Press, 1991.

Stepto, Robert B. *From Behind the Veil: A Study of Afro-American Narrative.* 2nd ed. Urbana: University of Illinois Press, 1991.

Wright, Richard. *Early Works.* Ed. Arnold Ramersad. New York: Library of America, 1991.

Reading 5.3

"We Were Never Immigrants"
Oscar Micheaux and the Reconstruction of Black American Identity

Jacqueline Najuma Stewart

G EORGE P. JOHNSON TOOK CREDIT FOR getting Oscar Micheaux started in the film production business. After reading Micheaux's third novel, *The Homesteader* (1917), Johnson approached Micheaux about the possibility of the Lincoln Motion Picture Company purchasing the film rights to his book. Correspondence ensued, and contracts were drawn up and ready to be signed when Micheaux demanded that the film be at least six reels in length and insisted on supervising the production himself. When Lincoln refused these terms, Micheaux produced the film on his own. He went on to make more than forty films between 1918 and 1948, becoming race film's most famous and prolific director.[1]

It is obvious why the Johnson brothers were attracted to *The Homesteader*. Like several Lincoln productions, Micheaux's novel is set in the wide-open spaces of the West, where a Black hero achieves personal and financial success that is

---

1 Micheaux's relationship with George P. Johnson is described in Henry T. Sampson, *Blacks in Black and White: A Source Book on Black Films,* 2nd ed. (Metuchen: Scarecrow, 1995) 149–50; Thomas Cripps, *Slow Fade to Black: The Negro in American Film, 1900–1942* (Oxford: Oxford UP, 1977) 184; Betti Carol VanEpps-Taylor, *Oscar Micheaux ... Dakota Homesteader, Author, Pioneer Film Maker: A Biography* (Rapid City: Dakota West, 1999) 96–97; and numerous documents in the George P. Johnson Negro Film Collection, Department of Special Collections, U of California at Los Angeles (hereafter referred to as GPJC). Micheaux turned to writing novels after the failure of his homesteading activities. The novels he published before he began filmmaking—*The Conquest* (1913), *The Forged Note* (1915), and *The Homesteader* (1917)—reveal a great deal about his biography, as well as his perspectives on western homesteading and interracial relationships.

prohibited in other sections of the country. Lincoln's and Micheaux's films demonstrate their shared conviction that the West was the ideal space for Negro self-improvement and self-definition. In this way, the West serves a mythic function for these Black film-makers much as it does in white-produced western films (which enjoyed great popularity among African American audiences). Like Lincoln, Micheaux juxtaposed western spaces with those settings in the North, East, and South where the vast majority of African Americans lived. But even in his earliest work, Micheaux's narrative voice assumes a much more didactic tone than seems to have been the case in Lincoln films. As Pearl Bowser and Louise Spence have argued, Micheaux considered himself not so much a spokesman *of* African American viewpoints as "an instructive voice and an empower-ing interpreter of Black life *for* the community."[2]

Although Micheaux carries his moralizing literary voice into his film practice, his views about how African Americans should earn and enjoy their rights as full American citizens are presented in complex and often contradictory ways on screen. Micheaux's construction of setting, in particular, reflects the range of challenges facing diverse and migrating African American communities, as well as the multiple modes of Black repre-sentation that were available for representing and addressing those challenges. Micheaux's first four films—*The Homesteader* (1919), *Within Our Gates* (1920), *The Brute* (1920), and *The Symbol of the Unconquered* (1920)—sketch out Black life in the West, the urban North, and the South, as well as migrations between these spaces, illustrating how various geo-graphically based "types" of Black characters function to help or hinder the projects of individual and race uplift.[3] [...], Micheaux presents migration and patriotism as vehicles for Black uplift; but his films also point to their limitations both as actual practices and as cinematic constructions. Micheaux's early melodramas leave open the contradictions of trying to uplift and entertain a national Black viewership by staging geographic con-flicts and comparisons at the levels of content and style, as well as in the promotion of

2   Pearl Bowser and Louise Spence, "Identity and Betrayal: *The Symbol of the Unconquered* and Oscar Micheaux's 'Biographical Legend,'" *The Birth of Whiteness: Race and the Emergence of U.S. Cinema,* ed. Daniel Bernardi (New Brunswick: Rutgers UP, 1996) 67.

3   Of the Micheaux films I discuss here, only versions of *Within Our Gates* (1920) and *The Symbol of the Unconquered* (1920) are extant. As yet, no prints of *The Homesteader* (1919) or *The Brute* (1920) have resurfaced. For descriptions of these films, I rely on advertisements and reviews, as well as summaries in Bowser and Spence, "Identity," and their exemplary book-length study, *Writing Himself into History: Oscar Micheaux, His Silent Films, and His Audiences* (New Brunswick: Rutgers UP, 2000); Sampson; Cripps; and Bernard L. Peterson Jr., *Early Black American Playwrights and Dramatic Writers: A Biographical Directory and Catalog of Plays, Films, and Broadcasting Scripts* (New York: Greenwood, 1990). Release dates and exhibition venues are also gleaned from "An Oscar Micheaux Filmography: From the Silents through His Transition to Sound, 1919–1931," compiled by Charles Musser, Corey K. Creekmur, Pearl Bowser, J. Ronald Green, Charlene Regester, and Louise Spence in Pearl Bowser, Jane Gaines, and Charles Musser, eds., *Oscar Micheaux and His Circle: African-American Filmmaking and Race Cinema of the Silent Era* (Bloomington: Indiana UP, 2001) 228–77.

his films. Micheaux's aesthetic intentions can be difficult to determine given the incomplete, heavily censored, and inaccessible status of much of his work. Still, what survives of his films and records of their circulation, particularly in the case of *Within Our Gates*, indicates how his early efforts to represent Black American mobility and identity in cinematic terms not only respond to racism and race pride as expressed through mass culture but also raise questions about the reliability and efficacy of cinematic representation for Black subjects and viewers.

West Is Best

Micheaux's first production, *The Homesteader*, released in Chicago in February 1919 (and shot, in part, at the Ebony studios in Chicago), was the first feature-length film produced by a Black-owned company. The eight-reel feature combined references to Micheaux's own early adult life in the West with an interracial love story. A young Black man, Jean Baptiste (Charles D. Lucas), moves from Chicago to South Dakota, where he becomes prosperous and falls in love with a woman, Agnes Stewart (Iris Hall), whom he believes is white. Thinking their love is doomed, Jean returns to Chicago, where he marries Orlean (Evelyn Preer), the daughter of a prominent Black minister (fig. 5.3.1). This marriage proves to be an unhappy one, and Jean returns to South Dakota, where he is reunited with Agnes upon discovering that she has Black heritage.[4]

The Homesteader seems to have been well received by urban audiences, despite its bias toward life in the West and against corrupt, hypocritical ministers who enjoyed positions of power in Black communities, not to mention the censorship his anticlerical themes elicited.[5] Micheaux staged an elaborate premiere, with live musical performances, at the Eighth Regiment Armory on Chicago's South Side as the all-Black unit made its triumphant return from Europe [...]. Micheaux's promotional materials cited O. C. Hammond, owner of Chicago's newly constructed Vendome Theater, remarking on the

---

4 Micheaux's obsession with this tale—which closely parallels his own life experiences—resulted in two sound versions of this story, *The Exile* (1931) and his last production, *The Betrayal* (1948). For an extended discussion of the relationships between Micheaux's biography and his novels and films, see VanEpps-Taylor. Shooting at Ebony Studios noted in "An Oscar Micheaux Filmography" 231.

5 On the popularity of *The Homesteader* upon its release in Chicago, despite objections raised by ministers, see Bowser and Spence *Writing Himself* 13. Micheaux's repeated castigations of ministers in many of his novels and his films are thinly veiled criticisms of his father-in-law, the prominent Chicago minister Elder N. J. McCracken, whom Micheaux blamed for the dissolution of his marriage. See VanEpps-Taylor 63–71. The compilers of the "Oscar Micheaux Filmography" note that the Chicago Censor Board "ordered substantial cuts, including the complete elimination of the characters Orlean and Ethel," prompting Micheaux to advertise the film (in the *Defender* 1 Mar. 1919: 11) as "Passed by the Censor Board Despite the Protests of Three Chicago Ministers Who Claimed That It Was Based upon the Supposed Hypocritical Actions of a Prominent Colored Preacher of This City." "An Oscar Micheaux Filmography" 233.

film's continued strong drawing power: "A line had formed at our box office and from 2pm to midnight 5700 paid admissions, at an advance price of 10c over our regular admission had been recorded."[6]

Figure 5.3.1   Jean Baptiste (Charles D. Lucas), the virile western frontiersman, with his soon-to-be-estranged wife, Orlean (Evelyn Preer). *The Homesteader* (dir. Oscar Micheaux, 1919). African Diaspora Images Collection.

Micheaux solicited African American viewer interest by cultivating pride in his achievement as a Black artist and entrepreneur and by tying *The Homesteader*'s release into Black patriotic feeling. But the film also drew audiences because it offered melodramatic juxtapositions of urban and western life that drew from both real life and cinematic fantasy. By the time *The Homesteader* was released, Micheaux was already well known to readers of the *Defender*, which published his letters advocating Black migration to the West and reported on his marital problems, which were related, in part, to the long distance between his wife's roots in Chicago and his homesteading enterprises in South Dakota.[7] Thus the film evoked comparisons between the city and the frontier

---

6   Oscar Micheaux, letter to exhibitors, Mar. 1919, GPJC.

7   See Micheaux's treatise on the West as the space for the Race's best chances for the future in "Where the Negro Fails," *Defender* 19 Mar. 1910; Micheaux's unsuccessful attempt to visit his wife at her father's home in Chicago made front-page headlines: "Mr. Oscar Micheaux in City, Seemed to Be in Family Mix-Up Yet Would Not Speak; Seen with Dr. Daily at Father-in-Law's Door, but Neither He nor the Doctor Were Admitted," *Defender* 29 Apr. 1911.

that were familiar from Micheaux's biography (as rendered in the Black press) and from other Western films.

Although censor boards raised objections to *The Homesteader*, Micheaux's combination of appeals to race pride and popular western themes seems to have fostered Black support of the film across regional lines. A gushing review in the October 1919 issue of *Master Musician* magazine indicates that *The Homesteader* was a huge hit with Black Philadelphia audiences, who had begun to recognize that "[they] can be entertained to the fullest extent by [their] own movie actors and actresses."[8] As might be expected, *The Homesteader* was quite popular among Black audiences in the West. An advertisement in the July 29, 1920, issue of the *Monitor*, an Omaha weekly, announces that *The Homesteader* is returning for a repeat engagement at the Loyal Theater. As in the *Master Musician* review, the experience of patronizing Micheaux's film is described in terms of expressing a race pride that benefits other Blacks associated with the industry, this time including theater owners: "The management of the Loyal Theater is sparing neither expense nor trouble in their efforts to colored and white movie 'fans' who appreciate first class photoplays, courteous treatment and good order. If you appreciate our effort, come out and see a Negro Photo-play, written and produced by Negroes, acted by Negroes, owned by Negroes and shown in a Negro theater catering to Negro patronage."[9] Thus it would seem that Micheaux's treatment of westward migration in *The Homesteader* struck a chord with audiences in different parts of the country and provided an occasion for mustering up broad support for Blacks who worked in all areas of the race film industry (including theater owners who would welcome white viewers).

Micheaux would again take up the story of western migration in his fourth feature, *The Symbol of the Unconquered*. Released in November 1920 in Detroit, this eight-reel drama told the story of Evon (Eve) Mason (Iris Hall), a "quadroon" from Selma, Alabama, who moves to the Northwest to claim a mine that was willed to her by her grandfather. In the West she meets Black homesteader Hugh Van Allen (Walker Thompson), who is afraid to confess his love for Evon because he believes that she is white. When Hugh discovers oil on his property, he is harassed by a white swindler, August Barr (Louis Déan), and his cohort, Jefferson Driscoll (Lawrence Chenault), a Black man passing for white who hates his own race. Barr and Driscoll arrange for the Ku Klux Klan to attack Hugh and drive him off of his valuable land.[10] With Eve's assistance, however, Hugh effectively

---

8   "Photoplay" section, *Master Musician* Oct. 1919: 15.

9   Advertisement, *Monitor* 29 July 1920: 3.

10   Although the currently circulating print of *Symbol* (restored by the Museum of Modern Art and Turner Classic Movies, with a score composed and performed by Max Roach) lists the film's white antagonist as "August Barr" and played by Louis Déan, the compilers of "An Oscar Micheaux Filmography" cite sources naming this character "Tom Cutschawl," played by Edward E. King. "An Oscar Micheaux Filmography" 238–39.

protects his property. Eventually Hugh and Eve can acknowledge their mutual attraction after her true racial identity is revealed.

The surviving, incomplete print of *The Symbol of the Unconquered* indicates that Micheaux has made some significant changes to his representation of westward migration, perhaps to expand its particular appeals to different segments of his audience—women and southerners. *Symbol* represents the movement of a woman to the Northwest. Eve's determination to travel alone to distant country makes her a uniquely strong and independent female character, and her bravery during the Klan attacks further distinguishes her from weaker, more dependent heroines found in other race films, and potentially more exciting to female viewers. All decked out in a buckskin cowgirl outfit, Eve jumps onto her rearing horse, determined to help Hugh fend off the Klan (fig. 5.3.2). Another important variation in this tale is that Eve migrates west from Selma, a southern city. For Micheaux, then, neither the North nor the South provided adequate opportunities for the Race's most enterprising young adults. As Bowser and Spence have noted, for Micheaux the western frontier is "the mythic space of moral drama and the site of opportunities seemingly free of the restrictive and discriminatory laws and social arrangements of the rural South and the urban metropolis."[11] Thus, whereas Micheaux shares Booker T. Washington's skepticism about Black urban migration, he revises Washington's program by advocating that Blacks plant themselves in western, rather than southern, soil. And while many southern Blacks were considering the appeals made by northern Black media, like the *Chicago Defender*, to migrate to industrial centers, Micheaux seems to advocate bypassing the city altogether.

The western frontier of *The Symbol of the Unconquered* also provides Micheaux with a novel setting from which to counter the heroic treatment of the Klan in *The Birth of a Nation. Symbol* exposes the fact that night riding is not limited to the seemingly more repressive southern districts. Micheaux's dramatic scenes of Klan violence directly addressed the sharp rise of Klan activity in many parts of the country, including New England and the Midwest as well as the South, after World War I.[12] *The Symbol of the Unconquered* attempted to capture and capitalize on the sensational, real-life topic of Klan violence, which enhanced the film's popularity well after its initial release. A front-page story in the October 1, 1921, issue of the *Chicago Star* featured an interview with Swan Micheaux, Oscar's brother and business manager, who obliquely suggests that *Symbol's* second run could prove to be more successful than the first: "Just what the harvest will be from the new demand for the 'Symbol of the Unconquered' bookings in America since the resurrection of the Ku Klux Klan can not yet be estimated. ... [Swan Micheaux] stated that he cannot determine on the receipts abroad as to how the people

---

11   Bowser and Spence, "Identity" 61.
12   John Hope Franklin and Alfred A. Moss Jr., *From Slavery to Freedom: A History of Negro Americans*, 6th ed. (New York: McGraw, 1988) 311–12.

in France and England will be attracted by their great Ku Klux Klan scene in all its haggard splendor."[13] Micheaux's threat to expose America's rampant, violent racism to a European audience, like his frequent use of interracial romance, was calculated to generate publicity. By broadening the scope of the setting in which Klan activity is represented—both within the film and in its potential viewership—Micheaux seeks to increase political awareness and his box office receipts.

Figure 5.3.2 Eve Mason (Iris Hall) rides to warn Black frontiersman Hugh Van Allen of an impending Ku Klux Klan attack on his property. *The Symbol of the Unconquered* (dir. Oscar Micheaux, 1920). Frame enlargement by Charles Musser.

In addition to films representing westward migration, Micheaux did produce a number of films set in northern cities such as Chicago and New York, where significant portions of his audience and his publicity were centered. Although most of his "city" films date from the sound era (presenting song and dance numbers associated with urban cabaret and nightlife), Micheaux's third feature, *The Brute* (released in August 1920 at Hammond's Vendome Theater in Chicago), is set entirely in the city. Shot in Chicago, *The Brute* depicts a young Black woman, Mildred Carrison (Evelyn Preer), who is forced to marry "Bull" Magee (A. B. Comanthiere), a brutal underworld gambling kingpin. *The*

---

13   "'Symbol of the Unconquered,' Oscar Micheaux Great Picture to Show the KuKlux in Europe," *Chicago Star* 1 Oct. 1921: 1. Antilynching activist Ida B. Wells used similar tactics by embarking on lecture tours in Europe to expose the atrocities white Americans perpetrated against African Americans. See *Crusade for Justice: The Autobiography of Ida B. Wells,* ed. Alfreda M. Duster (Chicago: U of Chicago P, 1970).

Brute depicts domestic violence as being directly linked to a depraved urban environment in which alcohol, gambling, and physical violence are the norm.[14] Micheaux drew fire from Black critics for his representation of the unseemly side of Black urban life (as he would throughout his career). *New York Age* critic Lester A. Walton complained, "As I looked at the picture I was reminded of the attitude of the daily press, which magnifies our vices and minimizes our virtues."[15] Micheaux's use of sensational topics, [...], reflected both "yellow journalism" trends in urban newspapers and topics covered in white-produced "pink slip" films. Though no print of *The Brute* is extant, descriptions and stills suggest that while the film criticizes violence against women, Micheaux's commentary on the cultural life African Americans were developing in urban centers also glamorizes many less "uplifting" aspects of fast city living, such as drinking, boxing, craps shooting, and the wealth one can accumulate, particularly by illegal means (fig. 5.3.3).[16] One can imagine that Micheaux's representations of urban life in *The Brute* and later films might accommodate a range of interpretations by his diverse audiences—as welcome reflections of urban (underworld) realities, as instructive preachments against greed and violence, and as warnings against city life altogether.

Although Micheaux frequently argued that the western frontier, not the city, was the ideal space where African Americans could succeed morally, financially, and socially and stake their most convincing claim to American citizenship, his filmmaking relied heavily on Black urban themes, audiences, and presses. Micheaux constructed dangerous but exciting urban landscapes in which young Black women are threatened by unscrupulous men and where promising Black men risk losing their integrity. In doing so, his films not only reflected many of the social and moral dilemmas Black urban audiences faced in their daily lives but also provided Black newspapers with the contradictory material on which they thrived—opportunities to celebrate his artistic and entrepreneurial achievements and to attack his often scandalous and unflattering representational choices.[17] Micheaux's films may not have advocated Black migration to the urban North, but in many ways they depended on the markets, cultural practices, and debates that had been produced by the Great Migration.

---

14   According to Bernard L. Peterson, "The film was considered too sensational because of its erotic love scenes, racial violence, and realistic scenes of low life in black drinking and gambling joints, and failed to gain the censor's approval in Chicago." Peterson 135.

15   *New York Age* 18 Sept. 1920, qtd. in Bowser and Spence, *Writing Himself* 177.

16   See Bowser and Spence, *Writing Himself* 130, for a discussion of *The Brute*'s detailed illustration of a "well-appointed parlor" (perhaps that of gambling boss Bull Magee).

17   Charlene Regester outlines how the Black press shifted from offering almost uniform praise for early Black filmmaking to voicing more detailed criticism of its Black images and production values in "The African-American Press and Race Movies, 1909–1929," in *Oscar Micheaux and His Circle* 34–49. See also Anna Everett's discussion of Walton's response to *The Brute* in *Returning the Gaze: A Genealogy of Black Film Criticism, 1909–1949* (Durham: Duke UP, 2001) 161–62.

Figure 5.3.3 In *The Brute* (1920), Oscar Micheaux depicts city life as materially opulent but morally impoverished. African Diaspora Images Collection.

A Circuitous Journey to Citizenship: *Within Our Gates*

Micheaux may have privileged western spaces over both northern and southern ones for Black moral and material progress, but he always acknowledged the fact that most African Americans lived in the South or had migrated to urban industrial centers. Micheaux's second feature, *Within Our Gates* (released in January 1920 at Hammond's Vendome Theater in Chicago), concerns itself with the movement of its African American heroine between the South and the urban North. In *Within Our Gates,* Micheaux stays within the dominant pattern of the Great Migration in order to address issues of racism, intraracial conflict, gender politics, and patriotism as experienced and recognized by the majority of his audience. *Within Our Gates* dramatically illustrates the significance of migration and patriotism not just as themes but also as key formal influences in Black filmmaking practices as they developed in relation to Black efforts to construct modern African American identities. In light of such recent events as the 1919 riots, the failure of World War I to bring about racial "democracy" at home, and the extraordinary popularity of Griffith's racist version of American history in *The Birth of a Nation,* Micheaux presents a picture of the country as deeply fragmented—regionally and racially—beyond complete political or aesthetic repair.

Within Our Gates represents Micheaux's most ambitious attempt to fashion a discourse on the meaning of Black American identity. The film features a large cast of Black character types, demonstrating that the Black population is made up of individuals from a wide variety of backgrounds and with very different goals and lifestyles. The film's heroine, Sylvia Landry (Evelyn Preer), is an educated southern belle who believes in doing what she can to uplift the less fortunate members of her race; Sylvia's cousin, Alma Pritchard (Flo Clements), and Alma's stepbrother, Larry (Jack Chenault), are dishonest city dwellers who misrepresent Sylvia's past in order to manipulate her; Conrad, Sylvia's fiancé (James D. Ruffin), is an educated man who holds a prestigious position that sends him to remote regions of Canada and Brazil; the Reverend Wilson Jacobs (Sam T. Jacks) and his sister, Constance (Jimmie Cook), are honorable Black southern teachers who run the impoverished Piney Woods School; Dr. V. Vivian (Charles D. Lucas) is a Boston physician-intellectual who intently studies race questions; Ned is a sellout southern Black preacher; Sylvia's adoptive parents, Mr. and Mrs. Jasper Landry (William Starks, Mattie Edwards), are struggling but upstanding southern sharecroppers; Efrem (E. G. Tatum) is an ignorant, gossiping southern servant who turns against members of his own race. Micheaux makes it clear that the environments from which these characters hail, and to which they migrate, say a great deal about what kinds of people they are and what impact their type will have on the progress (or failure) of the Race as a whole. But Micheaux presents no simple northern/southern, positive/negative, or New Negro/Old Negro dichotomies. Instead, by structuring *Within Our Gates* along a complex topography of narrative and character relations, Micheaux creates a film that mirrors the diverse but interconnected experiences of his African American characters and audiences.[18]

The meandering, melodramatic plot of *Within Our Gates* details the experiences of southerner Sylvia Landry as she moves between the North and the rural South in an attempt to figure out her rightful place in (Black) American society. The film opens in a northern city where Sylvia is visiting with her cousin Alma. After being spurned by her fiancé, Conrad, Sylvia returns to the South in response to a call for teachers at the Piney Woods School. Upon learning that Wilson and Constance Jacobs need $5,000 to keep the school running, Sylvia goes back up North, to Boston, to try to raise funds from the city's wealthy people. While in Boston, Sylvia meets Dr. Vivian, a "race man" with whom she grows quite close. One day Sylvia is accidentally hit by a car while saving a child's life. As luck would have it, the car belongs to a wealthy white woman, Mrs. Elena Warwick, who after much thought decides to donate not $5,000 but $50,000 to Piney Woods. Sylvia returns South with the funds but is forced to run away when Larry

---

18   In later films, Micheaux would continue to use a North/South contrast to explain character motivations (*The Notorious Elinor Lee,* 1940) or to clear up misunderstandings that threaten narrative closure (*Lying Lips,* 1939). Other Micheaux films that feature other migration narratives include *The Exile* (1931; sound remake of *The Homesteader,* about a man who moves from Chicago to homestead in South Dakota); *Birthright* (1924; a Harvard graduate tries to start a school for Negro children in the Deep South; remade with sound in 1939); *The Spider's Web* (1926; a Harlem woman travels to a small town in Mississippi and back again; remade with sound as *The Girl from Chicago,* 1932); *Swing* (1938; a couple travels from Birmingham to Harlem).

Pritchard, the criminal stepbrother of her cousin Alma, threatens to disclose unflattering information about Sylvia if she does not consent to a sexual relationship with him. Meanwhile, Dr. Vivian searches for Sylvia in the North, where he meets up with Alma. Alma recounts to Dr. Vivian the story of Sylvia's past, which, presumably, helps to explain why she has not committed to Dr. Vivian or any man since breaking up with Conrad.

Sylvia's painful southern story involves the false accusation of her adoptive father, Jasper Landry, of the murder of a tyrannical white landowner, Philip Gridlestone. The Landrys hide in the woods while a white lynch mob assembles to find them and exact revenge. As Sylvia's parents are captured, hung, and burned, Philip Gridlestone's brother, Armand (Grant Gorman), corners Sylvia in an empty house and tries to rape her. At the last minute, Armand stops his attack when he discovers a birthmark on Sylvia's breast, which indicates to him that she is his daughter, the product of his sexual relations with a Black woman.

Micheaux's revelation of Sylvia's interracial parentage helps to explain why she is repeatedly subjected to social, psychological, and moral dangers that prevent her from maintaining a stable family, home, and identity. This characterization of Sylvia draws on the long tradition of "tragic mulattoes" in Black cultural production, as well as the tradition of the African American migration narrative, with themes of exile, alienation, and reinvention.[19] In many ways, *Within Our Gates* resembles three roughly contemporary Black novels that combine mulatto and migration themes. Sylvia's multiple journeys north and south echo the movements of the title character of Frances Ellen Watkins Harper's *Iola LeRoy, or Shadows Uplifted* (1892), the protagonist of James Weldon Johnson's *The Autobiography of an Ex-Coloured Man* (1912), and Helga Crane in Nella Larsen's *Quicksand* (1928).[20] These characters similarly struggle with their interracial heritage, moving from place to place as they try to fit into different kinds of communities. The experiences of these characters serve as limit cases for the political and psychological status of the Race as a whole. Sylvia, Iola, the Ex-Colored Man, and Helga share a sense

---

19   On miscegenation and the "mulatto" figure in American literature, see Werner Sollors, *Neither Black nor White yet Both: Thematic Explorations of Interracial Literature* (New York: Oxford UP, 1997); and James Kinney, *Amalgamation! Race, Sex, and Rhetoric in the Nineteenth-Century American Novel* (Westport: Greenwood, 1985). On the African American migration narrative, see Farah Jasmine Griffin, *"Who Set You Flowin'?": The African American Migration Narrative* (New York: Oxford UP, 1995); and Lawrence R. Rodgers, *Canaan Bound: The African-American Great Migration Novel* (Urbana: U of Illinois P, 1997).

20   Like Sylvia, all three characters diverge from the one-way pattern of many migration narratives (the move from South to North) by making several journeys between South and North. The Ex-Colored Man and Helga Crane also migrate to Europe and back. Frances Ellen Watkins Harper, *Iola LeRoy* (1892; Oxford: Oxford UP, 1988); James Weldon Johnson, *The Autobiography of an Ex-Colored Man* (1912) in *Three Negro Classics* (New York: Avon, 1965) 391–511; Nella Larsen, *Quicksand* (1928; New Brunswick: Rutgers UP, 1986).

of estrangement in the urban North, as well as a complex relationship with the South as both "home" and the site of Black victimization and demoralization.[21]

Micheaux clearly marks the South as the source of far-reaching white racism and Black American trauma, which continue to have profound effects on Blacks despite their efforts to move forward with their lives via education and migration. In the restored Library of Congress print of *Within Our Gates*, it seems that Micheaux deliberately withholds pertinent information about Sylvia's southern experiences until the very end; the lengthy flashback does not occur until fifty-three minutes into the sixty-five-minute film. If this print reflects Micheaux's intended structure, he conspicuously extends the viewer's curiosity about the background and "true" character of his seemingly ideal Black heroine as they were shaped in the South. Indeed, when Larry warns Sylvia that he will tell her friends at the Piney Woods School "just what sort of person you are," it is not yet clear to the viewer what he means. Larry's threat seems to resonate with a brief scene very early in the film in which Sylvia's cousin, Alma, leads her fiancé, Conrad, to a room in which Sylvia is engaged in an emotional meeting with a white man whom we later learn is her father, Armand Gridlestone. At this early point in the film, we, like the enraged Conrad, are led to believe that Sylvia is having an affair with this unidentified white man. Micheaux does not explain Sylvia's relationship with him until the "rape" scene at the film's climax, and he never completely explains the circumstances of Sylvia's interaction with Armand Gridlestone in the North.[22] The "sort of person" Sylvia is, as represented in the main body of the film (an honorable woman dedicated to racial uplift), takes on different meanings when understood in the context of the flashback to her past, in which she is orphaned, rendered homeless, sexually attacked, and revealed to be biracial. She is the product, and victim, of illicit interracial relations, a southern legacy she can never escape. Placed at the end of the film, Micheaux's representation of southern life—characterized by sharecropping (which was an attempt to preserve the social and economic hierarchies of slavery), lynching, and the rape of Black women

---

21 Although Iola grew up comfortably in the South believing that she was white, her return there after the revelation of her Black heritage is fraught with traumatic events, not the least of which is being remanded into slavery. The Ex-Colored Man witnesses a lynching in the South that impels him to renounce his Black heritage and pass for white. Helga Crane feels alienated in the repressive, upwardly mobile atmosphere of a southern Black college at the start of the novel. When she returns to the South at the novel's conclusion—with hopes of "uplifting" a poor, rural Black population— she again feels woefully out of place, but this time she becomes too physically and psychologically drained to escape.

22 The end of the scene in which Conrad sees Sylvia with Armand Gridlestone is missing from the restored print of the film. Perhaps there was more footage (and more explanatory intertitles) in original prints of the film that would have included a more detailed account of what happened between Armand, Sylvia, Conrad, and Alma at this point in the narrative. Still, the Library of Congress's explanatory note that Conrad leaves the room without hearing Sylvia's explanation suggests that Micheaux did not yet reveal Sylvia's "secrets" to the viewer.

by white men—demonstrates that these are powerful and constant undercurrents of "modern" Black life, making it difficult for many Blacks (including educated, upstanding migrants) to feel "at home" anywhere in the United States.

The flashback to Sylvia's southern past contains many of Micheaux's most scathing criticisms of American racism, particularly as it had been practiced and rationalized (or ignored) in a spate of romantic antebellum-themed films of the 1910s, culminating with *The Birth of a Nation*. For instance, several scholars have pointed out that the "rape" scene involving Sylvia and Armand Gridlestone is staged as a direct response to the "rape" scene involving Gus and Little Sister in *Birth*. As Toni Cade Bambara observes, Micheaux sought to "set the record straight on who rapes who."[23] Black men were regularly accused of raping white women in order to justify their lynching, when, in fact, white men routinely raped Black women as a form of social and political terrorism as African Americans expressed political and economic self-determination.

Certainly, Micheaux's film has broader aims and significance beyond its function as a critique of or corrective to *Birth*. Among its interventions, *Within Our Gates* provides an African American perspective on Black migration and citizenship that challenges southern white warnings and northern white paranoia about the transformation of the "race problem" from a regional to a national concern. Micheaux's film addresses both the kind of southern anti-Reconstruction sentiment represented by Thomas Dixon's novel *The Clansman* and the national appeal of Griffith's cinematic adaptation, which combined antebellum nostalgia with innovative visual and narrative styles. "Answering" *Birth* is not Micheaux's sole objective, but the film does mobilize Black American cosmopolitanism and patriotism to refute the racist discourses (and the powerful stylistic means of conveying them) that Griffith's landmark film represents.

Take, for instance, the way Micheaux constructs the coupling of Sylvia and Dr. Vivian as a union of South and North, a marriage that echoes and challenges the white Cameron/Stoneman union at the close of *Birth*. Sylvia has a number of suitors representing various Black male types as they perform in particular geographic contexts. Larry is obviously not the right mate for Sylvia because he is manipulative and dishonest. Whether he is running crooked poker games in the North or selling costume jewelry to Black laborers in the South, Larry exploits members of the Race, and he is therefore killed off. Conrad is not a viable husband for Sylvia because his job keeps him outside of the United States. If Sylvia were to live with Conrad in Canada or Brazil, she would not be in a position to claim her American birthright and work toward race equality at

---

23   Toni Cade Bambara quotation from the documentary film *Midnight Ramble: Oscar Micheaux and the Race Film*, dir. Bestor Cram and Pearl Bowser, The American Experience, 1994. For a discussion of *Within Our Gates* as a response to *The Birth of a Nation* (particularly in its representations of rape and lynching), see Jane Gaines, "Fire and Desire: Race, Melodrama, and Oscar Micheaux," *Black American Cinema*, ed. Manthia Diawara (New York: Routledge, 1993) 49–70.

home. Finally, Reverend Jacobs, the principal of Piney Woods School, is eliminated from competition because, it seems, he is from the South. Although Jacobs is an intelligent man with honorable intentions, Micheaux chooses not to match southern Sylvia with a southern husband. She brings northern white capital down to Piney Woods (much like Booker T. Washington's method of financing his Tuskegee Institute), and that seems to fulfill her obligation to Reverend Jacobs.

The winner of Sylvia's hand is Dr. V. Vivian, the Boston physician who is never shown examining patients but is instead seen examining race issues in various highbrow publications. From his first appearance, when he recovers Sylvia's stolen purse from a thief, Dr. Vivian is revealed to be a rare, respectable Black urban man.[24] Micheaux deliberately chooses to match Sylvia and Dr. Vivian because they represent the educated elite of the Black South and North coming together to study and work for uplift. Perhaps one of the reasons Rev. Jacobs cannot become Sylvia's husband is that his southern, religious upbringing and his social position as a race educator would not allow him to fully and/ or publicly accept her relationship with her white father/near-rapist. Though Sylvia's bespectacled fiancé, Conrad, has an adventurous professional life that might suggest his progressive New Negro status, we witness his violent reaction to finding her in "compromising" proximity to a white man—after seeing Sylvia with Armand Gridlestone, Conrad chokes her and throws her to the floor. Dr. Vivian, on the other hand, is represented as a sensitive, sophisticated, modern race man who can understand the contradictions of Sylvia's position. When he learns the whole truth about Sylvia, he is more convinced than ever that he wants to spend his life with her.

In light of Micheaux's attention to questions of racial uplift, community building, and Black American citizenship, his representation of Sylvia's impending marriage gestures both forward and backward in its political and stylistic construction. Like Griffith, Micheaux attempts to link traditional values and discursive modes with modern social and aesthetic possibilities. J. Ronald Green has argued that Micheaux's formulation of the Black "bourgeois marriage icon" in *Within Our Gates* rejects Griffith's conservative politics of white heterosexual coupling, in which marriage was "a reaffirmation of classical liberalism (the [male] individual as free agent) and of patriarchy" based upon "an old vision of racial purity and white supremacism."[25] But although Micheaux's representation of the uplift marriage may seem more "progressive," community-minded, feminist, and inclusive than Griffith's ideal couples, in many ways it is also decidedly more traditional

---

24   Representations of urban criminals are common in the scenes of urban encounter in migration narratives. I should note, however, that the casting of a dark-skinned actor in the role of the thief, who is apprehended by the light-skinned Dr. Vivian, reveals Micheaux's frequent (but by no means universal) mobilization of color-based typing and hierarchies in his films.

25   J. Ronald Green, *Straight Lick: The Cinema of Oscar Micheaux* (Bloomington: Indiana UP, 2000) 29.

(and optimistic) than representations of heterosexual coupling for "mulatto" characters in contemporaneous African American literature. Unlike the Ex-Colored Man, who opts to pass for white and marries a white woman, Sylvia's marriage confirms her proud Black identity. And unlike Helga Crane, who marries a southern Black preacher, Sylvia will not perish in the traditional, oppressive confines of wife and mother. Micheaux's treatment of Sylvia does not demonstrate the kind of modernist skepticism Johnson and Larsen exhibit regarding the impossible position of biracial characters in a racially polarized society. Instead, Micheaux reaches back to the melodramatic conventions of the sentimental uplift novel, like Harper's *Iola LeRoy*. The pairing of Sylvia and Dr. Vivian as a "race couple" is strikingly similar to Harper's pairing of Iola and physician-intellectual Dr. Latimer. Hazel Carby has argued that Harper presents Iola's marriage as an egalitarian one, "based on a mutual sharing of intellectual interests and a commitment to the 'folk' and the 'race.'"[26] Micheaux suggests that with the race man Dr. Vivian by her side, Sylvia finally will be able to settle down in one location and proceed to fulfill her role as a member of the African American educated elite.

Micheaux combines sentimental and modernist approaches in his attempt to redeem the mulatto figure as she or he had been slandered in white supremacist discourse (e.g., Dixon, Griffith). Since, as Michele Wallace reminds us, the mulatto figure's "real-life counterpart had, after all, played a central and pivotal role in Reconstruction politics," this figure was used by Black and white artists to reflect upon the troubling implications of interracial intimacy and biracial identity in both the southern past and the modern present/future.[27] Micheaux works to redeem Sylvia the mulatta not only by presenting her as the kind of educated and uplift-minded heroine who seems to step out of the pages of nineteenth-century Black fiction but also by fragmenting the film's narration in ways that attempt to convey the complex social, psychological, and political dimensions of Sylvia's mixed-race background. He presents Sylvia's marriage as precipitated by a jarring and lengthy temporal discontinuity—the southern flashback. Green argues that Micheaux's view of marriage, unlike Griffith's "old vision of racial purity and white supremacism," affirms "the social self," "mutuality," and women's rights to "free agency" and "racial hybridity and equality."[28] These oppositions are clearly staged in the southern

---

26   Carby notes that Harper presents Iola's attraction to Dr. Latimer not in "base" physical, sexual terms but rather as "spiritual." I would argue that Micheaux's awkward treatment of Vivian's marriage proposal (as discussed later) functions to similarly circumvent sticky questions of Black sexuality. Like Harper, Micheaux "initially utilize[s] romantic convention and then discard[s] the romance." Hazel Carby, *Reconstructing Womanhood: The Emergence of the Afro-American Woman Novelist* (Oxford: Oxford UP, 1987) 79–80.

27   Michele Wallace, "Oscar Micheaux's *Within Our Gates*: The Possibilities for Alternative Visions," *Oscar Micheaux and His Circle* 58–59.

28   Green 29.

flashback at the story level. But at the plot level, Micheaux takes advantage of some of the innovative cinematic narrative techniques Griffith develops in *Birth*.

For example, Griffith expands previous uses of parallel editing from showing two actions occurring at one time to, in the infamous "rape" sequence, combining three actions—Little Sister running, Gus the Black brute in hot pursuit, and her brother, the "Little Colonel," following them both. Here, as in some of his previous work at Biograph (e.g., *The Girls and Daddy*, 1909), the rescue is delayed to suspenseful effect by keeping the white male rescuer at bay with a relay of cuts between him, the black aggressor, and the white female victims. In *Within Our Gates*, Micheaux not only intercuts the lynching and burning of the Landrys with the rape of Sylvia but also interpolates the framing narrative voice of Alma to draw out, in Griffithian style, Sylvia's ordeal. The "rape" of Sylvia is repeatedly "interrupted" (to use Gaines's term) by shots of the lynch mob's bonfire and, at the climax of the sequence, by a shot of Alma telling the story to Dr. Vivian (fig. 5.3.4) and a corresponding title card explaining that Sylvia is Armand's daughter. Micheaux's use of a third term here—a voice from the North/present—to rescue and redeem the mulatta victim suggests how his stylistic response to Griffith is not predicated on Griffith's aesthetic as simply an "old vision." Instead, Micheaux counters white supremacist accounts of Black character and race relations by acknowledging and adapting some of the narrative techniques from Griffith-dominant cinema.

Figure 5.3.4   Alma (Flo Clements) tells Dr. Vivian (Charles D. Lucas) the story of Sylvia's southern past. *Within Our Gates* (dir. Oscar Micheaux, 1920). Library of Congress, Motion Picture, Broadcasting and Recorded Sound Division.

Micheaux combines his interventions in dominant narrative film style with themes circulating in contemporary African American discourse. By joining the Black South and the Black North in matrimony, he produces an alternative narrative on national identity and belonging that resonates with Black patriotic expression. The white northern and southern characters who couple in *Birth* do so in defeat of African Americans who lust after power (and white women), thereby restoring white supremacy. The only Black characters in Griffith's epic who might be eligible for a second-class American citizenship are the loyal and submissive Black servants (or "faithful souls"). Micheaux, however, ends *Within Our Gates* with a speech delivered by Dr. Vivian asserting that African Americans have more than paid their dues and, as an entire race, are entitled to their rights as American citizens. Dr. Vivian offers as evidence a number of specific instances of Black military service, including battles in Cuba and Mexico and campaigns in France during World War I.[29] "Be proud of our country, Sylvia," Dr. Vivian exhorts, as he explains why African Americans should take their rightful place in American society.

Dr. Vivian's closing speech is notable for the ways it attempts to paper over deep cracks in the logic of Black patriotic rhetoric. At one point, he tells Sylvia, "We were never immigrants," thereby distinguishing African Americans from European immigrants who are more recent arrivals to the United States, and who presumably have less of a claim to American identity. At the same time, though, Dr. Vivian (as Micheaux's mouthpiece) seems to gloss over the contradictions of being a proud Black American in light of the radically different circumstances that brought Blacks to the United States—the slave trade. Bowser and Spence argue persuasively that while such expressions of Black patriotism may seem shortsighted from our current historical vantage point, at the time they played a major role in countering the erasure of Blackness from dominant commercial media. By expressing their patriotism, African Americans were "declaring their own identity" and thereby "writing their world into existence."[30] The conclusion of *Within Our Gates*, as with many of the patriotic films produced and circulated by African Americans during this period, strategically does not take up the obvious contradictions (or commonalities) raised by comparing Black and European immigrant claims to American identity.

Instead, Dr. Vivian's speech seeks to designate a form of patriotic expression that is viable for Black women—he delivers it at the end of the film as he asks for Sylvia's hand in marriage (fig. 5.3.5). Sitting by her side in a drawing room, Vivian acknowledges the difficulties Sylvia must face when trying to take pride in her American nationality

---

29   In addition to its many other contradictions, Vivian's patriotic speech does not address the problem of advocating America's imperialist military actions against people of color abroad in light of its racist practices and policies at home.

30   Bowser and Spence, *Writing Himself* 109.

given her experiences with racial violence: "You ... have been thinking deeply about this, I know—but unfortunately your thoughts have been warped." Still, he concludes his proposal with: "In spite of your misfortunes, you will always be a patriot—and a tender wife. I love you!" This dual proposal—asking Sylvia to become a wife and patriot in the same breath—seems like an awkward, hurried attempt to achieve narrative closure, heterosexual union, and interracial harmony, all at once. But, more significantly, it attempts to create a positive, race-serving function for Sylvia at the precarious intersection of her racial and gender identities to counteract the history of rape and terrorism she has experienced and that she represents. If Micheaux can make a case for Sylvia to embrace her American identity, then by extension any African American (regardless of gender, location, family history, experience with racism) can make the same claim. To paraphrase Anna Julia Cooper, Micheaux is suggesting that only when and where Sylvia Landry can enter the American citizenry, then and there the whole Race enters with her.[31]

Figure 5.3.5   Dr. Vivian makes a passionate patriotic proposal to the skeptical Sylvia Landry (Evelyn Preer). *Within Our Gates* (dir. Oscar Micheaux, 1920). Library of Congress, Motion Picture, Broadcasting and Recorded Sound Division.

Dr. Vivian's speech suggests that Sylvia, like African Americans in general, honorably earned her patriotism through violence and victimization. Jane Gaines argues that the film's culminating expression of "optimistic nationalism" depends on the representation, in the southern flashback, of "racial injustice as relegated to the past,

31   Anna Julia Cooper, *A Voice from the South* (1892; Oxford: Oxford UP, 1988) 31.

not conceivable in the present of the film's contemporary story."[32] I would argue, however, that the revelation of Sylvia's family history late in the film actually emphasizes the grip that the southern past continues to have on its migrants, influencing their beliefs and actions as they attempt to shape themselves into New Negroes. Released not long after the bloody riots of 1919, *Within Our Gates* tries to demonstrate that African Americans will not endanger the security of the nation, despite (and possibly because of) all the pain and suffering they have individually and collectively experienced in their pursuit of U.S. citizenship. Their status as former slaves and their legacy of oppression trump claims to Americanism any white ethnic immigrant might make. And as a biracial woman, Sylvia has experienced, and represents, the most abject forms of racial discrimination, positioning her for the most sublime expression of American identity.

Perhaps Micheaux includes Vivian's patriotic speech, in part, to dampen the inflammatory potential of the lynching scenes presented earlier in the film. Indeed, *Within Our Gates* incited much controversy and was challenged (and cut) by numerous local censor boards that were concerned that its depictions of lynching and interracial rape might reanimate the racial antagonisms displayed during the 1919 riots.[33] But when Micheaux uses patriotism to try to rebury the traumas unearthed in the southern flashback, suggesting that Blacks can and should be well-behaved patriotic citizens, his rhetoric is hardly convincing. Sylvia's pained expression during Vivian's speech heightens the incongruity of this moment; her experiences in the North and South do not bear out the false promise of full American citizenship for Black people.

Seeing and Believing

The unsatisfactory ending of *Within Our Gates* actually functions to emphasize what I would argue is the film's most compelling stylistic quality—its repeated demonstration that competing discourses about African Americans (as individuals and as a group) render Black representations, including Micheaux's, extremely inconsistent and unreliable. Although the film presents a thoroughly didactic message against white racism and in favor of African American uplift and equality, it also displays numerous ambiguities and misrepresentations, thereby calling modes of rendering Blackness, including cinematic realism, into question.

Some of the stylistic qualities I have in mind may not be intentional on Micheaux's part; we cannot know for sure how closely the print currently available for analysis reflects versions of the film that were shown at the time of its original screenings. This

---

32   Gaines, "Fire and Desire" 52.

33   Gaines, "Fire and Desire" 50; Bowser and Spence, *Writing Himself* 15–16.

is always an issue with Micheaux's work because his films were so routinely censored and reorganized. Micheaux regularly made cuts, restored scenes, and changed the order of sequences, making it difficult to know what version(s) audiences saw when they were first shown. *Within Our Gates* was heavily censored, and newspaper accounts of screenings during the film's initial exhibitions suggest significant variations from what we see in the print currently in circulation. For example, Bowser and Spence cite a letter to Micheaux from George P. Johnson that describes a lynching occurring in the film's second reel, leading them to question the intended placement of the southern scenes.[34] In addition, the intertitles included in the surviving print are reconstructions—the print was located in an archive in Spain, and its Spanish intertitles had to be translated back into English by researchers who relied heavily on Micheaux's novels to make sense of narrative and character details. What is more, the current print is full of text. The intertitles include character and plot description, dialogue, letters, and print media stories. We must wonder if Micheaux intended to require so much reading (given the illiteracy rate among his primary audience), or if perhaps more explanatory titles were added in Spain for a European audience unfamiliar with many of Micheaux's culturally specific details. Gaines, Bowser, and Spence discuss one of the most glaring problems presented by the translated text—Sylvia is described in the Spanish titles as the product of a "legitimate" marriage between Armand Gridlestone and a Black woman, but evidence from viewers and advertisements (including references to "concubinage" not evident in the available print) suggests that she is the product, as well as the victim, of forced sexual relations.[35] With these inconsistencies in mind, I would argue that the footage we have displays major tensions regarding the reliability of Black media representation, in both textual and visual terms. By challenging the idea that one can believe what one sees, particularly with regard to Black character and actions, Micheaux's film points to the limitations of the very medium he is using, despite claims he (and other filmmakers) might make that cinema represents a powerful modern means of truth telling and intelligibility.

Within Our Gates contains various suspicious and contradictory elements at textual and visual levels. Corey Creekmur has pointed out that Micheaux, drawing from the writings of Charles Chesnutt, fills *Within Our Gates* with "white lies"—that is, white versions of events and perspectives on African Americans that deliberately

---

34   Before arranging for a second run of the film in Omaha, Johnson asks Micheaux to "kindly eliminate from the second reel all the objectionable lynching scenes such as has caused trouble in other communities." Letter, George P. Johnson to Oscar Micheaux, 4 Oct. 1920, GPJC. Bowser and Spence wonder "if the film was, at one point, arranged in chronological order," or "maybe there had been other lynchings in the second reel." Bowser and Spence, *Writing Himself* 146.

35   Jane Gaines, "*Within Our Gates:* From Race Melodrama to Opportunity Narrative," *Oscar Micheaux and His Circle* 75; Bowser and Spence, *Writing Himself* 134.

misrepresent the "truth."[36] In a couple of instances, Micheaux demonstrates how such "white lies," told to maintain Black subjugation, circulate in print. Just after a scene in which we see Dr. Vivian reading an article about a prominent reverend seeking federal funding for Negro schools, Micheaux cuts to the prejudiced white southerner, Geraldine Stratton, reading a racist newspaper's account of the Negro's inherent ignorance and unfitness for the vote. Later in the film we see the restless southern white mob surround Efrem (the gossipy servant to Philip Gridlestone), with the intention of lynching him simply because he is the nearest Black victim. But later, when the town newspaper reports Efrem's death, it describes his murder as "an accidental death at unknown hands." While both scenes illustrate the powerful and historical role that white print media have played in sustaining racist policies and violence, the second is notable because the newspaper account clearly contradicts the visual representation of Eph's death dramatized earlier in the narrative. In fact, *Within Our Gates* features numerous moments in which the image presented on screen is later contradicted or is entirely misleading in its own right, providing a false picture of particular characters or events.

Creekmur describes Micheaux's repetition of events as representing the discursive demands of a segregated society, which "reinforced the regular construction of alternative *public narratives*, demanding at least two versions of every story" (emphasis in original).[37] What is particularly striking in *Within Our Gates* is the way in which Micheaux structures the relationships between how truth and lies are told (verbally or visually) and where they are staged and/or narrated (in the North or in the South). Sylvia's backstory, in particular, contains and is associated with various moments of misrepresentation and misrecognition. I have already indicated how the story of Sylvia's southern past, constructed through flashback, creates some extremely confusing moments in the film, such as her initially unexplained relationship with Armand Gridlestone. The confusion about what really happened in Sylvia's past, and how much of the truth various characters think they know, makes Sylvia's story (even if not intended as a last-minute flashback) a compelling statement about the unreliability of cinematic representation of Blackness in general, particularly how the South (its history and its contemporary representatives) obscures the picturing of Black truths.

For example, a striking instance of misrepresentation occurs when Sylvia's adoptive father, Jasper Landry, is accused of murder. The Landrys are lynched because the servant Efrem mistakenly accuses Jasper Landry of shooting white landowner Philip

---

36   Creekmur's insightful analysis of the politics of adaptation in Micheaux's work describes *Within Our Gates*'s relation (at the levels of content and form) to Charles Chesnutt's *The Marrow of Tradition* (1901). Corey Creekmur, "Telling White Lies: Oscar Micheaux and Charles W. Chesnutt," *Oscar Micheaux and His Circle* 147–58.

37   Creekmur 156.

Gridlestone. The first time the murder is shown, it is represented from an omniscient narrative perspective that shows what really happened inside and outside of Gridlestone's office: a disgruntled white farmer shoots Gridlestone from a window; Gridlestone picks up his own gun to attempt to defend himself; Landry takes the gun out of the dead Gridlestone's hand. When the murder is actually committed, Efrem's head is turned away from his peeping vantage point, and when he turns his gaze back into the room, he sees only Landry holding a smoking gun. Landry then flees the scene in fear (fig. 5.3.6). Therefore, when Efrem recounts the murder to the white townsfolk, his version is based on circumstantial evidence. It is Efrem's account of Gridlestone's murder that is printed in the town newspaper. Micheaux graphically illustrates the power and pervasiveness of Black misrepresentation not only by conveying the false version of the murder in intertitles depicting the town's newspaper text but also by intercutting this text with a visual restaging of the murder. In this white reconstruction (informed by Black Efrem's false evidence), we see a drunken Landry pull the trigger (fig. 5.3.7). In this instance, as well as in the fleeting image of Sylvia with Armand Gridlestone, the film presents visual "evidence" that illustrates the manipulations of characters who bear false witness and precipitate violent consequences.

By visually restaging false versions of Black actions, *Within Our Gates* challenges rhetoric advanced by D. W. Griffith in *The Birth of a Nation*, in which the cinematic apparatus is imbued with the power to objectively and accurately represent life, including historical personages and events. Unlike live theater, Griffith claimed, "the motion picture is what technique really means, a faithful picture of life."[38] To be sure, Griffith's sense of realism was not a naturalistic or journalistic one; there was room for allegory, fantasy, and hyperbole in his cinematic practice. But Griffith's claims that the cinema could get at life's emotional truths were tied to his many gestures toward historical accuracy, particularly in *The Birth of a Nation*, which is filled with historical "facsimiles"—from Lincoln's assassination to the activities of newly elected Black state representatives. By inserting racist imagery into his facsimiles—like depicting Black legislators drinking alcohol and eating fried chicken while repealing laws against interracial marriage—Griffith amplified Black concerns about the cinema's damaging potential [...]. More than the Black spectacles in early cinema, or the recirculation of minstrel figures in short comedies, Black representations in narratively integrated dramatic cinema (largely crafted by Griffith) were seen as politically dangerous because they were mounted in an aesthetic framework that gave the medium new artistic and cultural legitimacy. Micheaux foregrounds the deceptive (as opposed to the "faithful") representational potential of the cinema, demonstrating repeatedly that the dominant media can (and

---

38   Griffith quoted in Michael Rogin, "'The Sword Became a Flashing Vision': D. W. Griffith's *The Birth of a Nation*," *Representations* 9 (1985): 157.

does) lie, and showing how such lies result in the demoralization, disfranchisement, and death of innocent Blacks.

Figure 5.3.6   The murder of Philip Gridlestone (Ralph Johnson), as it really happened: Jasper Landry (William Starks) is a shocked, innocent bystander. *Within Our Gates* (dir. Oscar Micheaux, 1920). Library of Congress, Motion Picture, Broadcasting and Recorded Sound Division.

But Micheaux does not restrict his critique to white characters and media practices. Significantly, he also implicates African Americans in misrepresenting the "Black" truth. Jane Gaines observes that the notion of betrayal—of wronging one's own—is a recurring theme in silent-era race cinema, and that "in Micheaux's world, the crimes committed against one's own people explain the failure of those people to rise higher and go further."[39] When Micheaux chooses to visualize the stories that unreliable Blacks tell about upstanding ones, he stresses how obstacles to Black progress and mobility should be read as interracial constructions. For example, in a key scene Philip Gridlestone imagines that his Black tenants, the Landrys, are becoming too uppity because their daughter Sylvia has received some education. Gridlestone pictures the Landrys at home discussing their yearly account, with Mrs. Landry advising her husband: "[Sylvia] is as educated as white girls now—so when you go pay the boss you tell him that." However, another title card introduces "what they

39   Gaines, *Within Our Gates* 80.

really said": we see the Landrys again at their table, and Sylvia advises her parents to "keep an account of all your purchases, sales, and debts so that … when you go to the Gridlestone house you can take the accounts and settle without argument." Here Micheaux again presents two visual stagings—one white and one Black—of the same event (fig. 5.3.8). And like the newspaper's false account of Gridlestone's murder, Gridlestone's false sense of the Landrys' audacity is instigated by his Black servant, Efrem. Efrem taunts his employer by telling him, "Dat Landry gal been ta school 'n' keeps her pappy's books now—so ya won't git ta cheat him no mo'." Thus, Micheaux illustrates repeatedly how Efrem enables white misrepresentations of the truth by fanning the flames of racial antagonism—first suggesting that Black share-croppers will educate themselves out of subservient social and economic roles, and then falsely accusing a Black man of murder, inciting the retaliation of a white lynch mob. When Micheaux presents Eph imagining his own murder by lynching before it happens, and stages white fears about violent and educated Blacks, he marks the power of the visual to make even lies and fantasies "real," as supported by print media and facilitated by Black liars.

Figure 5.3.7   The murder of Philip Gridlestone, as told by Eph and the white press: Jasper Landry is a drunken murderer. *Within Our Gates* (dir. Oscar Micheaux, 1920). Library of Congress, Motion Picture, Broadcasting and Recorded Sound Division.

Figure 5.3.8 The Landry family discusses its annual sharecropping accounts; the same discussion is rendered from conflicting white and Black perspectives. *Within Our Gates* (dir. Oscar Micheaux, 1920). Library of Congress, Motion Picture, Broadcasting and Recorded Sound Division.

Micheaux implicates another Black character in the film's politics of truth and fabrication when he frames the entire flashback to Sylvia's southern past within the narrative voice of Alma, Sylvia's dishonest cousin. Micheaux invests considerable narrative authority in this unreliable character; there is never any diegetic reason, once the flashback starts, to disbelieve the events depicted. In some ways, Alma's role in keeping Sylvia running between North and South links her abuses with the revelation of those perpetrated by whites within the lengthy southern scenes framed by her narrative voice. Although Alma initially stood in the way of Sylvia's happy ending (orchestrating her breakup with Conrad), she introduces Sylvia's backstory to Dr. Vivian (and the viewer) by confessing her previous deceptions, so that her narration functions as an opportunity for her to redeem herself. Old Ned, the dishonest, white-serving Black reverend, gets a similar moment of redemption when he acknowledges his wrongs to himself (and the viewer), despite the fact that he is presented within the framework of racist Geraldine Stratton's myopic narration. At these awkward and striking moments, along with Eph's vision of his own lynching, Micheaux foregrounds his role as narrator, passing judgments and designating fates in ways that require some bending of the rules of classical narrative logic.

In these ways, *Within Our Gates* goes beyond criticizing the racist tendencies in white American filmmaking and the dominant society in general. The film also demonstrates stylistically that there are various and contradictory modes available for representing

African Americans—textual and powerful new cinematic ones, for use by white people and Black people—complicating any claims that this mobile and diverse population can ever be represented entirely "realistically." Micheaux suggests that while Blacks were never immigrants, they are not completely innocent either. He implicates African Americans in the negative and positive directions that modern Black life and its representations are taking. Micheaux challenges his viewers to tell and to face the many truths about African Americans despite southern and northern temptations to put individual self-preservation before the advancement of the Race as a whole. What is more, his own narrative style betrays the difficulties of speaking to, speaking of, and particularly speaking for a Black population in the midst of dramatic social, psychological, and geographical transformations.

It was clear when *Within Our Gates* was released that the racial situation in the United States had reached an acrimonious state and that African Americans of all classes in all parts of the country were still the targets of virulent white attacks. Micheaux's attempt at the film's conclusion to construct proud Black American characters, unified in patriotism, certainly provides a compelling response to the racist and exclusionary image of America presented in *The Birth of a Nation*. But the film's use of patriotic rhetoric also reflects the often unresolved conflicts within and between diverse African American individuals and communities that were exacerbated by migration and persisted even as African Americans seemed to face a common enemy. Ultimately, the film cannot fully reconcile its controversial exposure of unspeakable white crimes (rape, lynching, media misrepresentation) and disgraceful Black betrayals (dishonest relatives, urban criminals, false religious leaders). By mobilizing the multiple appeals of migration narrative, patriotism, melodrama, and uplift tale, the film's awkward conclusion heightens our awareness of its contradictory discourses on the notion of Black progress and the variable nature of Black cinematic representation.

The inconsistent, fragmented narrative voices contained in *Within Our Gates* bear an important relation to the disharmonious Black environments and disruptive slapstick "heroes" featured in the comedies produced by the Ebony Film Corporation. Both reflect the new social possibilities that urban migration presented for Black individuals and communities. But they also illustrate the risks of subjective dispersion and instability in Black life and in African American cultural production. Micheaux, Luther J. Pollard at Ebony, and other early African American filmmakers attempted to take advantage of the cinema's uplift and commercial potential. However, the Black diversity they relied upon—that is, audiences in various regions, viewer tastes for different genres, models for numerous character types—also threatened their efforts to use the cinema to produce political consensus or a stable, national Black audience. By responding to pressing issues in modern Black life, such as migration and patriotic feeling, early Black filmmakers reached many segments of the African American audience, but they also broached the very topics that critics used against the movies, such as the breakdown of traditional values, the city's immoral temptations, and false media representation of the Race.

From their first filmmaking efforts and throughout the silent period, African American producers struggled with a series of financial and representational challenges. Although they often felt ill equipped to compete with the mainstream film industry, the comedies, westerns, nonfiction films, and melodramas they produced from the mid-1910s through the World War I and Great Migration years reveal the complexity of defining, claiming, and representing Black American identity at this historical moment. With the release of Micheaux's *Within Our Gates,* with its multilayered discourses on Black migration and patriotism, African American identity, and cinematic representation, we see an assertive post-*Birth,* postwar, post-riots Black filmmaking practice. By extension, this film announced the emergence of an African American film culture no longer in its "infancy" but exhibiting the acute self-consciousness of adolescence.

Bibliography

Bowser, Pearl, Jane Gaines, and Charles Musser, eds. *Oscar Micheaux and His Circle: African-American Filmmaking and the Race Cinema of the Silent Era.* Bloomington: Indiana University Press, 2001.

Bowser, Pearl, and Louise Spence. "Identity and Betrayal: *The Symbol of the Unconquered* and Oscar Micheaux's 'Biographical Legend.'" *The Birth of Whiteness: Race and the Emergence of U.S. Cinema.* Ed. Daniel Bernardi. New Brunswick: Rutgers University Press, 1996. 56–80.

_____. *Writing Himself into History: Oscar Micheaux, His Silent Films, and His Audiences.* New Brunswick: Rutgers University Press, 2000.

Carby, Hazel. *Reconstructing Womanhood: The Emergence of the Afro-American Woman Novelist.* New York: Oxford University Press, 1987.

Cooper, Anna Julia. *A Voice from the South.* 1892. Oxford: Oxford University Press, 1988.

Cripps, Thomas. *Slow Fade to Black: The Negro in American Film, 1900–1942.* Oxford: Oxford University Press, 1977.

Everett, Anna. *Returning the Gaze: A Genealogy of Black Film Criticism, 1909–1949.* Durham: Duke University Press, 2001

Franklin, John Hope, and Alfred A. Moss Jr. *From Slavery to Freedom: A History of Negro Americans.* 6th ed. New York: McGraw, 1988.

Gaines, Jane. "Fire and Desire: Race, Melodrama, and Oscar Micheaux." *Black American Cinema.* Ed. Manthia Diawara. New York: Routledge, 1993. 49–70.

Green, J. Ronald. *Straight Lick: The Cinema of Oscar Micheaux.* Bloomington: Indiana University Press, 2000.

Griffin, Farah Jasmine. *"Who Set You Flowin'?": The African-American Migration Narrative.* New York: Oxford University Press, 1995.

Harper, Frances Ellen Watkins. *Iola Leroy*. 1892. Oxford: Oxford University Press, 1988.

Johnson, James Weldon. *The Autobiography of an Ex-Colored Man. Three Negro Classics*. 1912. New York: Avon, 1965 391–511.

Kinney, James. *Amalgamation! Race, Sex, and Rhetoric in the Nineteenth-Century American Novel*. Westport: Greenwood, 1985.

Larsen, Nella. *Quicksand*. 1928. New Brunswick: Rutgers University Press, 1986.

Micheaux, Oscar. *The Conquest*. 1913. College Park: McGrath, 1969.

_____. *The Homesteader*. 1917. College Park: McGrath, 1969.

Peterson, Bernard L., Jr. *Early Black American Playwrights and Dramatic Writers: A Biographical Directory and Catalog of Plays, Films, and Broadcasting Scripts*. New York: Greenwood, 1990.

Rodgers, Lawrence R. *Canaan Bound: The African-American Great Migration Novel*. Urbana: University of Illinois Press, 1997.

Rogin, Michael. "'The Sword Became a Flashing Vision': D. W. Griffith's *The Birth of a Nation*," *Representations* 9 (1985): 150–95.

Sampson, Henry. *Blacks in Black and White: A Source Book on Black Films*. 2nd ed. Metuchen: Scarecrow, 1995.

Sollors, Werner. *Neither Black nor White yet Both: Thematic Explorations of Interracial Literature*. New York: Oxford University Press, 1997.

VanEpps-Taylor, Betti Carol. *Oscar Micheaux ... Dakota Homesteader, Author, Pioneer Film Maker: A Biography*. Rapid City: Dakota West, 1999.

Washington, Booker T. *Up from Slavery. Three Negro Classics*. 1901. New York: Avon, 1965. 23–205.

Wells, Ida B. *Crusade for Justice: The Autobiography of Ida B. Wells*. Ed. Alfreda M. Duster. Chicago: University of Chicago Press, 1970.

CRITICAL REFLECTIONS

- Were you aware of the cultural importance of music within African and African-American culture? After reading Martin's article, what is your perception of African-American music now?
- Why are writers such as Toni Morrison, Maya Angelou, and Richard Wright considered influential contributors to American literature? What are your thoughts about Black literature's influence on America's literary landscape?
- In your opinion, why were Oscar Micheaux's films important to cinema and to the Black community?

Unit VI

Black Education

Introduction to Unit VI

Black education in America has suffered for a long time. With the apparent defunding of public education, the ever-increasing achievement gap between White students and students of color, the infamous school-to-prison pipeline, and low graduation rates, it appears that the American education system has failed to make education equitable for all segments of society, especially Black society. Therefore, many scholars have elected to highlight this disparity to assist with the much-needed transformation of American education. The readings within this unit were selected to present some of the racial, cultural, and societal reasons for the educational inequality within the Black educational experience.

Laurel Puchner and Linda Markowitz's "Do Black Families Value Education?" illustrates how white teachers following "racist scripts" inhibits the facilitation of an equitable education. Furthermore, Leonard Harris's reproduction of the late Alain Locke's article entitled "Negro Education Bids for Par" discusses the lack of parity between mainstream and Black education and suggests the moral burden and responsibility of equating Black education with White education rests upon the shoulders of the general public. Andrea Green-Gibson and April Collett's "A Comparison of African & Mainstream Culture on African-American Students in Public Elementary Schools" concerns the potential positive impact that infusing African culture into the current curriculum can have on improving Black education. Lastly, Cassandra West's writing in "Black Studies Programs Now Flourishing Despite Early Struggles" serves as a beacon of hope by chronicling the initial struggles and eventual successes of Black Studies programs within higher education.

Do Black Families Value Education?

White Teachers, Institutional Cultural Narratives, & Beliefs about African Americans

Laurel Puchner and Linda Markowitz

Introduction

> ... the value of education is different in a Black family than in a White family. And I think you gotta be aware of that ...

The above quote is from an interview with an effective, caring, seventh grade math teacher in a racially and socio-economically diverse school in the Midwestern U.S. She was one of six White teachers who were participants in our study of the evolution of preservice teacher understandings about race. All six of the inservice and preservice teachers in the study expressed the belief that African American families do not place a high value on education.

The problem of negative beliefs about African American families in schools is not a new idea, and many educators, including Delpit (2012) and Ladson-Billings (2000), have written much about institutionally racist beliefs held by teachers about Black families. However, many people still don't realize it's a problem, and teacher education programs in particular need to continue to figure out how to expose the reality of racism in our schools. Also relatively little recognized is the thesis of this [reading]: racism works via unconscious cultural narratives of which people are mostly unaware, even while those narratives have a major impact on their behavior within institutions.

Speaking recently about police shootings of unarmed Black men, FBI director James Comey (2015) acknowledged that law enforcement has a troubled history when it comes to race. Comey was speaking in relation to recent tragedies

Laurel Puchner and Linda Markowitz, "Do Black Families Value Education? White Teachers, Institutional Cultural Narratives, & Beliefs about African Americans," *Multicultural Education*, vol. 23, no. 1, pp. 9-16.

involving police officers killing unarmed Black men. In August 2014, not far from the Midwestern schools that provide the setting for this [reading], a White police officer killed an unarmed Black teenager in Ferguson, Missouri. In July 2014 in Staten Island a White police officer put an unarmed Black man in a chokehold and, despite the man's cries that he couldn't breathe, several New York Police Department officers continued to assault him until he died a few moments later. Grand juries failed to indict either of the police officers responsible for these deaths.

These are just two recent high profile cases, and we know the statistics are frightening. Comey attributed some of the trouble to unconscious racial biases that research has shown are held by all people. He also said that cops are no more racist than people in other professions.

Teachers are an obvious example of another profession where unconscious bias can have profound effect on the lives of African Americans, as negative beliefs about Blacks held by school staff have very serious consequences. Schools are primarily in the hands of Whites right now in the U.S. (Boser, 2014). As we train new White teachers, they go out into schools where teachers tend to hold (mostly unconscious) racist beliefs about African American families, and where the preservice teachers themselves are predisposed to hold such beliefs. These beliefs have a negative impact on teacher expectations, school climate, and the quality of the educational experience of students of color, leading to enormous negative consequences for the lives of thousands of children and youth in the U.S.

The dynamics underlying the problems of teacher beliefs about the value of education in Black families and of police mistreatment of Black men and boys are the same, and the question in both cases is one that Michael Gerson of the *Washington Post* asked, in relation to the Ferguson events, in a recent editorial:

> How people who do not regard themselves as biased can be part of a system that inevitably results in bias. How men and women who view themselves as moral can comprise an immoral society. (Gerson, 2015)

Individual beliefs and actions such as those of the teachers in our study and the police officers in Ferguson and Staten Island are individual acts and beliefs that both maintain and are maintained by institutional racism. The negative beliefs are very resistant to change partly because teachers and others in the institution think the beliefs are a rational conclusion based on logic and personal experience.

In fact, however, the beliefs actually stem from unfounded and untested assumptions about the way the world works and comprise the individual narratives that are engrained in institutional culture. In this [reading] we illustrate the racist background stories embedded within institutions and how those background stories become expressed in individual cultural scripts about race. We use Haney López's (2000) and Bonilla-Silva's (2003) theories and some of the data from our 2010–2011 study. Specifically, we use the six teachers' expressions of the belief that Blacks place a low value on education to explicate the relationship between institutional and individual racism in schools. We also argue that greater recognition of racism needs to be acknowledged by teacher educators and by society at large.

The examples and anecdotes we describe in this [reading] emerged from a qualitative study that we carried out in 2010-2011 focused on evolution of beliefs about race of two preservice teachers, Amber and Michelle.[1] We conducted about six hours of interviews each with Amber and Michelle over an eight-month period, in addition to interviews with the four inservice teachers with whom Amber and Michelle were placed for field experiences. We also did about 38 total hours of observation in the inservice teachers' classrooms. However, this is not an empirical research report. This [reading] uses study data to explore the intangible place where institutions and individuals meet in propagating and perpetuating racism.

We begin below by illustrating the first theme of our argument, that racism, largely unconscious and unintentional, gets embedded within institutional background stories and expressed in individual racist scripts. Then we illustrate the power of the cultural narratives that feed the racism. Finally, we explore the role played by social class in these unconscious cultural narratives.

Background Stories and Racist Scripts

Our first illustration of White teacher beliefs about African American families comes from Amber's cooperating in-service teacher during her second field placement, Mrs. James. Mrs. James's school comprised mainly middle and upper middle income students and her 4th grade class contained about 20 White students and about five students of color, who were mainly African American. The teaching episode in question occurred while Laurel Puchner was observing alongside Amber in Mrs. James's classroom in November.

Once the students had settled into their seats after returning from physical education, Mrs. James said she was going to tell them a story, and that the story was about her recent opportunity to help at a "soup bus" in a neighboring town. The following excerpt from Puchner's fieldnotes describes what Mrs. James told her 4th graders. (The quotation marks indicate quotes that Puchner felt she had written down close to verbatim, though she did not audio record the event):

---

1   All names are pseudonyms to protect the privacy of study participants.

She tells them that last night she went with some friends to [North City], to a "very very rough neighborhood called The Projects." And she got on a bus and they drove to the projects and served soup for a few hours to kids in this "very dangerous" neighborhood. Kids as young as three or four were there and the oldest was about 14 and they came out to the bus by themselves with no parents and it was their only meal. She stressed how these little kids were all by themselves. "We gave them food because they don't get food." "We had chili and hot dogs and buns we gave them. They don't have a family like yours that's fortunate enough. And every one of the kids said thank you and please ..."

WHITE GIRL raises hand: Do they go to school?

TEACHER: Yes they do. It was really scary because there were seven or eight year old kids taking care of their little siblings.

BOY OF COLOR in back of room raises hand: What happened to the families? ...

TEACHER: Well they were at home ... or they didn't care about their kids. There were two moms who didn't eat because they wanted to make sure their kids got food. But lots of kids were by themselves ...

TEACHER: We gave them each a book, too, so hopefully some of them will read their books to their kids but probably not because they don't have parents that read to them.

Mrs. James appears to be very well-intentioned here. In fact, she seems to be going out of her way to replace a regular academic lesson with a moral one that she feels is important for the students. At the level that we believe she was intending to communicate to the children (and also likely to Puchner) she seems to be attempting to model moral behavior (devotion of time and perhaps money to those less fortunate) and to teach the students a lesson about gratefulness and politeness. (The full transcript shows her several times comparing the soup bus children's high level of politeness to the class's often low level of politeness).

However, she was also communicating several more subtle but very dangerous messages to the students about Black people who are poor. The town that Mrs. James visited is well-known locally for its poverty and majority African American population. It is safe to assume from the story that Mrs. James did not know the children or the families of the children to whom she served food. It appears that all she witnessed was children eating food she served them. Yet her story implies that in her brief experience "in the projects" (code for Black) with them she decided the children's families were neglectful.

She communicated that to the students by stating or implying the following: poor Black parents don't care about their children; poor Black children have to raise themselves; poor Black parents don't read to their children; poor Black children need White "saviors" such as herself to survive. Each of these messages is a racist assumption that is part of a large packet of racist assumptions that are dominant in U.S. society (Delpit, 2012; Markowitz & Puchner, 2014). According to Haney López (2000), a set of assumptions embedded in a communication like this is an example of the use of a "racist script."

When people like Mrs. James use such scripts, they are not intentionally or consciously racist. Rather, Haney López argues, contrary to what is posited in rational choice theory, behavior is not determined by individuals choosing the best option for maximizing self-interest among a range of choices. Instead, people follow established patterns of behavior that are based on accepted, unquestioned, background understandings of how the world works and about what's true and not true about the world. Thus we mostly go through life with unexamined assumptions about the way things are and the way things work, and these unexamined assumptions become normal and natural for us, and in effect become reality.

Unfortunately, the unexamined assumptions or background understandings under which we behave in the U.S. are generally racist (Haney López, 2000). Similar to King's (1991) notion of "*dysconscious racism*," background understandings serve to rationalize discriminatory behavior and beliefs, hence most of the time individuals act in harmful and racist ways without realizing it or consciously intending to because they act according to these racist scripts.

Since these patterns are common within institutions, these background understandings are part of the culture of the institution, and to be a good member of our culture we act in accordance with them (Haney López, 2000). At times we are reflective and thoughtful to a degree, but our behavior is still heavily constrained by the background cultural understandings of the institution, which restricts our range of options (Haney López, 2000) and leads to the unintentional use of racist scripts.

There are several clues in the data from our study that support the idea that Mrs. James was not being intentionally racist in telling her story. First, Mrs. James admitted in a later interview with us that she was uncomfortable with the topic of race and believed in colorblindness:

> I try and stay away from the race factor. We don't mention it in the classroom ... I treat them as equal ... I don't know if there is a better way to do it. I know it is a problem but I really don't touch on it.

Further, she told the story while both the researcher and about five African American 4th graders were present. It seems unlikely that someone who tried to "stay away from race" and who was talking to such an audience would be conscious of how racist the story is. Rather, in telling that story she was likely unreflectively following a script. The background assumptions of that script, which made up reality for her, were racist, but she was not aware of it.

What makes this a particularly clear example of an individual following an unconscious script in Haney López's theory is that Mrs. James probably did not even know that she was talking about race in the story. She didn't mention race, and undoubtedly didn't realize how much her story was fueled by what Haney López (2000) calls "racial institutions" (p. 1806), or "any understanding of race that has come to be so widely shared within a community that it operates as an unexamined cognitive resource for understanding one's self, others, and the-way-the-world-is" (p. 1808). If you asked Mrs. James whether the families were Black, obviously she'd say yes. However, although she probably thinks the details in her story were shaped entirely by her experience on the soup bus, the shape the story took emerged in large part from unconscious assumptions about poor Black people that form a particular script that she was using in telling the story.

Importantly, Mrs. James is unintentionally *individually* expressing implicit racist beliefs even without mentioning race, but her individual expression of racist beliefs is a part of institutional racism because people "both inherit and remake racial institutions," and these beliefs need "group dynamics for their perpetuation" (Haney López, 2000, p. 1806). Following Haney López's theory we conclude that such beliefs are likely a part of the culture of her organization, the school, and with this soup bus story she contributed to the collective yet mainly unconscious project of the school to pass unconscious racist cultural understandings onto the students.

Finding that a single teacher such as Mrs. James holds racist beliefs might be considered an anomaly, but the fact that all six teachers in our study demonstrated racist beliefs is alarming. It's not inconsistent with past research, but it is inconsistent with most people's beliefs about teaching and teacher education. How can teacher education be effective if institutional racism pervades schools? Individual police officer and individual teacher beliefs and actions vary. But in both professions we need to recognize that racist background stories are the prevailing truth. And, as we'll focus on more later, we need to recognize that in schools (as in policing) the intersection of race and poverty magnify the problem.

The Power of Cultural Scripts

As mentioned earlier, all six teachers included in this study expressed views indicating that they believe African American families do not prioritize education. In the case of

Mrs. James, as we've already seen, the view manifested during a story she told to her students while teaching. With the other teachers, these views came across in the individual interviews that we conducted.

In the case of the two preservice teachers (PTs), we have extensive interview evidence of their beliefs about race. In many respects, Amber and Michelle were similar. They fit the demographic of typical PTs nationally in being young, White women (both were 21 years old in Fall of 2010). They also fit the demographic of typical PTs at the university as they were both from working class families and grew up in small, homogeneous, White rural towns. Their parents had high school diplomas but did not have college degrees.

In talking about race, they both generally used racial discourse that fit within the *new racism* described by Bonilla-Silva (2003), characterized by minimization of racism, use of culturally based arguments, and blindness to structural racism. Their views were also consistent with prior research on typical White PT racial discourse (c.f., Levine-Rasky, 2000), including blindness to White privilege and a belief in "reverse racism."

However, interview data also showed important differences between the two. Michelle appeared to truly value diversity, and felt that her lack of exposure to diversity as a child had done her a disservice. She was also highly engaged in all of her courses, and particularly loved the multicultural course. Amber was less engaged in coursework, and her interview responses betrayed a very negative emotional reaction to African Americans that was not present in Michelle's discourse.

In the interest of space, we are focusing here on interview evidence that illustrates their beliefs about the specific issue of the value of education in African American families. Amber spoke to this issue in our very first interview with her. She had made a comment regarding a video about Japanese math teaching that she had seen in her math methods class, and stated that Japanese people valued education more than people in the U.S. Then Linda Markowitz asked her a follow up question:

> MARKOWITZ: So do you think that it's true here for different racial groups or class groups that there's certain groups that value education more than others or might make it easier to teach to?

> AMBER: I think the Asian population would be easy to teach to because you know their parents still kind of like instill that upon them and then I would probably say the White community would be the next you know and then probably the African American community would be lowest to teach, though I don't really know why [I think that]

As can be seen in the excerpt, Michelle stated that she thought African Americans valued education less than Whites and Asians, but then indicated uncertainty about why she believed that. A similar phenomenon occurred in our interview with Mrs. Lester, a kindergarten teacher who was Michelle's second mentor teacher of the year. As seen in the quote below, Mrs. Lester said that she believed that African American students struggle more and have less involved parents, but then indicated that she didn't know why she thought that. Mrs. Lester had no students of color in her class that year:

MARKOWITZ: Have you thought about how it might be different to teach a class of students that was racially mixed?

MRS. LESTER: I don't want to be prejudice but I think there would be more behavioral problems if I had a class that was more racially mixed. Those kids tend to struggle more and it's harder to get hold of parents and I don't know why I think that. Because I know compared to the neighbor next door, the teacher next door, she has three [low performing] kids and hers are the African Americans ...

... That's why I think that. Because I'm not racist. I think I would have more lower kids if I had more African Americans. And she's always talking about how parental involvement isn't high but I had an African American kid last year and her parents were involved. So it's not always across the board ...

In the above quote Mrs. Lester says she'd have lower achievement, more behavior problems, and less parental involvement with a racially mixed class than she does with her all White class. Mrs. Lester's claim is not directly about value of education—rather, it's about the related topic of parent involvement. But as with Amber's quote, Mrs. Lester's statements fit with the culture of low expectations for African American students that is institutionalized in U.S. schools (Delpit, 2012). Interestingly, Mrs. Lester and Amber's statements about Black families/parents are followed by expressions of uncertainty about why they believed what they had just said. We contend that this uncertainty provides a particularly clear example of individuals making decisions based on unconscious and unexamined assumptions about the world. When answering the question about race, they didn't make a thoughtful, rational decision; rather, they followed a cultural script, and hence were not even sure why they'd said what they said.

Yet after making belief statements people don't usually express puzzlement about why they hold the beliefs, so why did Mrs. Lester and Amber wonder about their own beliefs? We speculate that the taboo nature of the topic of race meant that Mrs. Lester and Amber expressed ideas they were not even fully aware of. In other words, although people generally don't recognize the unconscious assumptions underlying their beliefs, they are usually accustomed to expressing their beliefs, so the beliefs don't come as a surprise. But since race is a taboo topic in much of U.S. society, Amber and Mrs. Lester probably very rarely, if ever, spoke directly about race, so some of their own racial ideas might not have been completely familiar to them.

Indeed, Amber's statement about values was in response to our first direct question about race in our very first interview with her. Likewise, Mrs. Lester's similar comment came in response to the interviewer's first question about race. Even though Amber and Mrs. Lester stated they did not know why they believed what they said they believed, they both quickly found a rationalization for their belief, with Amber saying "I think it's something I've seen in my [field placement] observations" (though in the next interview she claimed not to have noticed any racial differences in achievement or behavior), and Mrs. Lester deciding her belief came from reports from the teacher next door. Interestingly, Mrs. Lester appeared to place more stock in hearsay from next door than in her own personal experience with her actively involved African American parent from the year before, likely because she unknowingly held the beliefs she expressed long before she expressed them during the interview and long before she met the involved African American parent.

As Bonilla-Silva (2003) has argued, "cultural" arguments about deficiencies of African American families are currently relatively socially acceptable, and have replaced biological arguments about inferiority. So although many underlying assumptions that are part of the culture of institutions have no basis and are largely unconscious, we are not arguing that Whites are unaware of all of their negative beliefs about blacks. Indeed, Bonilla-Silva's research indicates that most are aware of their own cultural arguments about inferiority of Blacks (Bonilla-Silva, 2003). The unconscious part in many cases likely comes mainly in where they think the origin of those beliefs lies.

In other words, people believe their beliefs are based on evidence, when in fact they are simply part of an unconscious cultural narrative. Excerpts from two different interviews with Michelle provide a clear example of this phenomenon. In an excerpt from the April 2011 interview (at the very end of the study) Michelle told Markowitz that she felt the achievement gap between White and African American children was caused by family life in African American families and specifically the fact that African American parents are not as involved as White parents:

MARKOWITZ: Why do you think there is an achievement gap?

MICHELLE: I don't know. I think going off of my experience I have seen in placements a lot of it has to do with family life. I don't know why it is. Why just because you are of a certain color your family is just, but that is what I have noticed in Ms. [Rain's] class.

MARKOWITZ: What do you think families are doing differently, white families versus families of color?

MICHELLE: I don't think the parents are that involved as the parents that are white. ... I am basing this off of the parent conferences I had with Ms. [Rain]. Many of them [African American parents] she had to give packets for and say go over this at home and that is going to help your kid in the classroom and she didn't have to do that with a lot of the parents that were White.

Mrs. Rain was the teacher for Michelle's first field placement, several months earlier, and in this excerpt Michelle is referencing parent teacher conferences that she participated in during her time in that placement. In Mrs. Rain's third grade class 22 of 27 students (81%) were students of color, mostly African American. In the interview above, from April 2011, Michelle appears quite conscious of her belief that Black families are not involved in their children's education. She believes the reason she holds this belief comes from personal experience with the parent teacher conferences. However, we have good evidence that her belief does not come from the personal experience she cites. First of all, the Black/White student ratio in the class was such that even if the teacher had given homework packets to one White parent and six Black parents the proportion would be about the same, indicating that she wasn't using logic or rational thinking.

However, the clearest evidence that her belief about low involvement among the African American parents did not come from her observation of parent teacher conferences is that five months earlier she had used the same parent teacher conference experience, at that point much fresher in her memory, to argue that African American families did value education as much as Whites. Here is an excerpt from the November 2010 interview in which she is responding to a direct question about whether African American families value education less than White families:

I'm going to relate back to the parent teacher conferences because that was really eye opening hearing how they [African American parents] think of their kid as a student and how they think of the homework and things like that. I don't think they value it any differently at all. I didn't see a difference the entire time I was there. All of them want their children to get good educations and learn.

The quote indicates that directly following the parent teacher conferences the experience had convinced Michelle that African American parents valued education as much as her White students. The quote betrays the fact that she held low expectations for the families prior to meeting them; yet, the experience had proven her wrong. By the

April interview, however, five months later, the underlying cultural assumptions of the institution apparently proved stronger than her memory of the actual behavior of the African American parents.

As indicated earlier, the belief that African Americans don't value education is a prominent part of the institutional racism package experienced by African American children in schools. Since this belief is a focal point for the current analysis, here we describe prior research on the topic as well as the relationship between this focal issue and some of the related ideas that play important roles in institutional racism of U.S. schools and society.

Beliefs about the value of education are linked to beliefs about the heavily researched topic of parental involvement. Parent involvement is related to student achievement (Banerjee, Harrell, & Johnson, 2011; Kerbow & Bernhardt, 1993), and studies show that when people perceive low parental involvement, they assume parents are not motivated and don't value education (Kerbow & Bernhardt, 1993; Lee & Bowen, 2006; Wong & Hughes, 2006).

However, teacher perceptions are not always accurate, and teachers often assume low parental involvement when it is not the case (Msengi, 2007; Wong & Hughes, 2006). Empirical research indicates that the belief that African American families are less involved than White families simply isn't true. For example, Kerbow and Bernhardt (1993) analyzed data from the 1988 National Educational Longitudinal Study, which included a U.S. sample of 26,000 8th graders, their parents, teachers, and administrators. They found that controlling for SES, African American and Hispanic families were more involved than White families, and that especially with African American families, involvement was much higher.

Parental involvement can take many different forms, including parents' home interactions with children that tell them what the parents' expectations are and what they feel is important; parent-initiated contact with the school; and participation in parent-teacher organizations at the school (Kerbow & Bernhardt, 1993). The first type of parental involvement is generally invisible to teachers, and parents who communicate high levels of expectations and values toward school might not communicate with school. Hence even when teachers and administrators don't see involvement in school it does not necessarily mean it isn't happening (Kerbow & Bernhardt, 1993; Lee & Bowen, 2006).

A further complicating factor is that the relationship between visible school involvement and value of education is not always direct. For example, school personnel often don't consider the multiple factors other than "value of education" that influence school involvement. Especially with low income families, low involvement often means lack of time and resources, and lack of comfort with school personnel, rather than low value placed on education (Geenen, Powers, & López-Vazquez, 2005; Wong & Hughes, 2006).

Kerbow and Bernhardt (1993) found that single parenting, being low income, and working full-time were the most significant variables negatively impacting parental involvement. For poor parents who are less comfortable in a school environment, the difficulties are compounded. Structural barriers to school involvement, such as time and transportation, may lead teachers to believe the parents lack motivation and do not value school (Lee & Bowen, 2006). This perception may lead school personnel to treat those parents in a negative manner, thus exacerbating the lack of comfort those parents felt with school involvement to begin with (Lee & Bowen, 2006).

One of the best predictors of a child's achievement is teacher expectations for that student (Brown & Medway, 2007; Hauser-Cram, Sirin, & Stipek, 2003), and the perception on the part of schools that African Americans don't value education is closely linked to low expectations for Black student performance that characterize U.S. schools (Delpit, 2012; Ladson-Billings, 2007). Indeed, research indicates that the teacher's perception of the parental value of education influences teacher expectation of that student (Msengi, 2007; Tyler, Boelter, & Boykin, 2008).

Hauser-Cram et al. (2003) found that when teachers perceived there to be a large difference between their own educational values and the values of students' parents, they had lower expectations for the students, even when students' actual skills were controlled. There was a trend toward greater discrepancy when children were African American as opposed to White or Hispanic (Hauser-Cram et al., 2003).

The research cited above indicates that the value of education is likely not lower among African American families than White families, but another question to consider is whether it would in fact be appropriate if it were. In other words, should African American children and families, especially if they are poor, value education as much as White families? Job discrimination, poverty in the community, and lack of models of individuals from the community who have used education to get ahead may mean that not valuing education would be an appropriate response to the life situation of many African Americans (Philipsen, 1993). Thus not only should teachers not assume a low value of education, but if they do perceive it to be true, it probably should be considered a rational and logical response to the reality of being poor and Black instead of as a character flaw or an aberration.

Another factor that may be linked to teacher beliefs about the value of education in Black families is student resistance. Resistance is "opposition with a social and political purpose" (Abowitz, 2000, 878). In the context of schools, resistance occurs when students struggle against the authority and organizing structures and norms of schools because of their own marginalization, lack of power, and poor treatment (Abowitz, 2000; Hendrickson, 2012; McLaren, 1985). Resistance theorists see resistance as a logical and often unconscious reaction to the recognition that instead of being the democratic institutions they are purported to be, schools are in fact places where social reproduction occurs.

In other words, contrary to dominant ideology, school is not a system that provides knowledge and opportunities equally to all, but rather a system in which higher social classes get what they need to maintain their position of power and lower classes are kept in their place (McLaren, 1985). Resistance can take active forms of misbehavior and overt defiance, but it also takes more passive forms such as sleeping in class, and failure to do assigned work. Either way, it is often interpreted by teachers and others "as their culture not valuing education" (Abowitz, 2000). Unfortunately, while adults who think outside the box and challenge marginalization are sometimes considered heroic, students are not, and resistance tends to make it even less likely that they will get any benefit from school and education (Abowitz, 2000; Gilmore, 1985; Hendrickson, 2012).

Race and Social Class

One question that often comes up in discussions of racial bias is whether the bias is about race or social class. The comments and observations that have been discussed so far, as well as past research, indicate that the beliefs held by the teachers in this study are likely about both. In the U.S., negative beliefs (conscious and unconscious) about poor people abound, and negative beliefs (conscious and unconscious) about Black people abound—these beliefs and assumptions are part of the dominant narrative.

When these categories are combined, negative narratives stringing negative sets of beliefs and assumptions tend to be magnified. Thus, for example, in their study of special education Harry, Klingner, and Hart (2005) found that families who were victims of unwarranted negative assumptions and mistreatment by teachers and administrators were not those who were poor and White, or those who were Black and middle class, but those who were both poor and Black.

The families that were the subject of Mrs. James's soup bus story were both poor and Black, and the script she followed in talking about them was likely a script that combined the two characteristics in a way that would be difficult to untangle. However, although students in our university courses sometimes argue that claims of racism are entirely about social class and not race, research indicates that race does act independently of social class.

This is supported by research, as in Skiba et al. (2014), who studied the discrepancy in suspension and expulsion rates in schools, and who wrote: "Multivariate analyses have consistently demonstrated that race remains a significant predictor of suspension and expulsion even after controlling for poverty" (p. 646). Interview responses of the remaining two teachers in our study also clearly illustrate the independent role of race above and beyond social class in their beliefs about families.

Mrs. Blair, Amber's first mentor teacher in Fall 2010, was a 7th grade math teacher. At Mrs. Blair's school, Whites made up almost two-thirds of the student body, and the rest were mainly African American, with Hispanic and Asian students each making up around 2% of the population. Fifty-four percent of the students qualified for Free or Reduced Lunch. A White teacher with 21 years of teaching experience, Mrs. Blair taught three regular and three honors sections of math each day. Our observations led us to believe she was a caring and effective teacher. Below Mrs. Blair was responding to a question about whether she believes one should try to ignore race as a teacher or to take it into account:

> MRS. BLAIR: I try not to ignore [race], obviously fru fru White female and I try to stay up with the hip hop world, try to make sure I can at least relate some way. Obviously I don't fall in their same socioeconomic background either, I was raised by two parents that lived together, I raised my kids by two parents so that part of it, I think because there are so many single parents there, and that's something you have to pay attention to and it's not necessarily just the Black community, that's probably all of the kids, but then the value of education is different in a Black family than in a White family ...

> PUCHNER: And why do you think there's that difference in education?

> MRS. BLAIR: ... I don't know why the parent won't say education is the best way to go and that you need to stay in school and that you need to get the education, not drop out and work ...

In the excerpt above, Mrs. Blair begins by referencing cultural differences ("the hip hop world") between herself and her Black students that necessitate her effort to make sure she can "relate in some way" to the students in order to be a good teacher. Then she explores the social class and family configuration differences and notes that single parent families are not unique to the Black community. However, she finishes the response by emphasizing that although single parent families are White and Black, there is a White-Black difference in "value of education."

The comments indicate that Mrs. Blair sees social class as an issue, but that when it comes to the specific question of value of education, in her reality there is a Black-White difference that transcends social class. As with the previous examples of teacher statements, Mrs. Blair likely does not realize the extent to which that idea is an untested background assumption that permeates the institutional culture of the school.

Mrs. Rain's interview even more directly addresses the role of race above and beyond social class. Mrs. Rain was a 3rd grade teacher for Michelle's first field placement. Seventy-five percent of the students in the school qualified for free or reduced lunch, and, as indicated earlier, 81% of Mrs. Rain's students were students of color. Mrs. Rain had been teaching for eight years, and had a friendly, open personality. Our observations of her classes indicated that she had a very difficult time with behavior management, primarily due to weak teaching skills, a conclusion also expressed by Michelle in our interviews with her.

In our interview with her, Mrs. Rain did not directly say that African American families don't value education, but this belief underlay much of what she said. The views that she expressed in the interview were in general quite disturbing, and because of space we are sharing just a few very brief excerpts from a much larger narrative. During the interview she derided two nearby school districts that are almost 100% African American, she derided families "on public aid" who request not to pay textbook fees, and she derided children who spoke African American dialect. (Regarding student use of the phrase "that's mines" instead of "that's mine," among other things she said: "... you can't say words that aren't real. And he's like, 'but that's just my language', and I said, 'so your language is unreal words?'")

We speculate that Mrs. Rain was very frustrated by the difficulties she had with behavior management, and that one way that she dealt with the frustration was to denigrate and blame her students' parents and families. We also speculate that because of institutional racism and classism, even though she admitted during the interview that one of her most difficult students was White, she placed the blame entirely on the families of her Black students and by extension on Black families in general, who she implied were irresponsible, selfish, and neglectful in how they raised their children.

At one point she lamented the fact that when she was growing up, parents volunteered in school and in the classroom, but that it's different now.

> I don't want to say that parents don't care, but sometimes it seems like that. Sometimes it seems like they have other priorities, and their kids aren't at the top of that priority list.

A little later Markowitz picked up on that statement:

> MARKOWITZ: You were saying you think parents have another, sometimes the kids aren't their first priority. Like what is their first priority, like in your experience?

> MRS. RAIN: Themselves. They want to dress nice, they want to look nice, they have other kids, maybe one other kid, or multiple other kids, so there's just so many kids I've seen, it's like let the kids fend for themselves, and the oldest one can deal with everybody else, and I'm going to sit back and do what I want to do.

We see here a repeat of one of the salient themes in Mrs. James's story, cited earlier, about bad parenting in African American families, illustrating commonalities among institutions. Mrs. Rain's responses demonstrate an underlying belief that African American students tended to have worse behavior and lower achievement than White students, and that it was due to family acceptance of bad behavior at home, selfishness of the parents, and low value placed on education. At one point Mrs. Rain acknowledged that since most of her students were African American, it's hard to tell whether race is the cause "... when the majority of your class is African American, it's hard to say." However, later in the interview this exchange occurred:

> MARKOWITZ: Like if this whole class was full of White kids who were just from a lower SES, do you think you'd see some of the same issues?

> MRS. RAIN: I think I would see some but I think it plays part with race, I really do. Just because of, like I said, because of their background, because of what they grow up with, and what they see at home, and what their parents are saying at home ...

> MARKOWITZ: So what else ... do you think would be different in [an all-African American] classroom?

> MRS. RAIN: Academics I think. I think that the way they perceive school would be different. I know that some kids come to school just because they have to, because their parents say they have to, because their parent brings them. It's like a daycare, here you go, keep my kid until you possibly can. I think that it would be different just because I think that the backgrounds of the people, or of those kids' families, really play a part of how they act here.

Mrs. Rain's interview responses show very negative beliefs about Black families in general, with the low value of education a prominent theme. Further, Mrs. Rain felt that the problems she experienced with some students were more likely to occur with lower income children, but she did not feel that being poor was the complete explanation.

Mrs. Rain also told us in the interview that parents have accused her of being racist, and although she denied that she is, it's not hard to understand why many parents would feel that way. Importantly, the fact that Mrs. Rain felt comfortable expressing the beliefs she did to the researcher is likely an indicator of the nature of the institutional culture.

Implications

The data we've provided from the six teachers portrayed in this [reading] do not prove that schools are institutionally racist, but they show us the faces of institutional racism that we know exists from other research (Levine-Rasky, 2000; Sleeter, 1994; Vaught & Castagno, 2008). An important message from this material is that teacher education has a bigger challenge than most of us realize. Both preservice teachers and teacher educators need to understand better the institutional background stories of the schools we are sending our teacher education students to, and figure out how to wrestle with it.

In Ferguson Missouri, although the police officer who shot and killed Michael Brown in August 2014 was not charged, U.S. Justice Department investigations found widespread abuse of African American citizens. This abuse was not usually lethal, but it caused great harm. The context of teaching and the context of policing are very different, but the underlying institutional dynamics are not.

School cultures permeated by a belief that African American families do not value education have multiple negative effects on students of color. Two of the most commonly discussed problems are low teacher expectations for students of color and disproportionate punishment (Hauser-Cram et al., 2003; Lee & Bowen, 2006; Skiba et al., 2014).

Social trust, or the extent to which the students, teachers, administrators, and parents of a school maintain relationships with each other characterized by respect, personal regard, competence, and personal integrity (Bryk & Schneider, 2003, pp. 41-42), is also effected. Social trust has been found to be more important to school improvement than many other frequently-cited factors (Bryk & Schneider, 2003), and of course when teachers don't value or respect parents and their opinions or hold them in high regard, social trust is low. Preservice teachers who do field experiences in schools with institutional cultures characterized by low social trust are likely to have a harder time moving away from that pattern.

Although the unintentional racism causes great harm, and lack of intention does not equal lack of responsibility, understanding intent is important in planning anti-racist education. Haney López's theory helps us see the need to factor in the role of agency but in a way that also keeps in mind the institutionalized nature of the racism.

One avenue is helping people understand how all of our thinking in daily life relies on unexamined assumptions about the world, and that we act with unconscious patterns of cognition and scripts in all areas, not just race. Haney López (2000) cites examples from prior research of non-race related assumptions people hold as they go through life. One such assumption is that communication is always meaningful, and one experiment showed how people go to great lengths to create meaning out of communication that is actually entirely random (Garfinkel, 1967, as cited in Haney López 2000).

Relatedly, Haney López's theory helps us see the role of attempts to change individual beliefs. Although "group interaction generates racial institutions, and … such institutions influence individual behavior through widely shared cognitive processes" (Haney López, 2000, p. 1808), not all individuals within an institution must act in accordance with the group.

Hence in the area of teacher education, educating individual teachers to resist a racist institutional culture could certainly change to a certain degree the experience of students within an individual teacher's classroom. The punishment for violating cultural norms often makes it very difficult to behave in ways outside of the normative background stories, but the closed doors of U.S. classrooms make some deviation possible. Thus quality teacher education for diversity will be useful, since even mild disruptions made by individual teachers can make a difference to the students they are teaching (Khalifa, 2012; Marriott, 2003).

Further, a critical mass of individuals with background assumptions that are less racist or anti-racist will alter the institutional culture; obviously there are some schools that meet the needs of all students better than others. That being said, though, the theory also helps us understand the limitations of attempting to change beliefs.

Conclusion

In this [reading] we illustrate a major problem in education and in teacher education, the underlying dynamics of which are a national problem. The Ferguson unrest has spurred a spate of newspaper editorials addressing unconscious racial bias. However, although the bias part is somewhat well-known, it is not well-accepted, and neither is institutional racism.

What Haney López's and Bonilla-Silva's theories show is how individual unconscious bias and institutional racism fit together to decrease the odds of African American students succeeding, especially if they are poor. In teacher education most people tend to think we are already doing what is necessary to deal with racial issues by incorporating multicultural education into our courses. However, the current study shows what happens when you scratch the surface.

The national reform agenda for the past 20 years has focused on test scores and teacher evaluation, with no improvement in educational equity (Lee & Wong, 2004; Ravitch, 2010). Addressing the problem illustrated by the teachers profiled in this [reading] would arguably have a greater positive impact on student learning and student achievement than recent or current major reform efforts.

In the case of policing, the very unfortunate recent events have placed a national spotlight on racial bias, which for the moment has the public's attention and might lead to some positive change. In teaching, negative beliefs about Black families don't directly kill people, and it's hard right now to get the public to pay attention to it. So we need to work harder to raise the alarm and take action.

References

Abowitz, K. K. (2000). A pragmatist revisioning of resistance theory. *American Educational Research Journal, 37*(4), 877–907.

Banerjee, M., Harrell, Z. A. T., & Johnson, D. J. (2011). Racial/ethnic socialization and parental involvement as predictors of cognitive ability and achievement in African American children. *Journal of Youth Adolescence, 40,* 595–605.

Bonilla-Silva, E. (2003). *Racism without racists: Color-blind racism and the persistence of racial inequality in the United States.* Lanham, NJ: Rowman & Littlefield.

Brown, K. E., & Medway, F. J. (2007). School climate and teacher beliefs in a school effectively serving poor South Carolina (USA) African-American students: A case study. *Teaching and Teacher Education, 23,* 529–540.

Boser, U. (2014). *Teacher diversity revisited.* Center for American Progress. Retrieved March 25, 2015. https://www.americanprogress.org/issues/race/report/2014/05/04/88962/teacher-diversity-revisited/

Bryk, A. S., & Schneider, B. (2003). Trust in Schools: A core resource for school reform. *Educational Leadership,* March, 40–44.

Comey, J. (2015, February). Hard truths: Law enforcement and race. Speech at Georgetown University, Washington, D.C. Retrieved March 23, 2015, for Federal Bureau of Investigation Website. http://www.fbi.gov/news/speeches/hard-truths-law-enforcement-and-race.

Delpit, L. (2012). *"Multiplication is for White people": Raising expectations for other people's children.* New York: The New Press.

Geenen, S., Powers, L. E., & López-Vazquez, A. (2005). Barriers against and strategies for promoting the involvement of culturally diverse parents in school-based transition planning. *The Journal for Vocational Special Needs Education, 27*(3), 4–14.

Gerson, M. (2015). Viewing Ferguson from Selma: Bloody Sunday anniversary. *St. Louis Post-Dispatch,* March 12, p. A15.

Gilmore, P. (1985). "Gimme room": School resistance, attitude, and access to literacy. *Journal of Education, 167*(1). 111–128.

Haney López, I. F. (2000). Institutional racism: Judicial conduct and a new theory of racial discrimination. *The Yale Law Journal, 109,* 1717–1884.

Harry, B., Klingner, J. K., & Hart, J. (2005). African American families under fire: Ethnographic views of family strengths. *Remedial and Special Education 26,* 101–112.

Hauser-Cram, P., Sirin, S. R., & Stipek, D. (2003). When teachers' and parents' values differ: Teachers' ratings of academic competence in children from low-income families. *Journal of Educational Psychology, 95,* 813–820.

Hendrickson, K. A. (2012). Student resistance to schooling: Disconnections with education in rural Appalachia. *The High School Journal,* Apr/May, 37–49.

Kerbow, D., & Bernhardt, A. (1993). Parental intervention in the school: The context of minority involvement. In B. Schneider & J. S. Coleman (Eds)., *Parents, their children, and schools* (pp. 115–146). Boulder, CO: Westview Press.

Khalifa, M. (2012). Caught between theory and reality: Positionality of a Black male teacher in urban Detroit. *Vitae Scholasticae, 29*(2), 5–31.

King, J. E. (1991). Dysconscious racism: Ideology, identity, and the miseducation of teachers. *Journal of Negro Education, 60,* 133–146.

Ladson-Billings, G. (2000). Fighting for our lives: Preparing teachers to teach African-American students. *Journal of Teacher Education, 51*(3), 206–214.

Ladson-Billings, G. (2007). Pushing past the achievement gap: An essay on the language of deficit. *Journal of Negro Education, 76,* 316–323.

Lee, J., & Bowen, N. K. (2006). Parent involvement, cultural capital, and the achievement gap among elementary school children. *American Educational Research Journal, 43,* 193–218.

Lee, J., & Wong, K. K. (2004). The impact of accountability on racial and socioeconomic equity: Considering both school resources and achievement outcomes. *American Educational Research Journal, 31*(4), 797–832.

Levine-Rasky, C. (2000). The practice of whiteness among teacher candidates. *International Studies in Sociology of Education 10*(3), 263–284.

Markowitz, L., & Puchner, L. (2014). Racial diversity in the schools: A necessary evil? *Multicultural Perspectives, 16*(2), 72–78.

Marriott, D. M. (2003). Ending the silence. *Phi Delta Kappan 84*(7), 496–501.

McLaren, P. L. (1985). The ritual dimensions of resistance: Clowning and symbolic inversion. *Journal of Education. 167*(2), 84–97.

Msengi, S. G. (2007). Family, child and teacher perceptions of African American adult assistance to young readers. *The School Community Journal, 17,* 33–60.

Philipsen, M. (1993). Values-spoken and values-lived: Female African Americans' educational experiences in rural North Carolina. *Journal of Negro Education, 62*(4). 419–426.

Ravitch, D. (2010). Why I changed My mind. *The Nation,* June, 20–24.

Skiba, R. J., Chung, C-G., Trachok, M., Baker, T. L., Sheya, A., & Hughes, R. L. (2014). Parsing disciplinary disproportionality: Contributions of infraction, student, and school characteristics to out-of-school suspension and expulsion. *American Educational Research Journal, 51*(4), 640–670.

Sleeter, C. (1994). White racism. *Multicultural Education, 1*(4), 5–8.

Tyler, K. M., Boelter, C. M., & Boykin, A. W. (2008). Linking teachers' perceptions of educational value discontinuity to low-income middle school students' academic engagement and self-efficacy. *Middle Grades Research Journal, 3*(4), 1–20.

Vaught, S., & Castagno, A. (2008). "I don't think I'm a racist": Critical Race Theory, teacher attitudes, and structural racism. *Race Ethnicity and Education, 11,* 95–113.

Wong, S. W., & Hughes, J. N. (2006). Ethnicity and language contributions to dimensions of parent involvement. *School Psychology Review, 35,* 645–662.

Reading 6.2

Negro Education Bids for Par

Leonard Harris

L OCKE WAS IN THE MIDST OF controversy at Howard University when this [reading] was published. He was promoting the teaching of a course on race relations, the teaching of African studies, and pay equity between black and white faculty. All were rejected by the white administration, and in June, 1925, Locke was fired from Howard and would not return until 1928.

There were student strikes at nearly every traditionally black college in the 1920s. The strikers protested the Calvinist rules regulating student campus life; the racially separate pay scales for faculty; the employment of conservative, usually white, faculty; and the exclusion from college life of public debate and research programs about racism and segregation. In this [reading], Locke argues that under a system of segregation the role of black colleges involves the right to provide an education that is in the Negro's interest such that that interest is consonant with the Negro's liberation. The [reading] provides us with important insight into Locke's understanding of what cultural groups should do to promote their interest under conditions of duress. It also provides insight into the way Locke treats various educational programs that seem ostensibly unreconcilable or were offered as *the* program for black education.

Negro Education Bids for Par

The stock of Negro education has a heavy traditional discount, and is chronically "under the market." Whatever the local variation, one can usually count upon a sag in both standard and facilities for the education of the Negro, section

Leonard Harris, "Negro Education Bids for Par," *The Philosophy of Alain Locke: Harlem Renaissance and Beyond*, pp. 239-252. Temple University Press, 1991.

for section, program for program, below the top current level, so that to reach relative parity with surrounding systems of education, Negro education must somehow "beat the market." This extra spurt to overcome its generation-long handicaps is the immediate practical problem in Negro education. Its gravity, even as affecting general educational standards, can be gauged if we stop to consider that, counting the regional concentration of the Negro population in Southern and border states legally committed to separate education, plus the large numbers in many large cities even of the North and middle West that maintain separate or partly separate teaching of colored children, separate race education prevails over more than two-thirds the total potential school population of Negro children.

Since we cannot say that this dual system is on the wane, what ought, theoretically, to be an anomaly in our democracy exists as a definite and inescapably practical educational problem. Further, by reason of its being in ninety per cent of the instances a discriminatory separation, and only in ten per cent a voluntary group arrangement or a special effort to compensate the handicaps of a socially disadvantaged group, the situation presents a problem of general public responsibility, and a clear issue of public justice and fair play. Fortunately the last few years have seen a marked change of public attitude on the matter, not merely renewed effort to remove some of the most outstanding disparities, but more promising still, a shift of the appeal from motives of charity to motives of justice and the "square deal." Particularly the last year has been a boom year for Negro educational interests, and there is some warrant for hope that with the momentum of special campaigns for improving the facilities of both private and public schools for Negroes, our educational stock may somehow in the near future approximate par.

Fifteen, ten, even as late as five years ago, in Southern states, the ratio of division of state expenditures, per capita, between white and Negro pupils ranged as high as twenty to one, and averaged fifteen to one, as the Jones report startlingly revealed; and that might be taken as a general index of the situation as it then was, except for large cities and a few favored privately reenforced centers. Though few such glaring discrepancies now prevail, the disparity is still very considerable: a recent appeal in the Tuskegee-Hampton endowment campaign estimates that "the Negroes constituting about one-tenth of the total population, receive less than 2 per cent of the billion dollars annually spent here for education; and of $875,000,000 spent annually on public schools, only a little more than one per cent is expended for Negroes." Certainly, even if allowance is made for the lumped expenditures of areas where no separate account is taken, there is enough in these figures to warrant our picturing the Negro school child as still wearing educational shoddy instead of wool, with the adolescent Negro youth inadequately provided for by threadbare educational "hand-me-downs" or spirit-rasping missionary clothes.

Indeed the missionary type of school, necessary and helpful as it has been, has nevertheless done much to conceal and palliate the fundamental lack in the common school system. Here where the greatest disparity has existed is just where basic parity must first of all be established. Philanthropy and private endeavor do a real dis-service even when they aid the education of the Negro if they assume the moral burden of the deficiencies of public state education. Fortunately the more enlightened philanthropic effort of today, as exemplified in the policy of the Jeannes and Slater funds and the Rosenwald grants, extends only cooperative aid in the improvement of public school facilities, and is thus based on the only sound principle.

A standardized public school education must become the standard in the education of the average Negro child. Otherwise, Negro education costs double and yields half. As an indirect, but heavily mulcted taxpayer, the Negro, under the present system in the South, either pays for some one else's education and himself goes without, or with the aid of the philanthropist pays twice, once through the public system, and once again through the special agency of the private school. After a trying period of vexing publicity in criticism of these conditions, a really constructive and public-spirited reaction has gradually gathered momentum in the South. A new social vision is really involved in this new feeling of local and public responsibility for the education of the Negro. State appropriations, private fund grants, and voluntary contributions of black and white citizens have been cooperatively enlisted in this movement, but the true gauge of its value has been not so much the considerable sums that have been added to the meager resources of the public schools for Negroes in the South, but the recommitment of the state to its fundamental duty, and the reawakening to the principle of local responsibility in matters of education.

An outstanding instance of this is the progressive North Carolina state program, which by special appropriations invested five millions in permanent school equipment for Negro schools in the four-year period 1921–1925, and practically doubled its maintenance expenditures for the same period. Another outstanding instance is reported from Atlanta, where through the interracial committee and the wise direction of the colored vote on the Atlanta school bond referendum, $1,250,000 of the $4,000,000 bond issue was by agreement devoted to the facilities of the Negro schools. The same sort of pressure and leadership wrote into the Kentucky state bond issue for education the provision of a fixed percentage for the uses of Negro education. Recent news of agreements under the auspices of an interracial commission for additional high school facilities for Negroes in Texas, the extensive sharing of the Negro communities in private educational benefactions such as the Duke gifts in North Carolina and the Du Pont improvements of rural schools in Delaware all point, in spite of a continuance of much unfair and reactionary practice, to a new era in public policy. In the existing situation, efforts of this sort are to be regarded as the greatest hope and the safest guarantee of progress in the education of the Negro. To foster it in its most constructive spirit, however, we must not consider such progress any more than the plain duty and common obligation of every community. The improvement of Negro education is overwhelmingly a public task and responsibility; never for any reason of temporary advantage or special appeal must it be allowed to assume in the public mind the aspect of a special responsibility, a private enterprise, or a philanthropic burden. Many a well-intentioned friend of the Negro and of educational progress still thinks of Negro education largely in terms of something special and private rather than something basically standard and public, but by the right insistence the public conception in this regard must be brought to par.

It has been an undesirable and not necessarily permanent condition, then, that has brought the education of the Negro so overwhelmingly into the control of private institutions of all sorts—good, bad and indifferent. Many of these are non-standardized missionary enterprises, conceived in sentiment rather than scientific pedagogy, supported by long-distance philanthropy, and in numerous instances not strategically located or wisely planned as to the division of educational labor with other schools. It is no particular marvel that the South has for so long considered Negro education an alien concern, and, allowing for the aberrations of prejudice, an unwelcome intrusion.

No friend of progressive education can afford today to take a sentimental attitude toward the motley crop of "colleges," "seminaries," and nondescript "collegiate-industrial" schools still in operation despite the weeding-out process of the last decade attendant upon the exposures of the Jones report and other survey agencies. Standardization is the paramount demand of Negro education. This must come about partly by ruthless curtailment of philanthropic support for unworthy institutions, partly by voluntary consolidation of competing schools, and partly through the absorption of students by the increased facilities of the land-grant colleges and state normal schools. All these forces are at present working, but not with the force of thorough conviction behind them. Undoubtedly the next important forward step in Negro education must be the long-delayed but urgently needed concentration of the type once proposed by one of the great educational foundations. It was suggested that the five rival collegiate institutions in Atlanta combine to form one standard and resourceful college and university center thereby pooling their plants, faculties, students and resources. Backed by heavy endowment grants, a few such liberal professional training centers must be provided at strategically placed points like Atlanta, Nashville, one for the great Southwest, one for Texas and one for the Mississippi Delta region, to bring a progressive and standardizing influence into every important region of the Negro population. It has been the history of American education that its schools have been standardized from the top down, and largely through the influence of the private colleges and universities—and there seems no reason for expecting Negro schools to be the exception. As the public education of the Negro expands the private schools concerned with his education must concentrate, which is their one great opportunity to lift themselves to modern standards of efficiency.

Within the group of private schools founded to aid the Negro, those that have been the outgrowth of the Hampton-Tuskegee program have had an influence and a public acceptance far beyond their relative number. Because of their spectacular success and unique appeal to practical Americanism, they have indeed in the public mind become the outstanding elements of Negro education. The reaction of this appeal and popularity upon other types of Negro school, especially the program of the Negro college, has led to a feud of almost Kentuckian duration and intensity in Negro educational circles. Support of the school with a liberal or academic curriculum of the collegiate or professional sort unfortunately came to mean antagonism to the school with the industrial-vocational or "practical" curriculum, and *vice versa*. The question resolved itself often into the question of "what kind of education the Negro most needed," or was "best fitted for," or was most "worthy of public support," instead of the position backed equally by the best educational idealism and common-sense, that the Negro, like any other constituency, needed all types of education that were not actually obsolete in American educational practice.

Only now, when the antagonisms of this issue are beginning to disappear, does a dispassionate analysis become possible. Certainly, whatever the justifications or grievances on either side, the cause of Negro education as a house divided against itself has been in anything but a favorable position before the public. One of the most hopeful recent developments has been the waning of this feud, and the growing realization that the Tuskegee-Hampton program and that of the traditional Negro college are supplementary rather than antagonistic. One factor in this new understanding has been the relinquishment by the younger generation of college youth of the traditional fetishes of so-called classical education that during the missionary period of Negro college management were nevertheless important compensations for an ambition struggling up against colossal odds. The general American college world in fact has had to pass through the same conversion of values, but the "genteel tradition" has its special sentimental hold in the mind of the educated Negro of the older generation. But with a more practical and modernized conception of education, on one hand, growing up in the younger generation of liberally educated Negroes, the program of the "industrial wing" of Negro education, on the other hand, has itself grown. This year Hampton Institute graduated its second and Tuskegee its first crop of degree graduates from standard collegiate courses in education, science and economics.

Thus the year that has so been signalized by the successful seven million dollar joint campaign for Hampton-Tuskegee endowment, and that promises to net resources of nine millions for those valuable institutions, has fortunately seen such a resolution of old antagonisms that in the near future a united front may reasonably be expected in the ranks of Negro education. With close cooperation and understanding established between its two equally important wings, we can optimistically look forward to a new era in Negro education, especially when the powerful forces of public opinion and of philanthropic benefaction come to realize the significance and promise of this understanding and cooperation and lend support generously to both types of educational effort. We shall then see the education of the Negro not as a conflict between two programs or types, but as a mutually supplementary program of collegiate-professional education on the one hand, and of the collegiate-economic, technical and agricultural training on the other, with the field of teacher and social-service training divided between them, that for the great urban centers and their needs on the one hand and that for the important rural situation on the other.

It was not the fault of the Hampton-Tuskegee idea that the so-called higher education of the Negro could not for a generation compete with it in dramatizing its own values. The conception of education back of that idea was original; indeed in its day it was in advance of American educational reform. Before the general vogue and acceptance of technical and vocational types of education and the widespread use of the "project method," its practical demonstration and application of their value was a contribution to American education at large. In addition to its appeal to the American sense of the "practical," the Hampton-Tuskegee program exerted, as it still does, a strong sentimental appeal through its race and community service, and through making all institutions and agencies that come under its influence missioners of the masses, galvanizers of "the man farthest down," and exponents of a naturally popular doctrine of economic independence and self-help. But for every adherent this program has won through what its critics have called its "concessions" to the popular American way of thinking, including the characteristic conciliatory optimism of its philosophy of race contacts, it has, I think, won ten by its concrete appeal and demonstration of results. These it was spectacularly able to offer through the personality and career of Booker Washington, who became, along with a host of other successful products of the system, convincing exhibits of its value. If the type of education that felt itself threatened and depreciated by the vogue of the "industrial program" had been able to stress its social results as dramatically— as is quite possible, considering the indispensable service of the professions—it would have shared liberally in public favor and support.

The essential difference in the relative public success of the two types of education was not in their intrinsic worth but in the quite different caliber of their propaganda and leadership. At the particular time of the strong competition of the Washington program, the higher education of the Negro was in far weaker administrative hands than those of the hardy and zealous missionary pioneers who a generation before had founded it. Having made a success of its initial appearance, Negro collegiate education in the last twenty-five years or more has made the mistake of allowing its social appeals to lapse, of making only an individualistic appeal to its adherents, and of trying to justify itself either by depreciating the rival program or merely by abstract self-appraisal of its own values. Its leadership has been vitally at fault.

Oddly enough, the administrative leadership of the "higher education" wing of Negro education has always been less native and racial than that of the "industrial-vocational." Contrary to general knowledge or expectation, therefore, it has been the so-called liberal education of the Negro that has suffered the heavier effects of the missionary blight. As a consequence what has been liberal in name and intention has not always been liberalizing in effect. When we consider that the great service of Booker Washington to the mass education of the Negro consisted in transforming charity-education into work-education, and in revitalizing missionary motives with the positive tonic of the ideals of self-help and practical community betterment, we can realize that missionarism, as a tradition either of attitude or of management in Negro collegiate education, is doubly out of place. Indeed missionarism and self-leadership are incompatible. And if we assess the success of the "vocational program" as due largely to the public demonstration of its ability to develop its own leaders and effect a marked racial awakening, we can readily see that the non-success of the Negro college of the traditional sort to hold public attention and favor and elicit general support is in part due to the coddling and emasculating missionarism which still traditionally controls it. The Negro college represents too largely yet a reactionary, old-fashioned program, distantly though idealistically administered, second-hand in aim and effect. In short, it has not yet produced its own leadership to give it a vital and distinctive program and to justify it according to its true relation to racial development and advance. It has not failed as a medium of supplying in increasingly adequate numbers well-educated men, but it has failed in recognized social leadership and reform. This branch of our education needs then more than a theoretical defense, or renewed public support: it needs a practical reform of the first magnitude to recover its social values and purposes, and thus bring itself to par again.

This is not to say that Howard, Fisk, Morehouse, Atlanta, Wilberforce, Virginia Union, Johnson Smith and Lincoln—to name the outstanding Negro institutions of college and university grade—are not increasingly important centers of a modernized collegiate education and standardized professional training. Since the war they have all increased considerably in student numbers, faculty strength and in equipment, and most of them have attained standard scholastic rating. But in strange, almost paradoxical contrast to their material expansion and advance, there has persisted a reactionary conservatism of spirit and atmosphere. The mind of Negro youth senses and describes it as "missionary paternalism." It is significant in this connection that at a forum conference of over one hundred Negro college students representing eighteen different institutions, held recently at Nyack, N.Y., it was voted as the consensus of opinion that "because of the paternalistic attitude so prevalent in Negro colleges and so offensive and uninspiring to their students, Negro colleges should be headed by Negroes selected strictly on the basis of efficiency, though the faculties should contain both white and colored teachers." What it amounts to, in last analysis, is really that along with the maintenance of the obsolete system of theological control in the Negro college there has persisted an autocratic and conservative tradition of management. Indeed it is a tradition so rooted in them that it persists in cases where there is direct race control; but the situation is naturally accentuated in psychological effect where, as in the great majority of instances still, there is white executive control. Certainly the regime that inspired a former generation with race zeal and courage only irritates and antagonizes the present clientage of the Negro colleges. A case in point is the recent protest of the alumni body of Lincoln University, Pennsylvania, against the election of Rev. Dr. Gaston to the presidency of that institution on the ground of his "having exhibited a reactionary attitude in his administration of the board controlling the Presbyterian schools for Negroes in the South, and of his not being in favor of a standard progressive program of college education for the Negro." The fact is, having outgrown the idealisms of the missionary impulse which once galvanized them, Negro colleges have not been free to develop a modern emancipated spirituality of their own. Indeed to do this requires more self-direction and autonomy than the present tradition and practice of control and management permits.

The widespread student and alumni unrest of the last eighteen months in one Negro college after another—Tallahassee, Lincoln University in Missouri, Fisk, and Howard, with the situation at Fisk resulting in the ousting by a student strike and alumni agitation of a conservative president in spite of his recent completion of a successful million-dollar endowment campaign—is significant evidence of this rising demand for liberal reform, educational self-direction and autonomy. For while these breaks occur nominally over questions of alumni control and student discipline, they all come to a head in a feeling of racial repression and the need for more positive and favorable conditions for the expression and cultivation of the developing race spirit. So obviously there is a set to Negro collegiate education that does not conform to the psychology of the young Negro. Partly as a negative reaction to conservative management, partly as a response to developing race consciousness, Negro student bodies are developing the temper of mind and mood that has produced the nationalist universities and the workers' colleges.

This development is as reasonable as it is inevitable. Negro education, to the extent that it is separate, ought to be free to develop its own racial interests and special aims for both positive and compensatory reasons. Otherwise it becomes a flagrant anomaly and self-contradiction. But without autonomy and race control there is little or no opportunity for developing any such compensating interest: in short, racial separation presents under these circumstances a negative and irritating challenge or disparagement instead of a welcomed and inspiring opportunity. As organized today for the most part, this type of education constantly reminds Negro youth, in the midst of a sensitive personal and racial adolescence, of the unpleasant side of the race problem, instead of utilizing it as a positive factor in this education. The very noticeable negative reactions on this issue ought to be taken as unmistakable symptoms of an urgent need for a profound change of policy to restore the lapsing morale of important centers of Negro education. The highest aim and real justification of the Negro college should be the development of a racially inspired and devoted professional class with group service as their integrating ideal. Certainly the least that can be expected and demanded of separately organized Negro college education is that in the formative period of life the prevailing contacts should he with the positive rather than the negative aspects of race, and that race feelings of a constructive sort should be the stimulating and compensating element in the system education. But this element, in solution in the positively saturated group feelings of Negro youth at these centers, is inhibited from expression and precipitation by atmospheric conditions that range all the way from spirit-dampening condescension at its worst to spirit-repelling moralism at its best. The mind of the average Negro youth under these conditions turns rebelliously individualistic, and the finest social products of his education are lost.

This loss in the social coefficient of the education of the most promising section of Negro youth, under the very conditions where it should be most carefully conserved and nurtured, is one of the tragic wastes of the race situation. If there is anything specially traditional and particularly needed in Negro education it is the motive and ideal of group service. And though the loss of it in the more capably trained Negro of the present generation is partly due to the influence of the prevalent materialistic individualism of middle-class American life, a still larger loss is due to an inevitable and protective reaction against the present atmosphere of his education.

The lapsing social values of higher education for the Negro can, I think, be recovered only under race leadership, for they must be tactfully coaxed back in an atmosphere of unembarrassed racial councils, charged with almost a family degree of intimacy and confidence. To provide such a positive-toned community ought to be one of the first aims and justifications of the Negro college. Under such conditions, the Negro problem itself can be taken up into the very substance of education, and made, from the informational, the disciplinary and the inspirational aspects, a matter of vital consideration. Occasionally in the atmosphere of very liberal inter-racial exchange this is possible, but under average conditions of the present, decidedly not. Like its analogue, the nationalist university or the class-conscious group, the Negro college of the present day requires and demands, if not group exclusiveness, at least group management and the conditions of self-determination—in brief, spiritual autonomy. Just so long as so obvious and reasonable an advantage is not available will the Negro college remain below the level of its fullest educational potentialities.

This brings the pressing current problem of the Negro college in close alignment with the contemporary movement for the liberal reform of the American college, but for a very special and perhaps more urgent reason. Whatever the needs for more adequate financial backing and support of the Negro college, the need for liberalizing its management and ideals is greater. The less free a people are socially, the greater their need for an emancipating atmosphere in their education. Academic freedom is nowhere any too secure, but to see it so exceptionally curtailed as to be almost non-existent in Negro education is to realize what revolutionizing reform must come about before these schools can hope to attain their full spiritual growth and influence, and function actively in general race development. Under present circumstances and management, few if any of the Negro colleges are in a position to realize these newer demands or even experiment toward catering to these special needs of an increasing body of Negro youth, who cannot be spiritually content with the present regime, however standardized and effective may be the education which it offers. Of course, some of this insistence is only the liberal urge of the youth movement and the common needs of the younger generation, which know no color line and seep over into Negro college life. But when we remember that the present generation of young Negroes is in process of moulting the psychology of dependence and subserviency, and if we stop also to consider that the Negro college student earns his education in far larger proportion than the general college population, the urgency of his requirement for a liberal program and sensitively responsive control becomes apparent. It is something more than a youth problem; there is a racial significance and insistence to these demands.

If they are ignored, reactionary management may drive from the Negro college the constituency which is psychologically most virile and may once again goad reform into revolution. Offered scope and constructive expression in a legitimate field, this spirit of Negro youth is capable under the right native leadership of transforming a half-dozen segregated centers of Negro professional education into radiant centers of Negro culture. As it is, without race control and self-expression the Negro college is more than an anomaly: it is a potential seedbed of unrest. It is the thwarted force that is dangerous. All who fear the truly vitalized Negro college, labelling it a radical menace, will, if they succeed in repressing it, have actually chosen the radicalism of the half-educated charlatan who makes a precarious vocation of revolution and agitation instead of the liberalism of the fully educated and responsible professional man who makes an avocation of social service and reform. The only alternative about the forces of race assertiveness today in America is whether they shall be allowed constructive channels of expression. Certainly education and the Negro college ought, of all agencies, to be able to use them constructively. Indeed without some special motive force, the Negro college cannot hope in the very near future to overcome its particular handicaps.

The safest guarantee of parity in the higher education of the race, finally, is the open and balanced competition of Negro institutions for race patronage with other institutions of higher learning accessible to Negro students. The ratio of the total enrollment of Negro college students in mixed as compared with separate institutions, allowing for a strictly collegiate grade of instruction in the latter, is nearly one to three, and the ratio of degree graduates, according to the careful yearly statistics of the education number of *The Crisis,* is roughly one to two; that is, for every two degree graduates from standard Negro institutions for the last few years, there has been one from the private and state universities of the country at large. These facts reenforce two important principles. First, the inter-racial contact that is lost at the bottom of the educational ladder is somewhat compensated for at the top. It is of the most vital importance to race relations and the progress of democracy in America that contact be maintained between the representative leaders of the white and black masses. The greatest danger of separate school systems would be the removal of these surfaces of contact, and the detriment would be mutual enough to be national. In the second place, the Negro college has yet to justify itself in the full estimation of the college-going Negro constituency. Even when it does, it will take care only of a fraction of Negro college students, but that its clientele should diminish or that its product should lack a justifying distinctiveness and racial effectiveness would be the only indictment of separate education for which the Negro might in any way hold himself accountable. Developed in modern ways to its full possibilities, however, the Negro college ought to become the prime agency in recruiting from the talented tenth the social leadership which is an urgent need, both racial and national, in the difficult race situation of America.

Reading 6.3

A Comparison of African & Mainstream Culture on African-American Students in Public Elementary Schools

Andrea Green-Gibson and April Collett

Introduction

The public educational system is comprised of diverse demographics wherein each student has a distinct cultural personal history (O'Brien, 1998). In America, the traditional perception was that a melting pot society existed. But deMarrais and LeCompte (1999) maintain that a stew pot or salad bowl would be a more appropriate analogy. Melting pot suggests a European-American, middle- and upper-class orientation, whereas stew pot or salad bowl implies that diverse demographics exist alongside one another with many distinctive cultures enhancing humanity across America (deMarrais & LeCompte).

The melting pot theory has dominated the education system, adversely affecting many African-American students who attend urban, public schools (Carruthers, 1995; deMarrais & LeCompte; Marks & Tonso, 2006; Pai & Adler, 2001). A growing body of researchers have reported that educational leaders are constantly searching to find the best methods for teaching African-American students who attend urban public schools (NCLB, 2002). Leadership stake-holders and educators alike are now beginning to explore the possibility that infusing the cultural history of African descent within the schooling process may help African-American students learn more effectively (Pai & Adler, 2001).

Literature Review

One of every 10 African-American students drops out of high school (U.S. Department of Education as cited by Cholewa & West-Olatunji, 2008) compared to one out of every five of their European-American peers (Chicago Public Schools, n.d). According to Shockley (2007), the American education system has failed to address properly the educational and cultural needs of African-American students who attend public schools, which has caused major behavioral, social, and academic problems (Cholewa & West-Olatunji, 2008; Shockley, 2007). Little research has been conducted regarding the way culture in general and African descendants' culture in particular is being applied to the educational experience for African American students who attend public schools in Chicago (Davis, 2005).

For decades African-American students who attend predominantly African-American public schools in their Chicago neighborhoods have not been able to experience a culturally relevant education and have continued to fall behind their European-American peers academically (Shockley, 2007; U.S. Department of Education, 2007/09). On the south side of Chicago, the principal of a predominantly African-American school recently adopted an African-centered approach to the Chicago Public School's curriculum (Finkel, 2007), but questions remain about the overall effectiveness of such an African-centered education.

Many educators realize that how education is transmitted to students affects their academic outcomes as well as their psychological and emotional well-being (Cholewa & West Olatunji, 2008). Experts argue that educators should teach students

> ... academic skills that are supposed to be taught using culturally relevant instructions that connect the content of the lessons to the children. Students should exit classrooms and school with some sociopolitical awareness as well as cultural knowledge about themselves. (Ladson-Billings, 1994a, as cited by Boutte & Strickland, 2008, p. 55)

Infusion of African culture has a positive effect on learning, so the ability to address effectively the cultural and educational needs of African-American students must require leadership stakeholders, teacher educators, teachers, and counselors to work collectively to reform education and develop appropriate educational approaches. Leadership stakeholders must examine teachers and teacher educators' readiness and capacity to ensure they cease to misrepresent history and culture in teacher education programs (Swartz, 2007). Finally, leadership stakeholders and their constituents must evaluate their schools' cultural infusion methods to ensure that the deliberate transmission of culture aligns with the educational and cultural needs of attending students (Shockley, 2007).

Educational leaders, scholars, teachers, and parents are working to find the best ways to teach African-American students who attend inner-city public schools (Carruthers, 1995). Advocates for compensatory education suggested that the most effective way to help improve African-American student performance is to teach the same values, beliefs, and skills that the middle-class White students learn (Pai & Adler), yet others argued that African-American students achieve better academically when African culture is infused in the curriculum (Nobles, 1990).

For decades, according to Marks and Tonso, (2006), African-American students have not been achieving well with the compensatory education approach currently reflected in NCLB, an approach which began as an important part of the Great Society programs intended to improve the quality of education for poor children of ethnic minorities, particularly African Americans (Pai & Adler).

Instead, compensatory education has had an adverse effect on cultural equality for African Americans by imposing traditional educational norms of schooling in America (Pai & Adler, 2001). The Great Society programs, even under NCLB, have continued to stress the melting pot goal (Pai & Adler, 2001), which deprives African-American students of a significant educational experience (Cholewa & West-Olatunji, 2008; Pai & Adler, 2001; Shockley, 2007) and has affected the AYP outcomes for African-American students who attend public schools in Chicago and elsewhere.

In 1991, educational leaders in Chicago started the Small Schools Movement Workshop as an attempt to create new learning environments in communities that were historically toxic (Ayers & Klonsky, 2006). As a result at least two public schools in Chicago have used an African-centered curriculum (Finkel, 2007). While the former public schools CEO signed a proposal to open new small quality schools in Chicago. Finkel suggests that questions have emerged about the effectiveness of an African-centered curriculum in improving test-scores.

While a small number of predominantly African-American elementary schools infuse African culture in the curriculum, most schools do not (Cholewa & West-Olatunji, 2008). The public education system has always been based on Eurocentric values that work to benefit the cultural backgrounds of European Americans. To ensure that education aligns with the norms of African-American students, African-centered education is necessary (Shockley, 2007), but advocates of African culture infusion have yet to convince the public, and even some African-Americans, of the benefits of African cultural infusion.

Methods

A causal-comparative design was used to compare the educational practices of two predominantly African-American public schools in Chicago based on their AYP reports. A thorough investigation of existing documents and statistical data from the two schools was performed to determine whether cultural infusion affected AYP for African-American students. Information was collected from the Chicago Public School website and the websites of both schools that were under investigation as well as 2009 AYP reports retrieved from the Illinois State Board of Education website's State Report Card.

Statistical reports and other pertinent documents, including Illinois School Report Cards and mission and philosophy statements, were used to help describe the process by which the two schools infused culture into the curriculum. The 2009 ISAT score-levels served as a comparison of the schools to reveal the effect of cultural infusion on AYP for African-American students.

The specific types of data collected included mission and philosophy statements of the schools, School Improvement Planning for Advancing Academic Achievement (SIPAAA), ISAT score-levels, and 2009 AYP reports for third, fourth, fifth, and sixth grade students from the two schools. One was a school that infuses African culture into the curriculum (school A), while the other school does not (school B).

Themes were found in the SIPAAA and parent-student handbook data from both schools A and B which showed significant differences in educational practices and AYP information. Themes found in both school's SIPAAA included mission statements, vision statements, and descriptions of curriculum. In addition, the parent-student handbooks from the schools included a welcome letter and general school information.

Although one of the two schools offered pre-kindergarten through eighth grade, the population for this study was limited to third, fourth, fifth, and sixth grade students because these were the grade-level's both schools had in common. In addition, testing was a mandate for students beginning in the third grade. Some class sizes were larger than other classes and might have produced conflicting results but that was remedied by choosing a common number of students in each class for this study.

Approximately 30 students were enrolled in each third, fourth, fifth, and sixth grade class, and the student's ISAT score-level values in reading and mathematics were identified for this study. The total number of students at school A and school B who performed at level 1 and level 2 on the ISAT were calculated and a t-Test was used to compare the two schools. The Illinois School Report Card data revealed the percentages of student scores in each of four performance levels, identified as Level 1—Academic Warning, Level 2—Below Standards, Level 3—Meets Standards, and Level 4—Exceeds Standards.

The two-tailed t-Test was appropriate for this study because the results would have been interesting in either direction, a significant difference either positive or negative between the schools' AYP results. The following hypothesis was established for the study: There is a significant positive causative relationship between cultural infusion and better AYP scores for African-American students in Chicago public schools.

The 2009 Illinois School Report Card data from school A and school B showed the classroom sizes ranged from 20-34 students per class. Third grade student's average class size at school A was 28 and the class size for third grade students at school B was 25. Fourth grade student's average class size during the 2009 school year at school A was 26 and school B had 34 students in the fourth grade. Fifth grade students at school A classroom size was 20 and at school B the classroom size was 32. Finally, the population of sixth graders at school A was 28 and 24 students in the sixth grade in 2009 was 24. Strategic statistical measures were taken to determine that ISAT score-levels of 1 and 2 were most likely in classes with more students.

Data analyses for the study involved observable and statistical data, comparing group differences and group results with former predictions and past research (Creswell, 2005). An in-depth analysis of mission and philosophy statements, prospectuses, SIPAAA, and 2009 ISAT score-levels were used to search for themes. Internal data including SIPAAA information revealed the manner in which both schools transmitted culture to attending students.

The two schools' cultural infusion methods were compared and significant educational differences were identified. The 2009 AYP reports from schools A and B revealed third, fourth, fifth, and sixth grade students ISAT score-levels, which were calculated and compared by using the t-Test to search for significant statistical differences. Comparative results were summarized and were used to explain the differences between cultural infusion practices and AYP for African-American students at the two schools.

To explain the statistical significance of the differences found in ISAT score-levels for School A and School B, both schools' 2009 Illinois School Report Cards were collected and analyzed. A t-Test was used to find the statistical significance and difference between the means of under performing third, fourth, fifth, and sixth grade students' 2009 ISAT score-levels from the two schools.

Results

Data from School A revealed significant evidence showing that school A seeks to infuse African culture and implement an African-centered curriculum in all classrooms. In comparison, data from School B revealed a lack of cultural infusion related to the background of the students and their community. According to the evidence from the data analysis, School B does not infuse African culture in the schooling process. Both schools' student populations are predominantly African American and both are located in predominantly African-American neighborhoods.

An independent t-Test was performed on the hypothesis to see if there was a significant difference between third, fourth, fifth, and sixth grade students' ISAT performance levels revealed in 2009 AYP results, which served as the dependent variable, with the focus on culture infusion methods. The hypothesis was tested and validated by setting the alpha level at.05 using a two-tailed test, calculating the appropriate statistics and stating the degrees of freedom.

The results of the statistical data analysis showed a significant lower performance in third, fourth, fifth, and sixth grade students' AYP results in the school that does not infuse African culture (School B), as compared to students who attend the school that infuses African culture (School A). Thus, there is a significant positive causative relationship between cultural infusion and stronger AYP for African-American students in Chicago public schools.

Discussion

Third, fourth, fifth, and sixth grade African-American students' ISAT score-levels in reading and mathematics at school A, the school that infuses African culture, were significantly higher when compared to African-American students at school B, which that does not infuse African culture in the curriculum. African-American students at school A benefited from African cultural infusion as evidenced by a significantly higher number of students meeting AYP standards compared to students at School B.

Currently many African-American children who live in predominantly African-American neighborhoods in Chicago and attend schools where the population is predominantly African American are not taught by means of an African-centered curriculum in which African culture is infused (Marks & Tonso, 2006). Rather, most schools in Chicago employ a European-centered curriculum to educate all students (Pai & Adler, 2001). As a result, African-American students score significantly lower on the ISAT compared to their European-American counterparts (Cholewa & West-Olatunji, 2008).

Infusing African culture in the educational experience of all students is significant to the well-being of humanity (Carruthers, 1995; Solomon, 1996). African cultural infusion places the educational and cultural needs of African-American students at the center of their education and serves to uplift them and help improve the quality of their education (Shockley, 2007). Unfortunately, currently the inner city of Chicago has only two predominantly African-American public schools that employ African cultural infusion methods (Finkel, 2007).

In this study a significant relationship has been shown to exist between African cultural infusion and African-American student achievement. Data from the research demonstrated that more African-American students in the African-centered public school (school A) met or exceeded 2009 AYP standards, with more students performing at level 3 and level 4 on the ISAT, as compared to students at the non-African-centered school.

The majority of African-American students who did not experience African cultural infusion at School B performed at level 1 and level 2 on the ISAT, not meeting 2009 AYP standards. When a curriculum that addresses the educational, cultural, social, and emotional needs of attending students exists and is implemented appropriately, African-American students will more likely perform better academically and meet or exceed the desired AYP standard requirements.

Conclusion

Mainstream core curriculum in Chicago schools is not designed for the cultural interests of African-American students, resulting in suboptimal academic performance by many of those students (Banks, 2008; Cholewa & West-Olatunji, 2008; Shockley, 2007). According to Hilliard (1997) and Hopkins (1997) as cited by Shockley, the inability to address the cultural needs of African-American students effectively is one of the most complicated problems facing American schools.

Currently, only two predominantly African-American public schools in Chicago infuse African culture in the schooling process (Finkel, 2007). Evidence from the data revealed that school B is a traditional educational institution serving a predominantly African-American student population which does not infuse African culture in the curriculum.

The vision for school B, as revealed in the school's mission statement, is for educators to design and maintain a safe learning environment that works to develop knowledgeable, healthy, and socially responsible students who will function effectively in the global community. School B reflects a compensatory education approach by offering basic academics as a means for students to attain skills needed to acquire better paying jobs (Pai & Adler, 2001). Students at school B might ultimately obtain better paying jobs, but may not be receiving a meaningful and effective education.

Evidence from the vision statement suggests that leaders of School B fail to recognize or use the richness and strengths of African culture to help attending students learn more effectively (Worrill, 2007). Results from the data analysis showed that students at School B continue to fall behind academically as compared to students who attend School A, where the curriculum is infused with African culture.

The way education is transmitted has an effect on student's psychological and emotional well-being as well as on AYP outcomes (Cholewa & West-Olatunji, 2008). Students at school B, as revealed in the mission statement, and many other African-American students who attend other public schools in Chicago, have not been able to experience indigenous culture while in school and consistently fall behind academically (Shockley, 2007). According to Pai and Adler (2001), the curriculum at schools like School B is designed for the cultural interests of European Americans without regard for African Americans' cultural needs.

If African-American students are to be successful in Chicago public schools and similar schools across the U.S., infusion of African culture in the curriculum is necessary. School leaders should collaborate with educators and curriculum development specialists to determine what is appropriate for students to know and understand about indigenous culture. In addition, to ensure that teachers are educated about authentic African history and culture, the school system must design an extensive curriculum plan addressing the cultural, educational, social, and emotional needs and interests of attending students. Such a plan should involve students in class activities and field trips that reflect an African-centered curriculum.

School leaders can use the results of this study to advocate that African culture be infused in the schooling process. The study shows how school A infused African culture in the Social Studies content learning area as well as the various assembly performances throughout the school year such as Kwanzaa, African Heritage, and Ma'at.

Nobles (1990) suggests various ways to infuse African culture in mathematics, language arts, and science content learning areas. Addressing the mathematics curriculum, he calls for educators to understand the role of mathematics in classical African civilizations, the significance of numbers in African theology and music, math games, and the central role of African traditional math in the development of modern mathematics.

When curriculum deals with language arts, information should include the content of African art, the historical development of African art, and the functional continuity in African art (Nobles, 1990). Nobles points to the significance of infusing the curriculum with science and technology from the Nile Valley, understanding the ancient ancestral meaning of Sacred Science, and the African development of the earliest discovered scientific paradigms. This involves infusing the curriculum with African cultural information that reveals the use of time and the calendar, Dogon astronomical sciences, African ancestral metallurgy and electrical engineering practices, and African psychoenergetics are significant to highlight when the curriculum deals with science.

Students will benefit from an African-centered curriculum if leaders and educators collaborate, create, and adhere to an effective plan, and design the curriculum using the framework Nobles (1990) suggests. This approach will help African-American students attain self-worth, self-esteem, and self-identity and will have a significant effect on AYP reports for African-American students who attend public schools in Chicago and elsewhere.

Little research has been conducted regarding the way culture in general, and African descendant's culture in particular, is applied to the educational experience for African-American students (Davis, 2005). The results from this research study should encourage educational leaders to infuse African culture and provide significant information regarding effective African-American culture infusion methods.

Curriculum specialists, educational leaders, and policy makers should work collectively to write the programs, guidelines, and policies for implementing African-centered curriculums in predominantly African-American public schools in Chicago and elsewhere. The ongoing struggle by leaders in the field of education to discover and implement the most appropriate teaching practices, strategies, models, and theories to uplift African-American students may be resolved if educational leaders take the necessary steps to collaborate, plan, develop, and infuse curricula with significant content and culturally relevant information.

Leaders in the field of education and policy makers should work in collaboration to assess all of Chicago's underperforming predominantly African-American student populated schools as well as the two schools that infuse African culture to determine the most appropriate teaching methods for African-American students. The findings of such an investigation are most likely to reveal that African-American students will gain a sense of self-worth, self-esteem, self-identity, and be more than likely to meet or exceed the AYP when curriculum is infused with culturally relevant content.

African-American students who attend mainstream (European-centered) public schools, schools that do not infuse African culture, are failing at a higher rate when compared to African-American students who attend African-centered schools. Current educational policies in the state of Illinois should be reevaluated and rewritten to impose a requirement for all Chicago public schools in predominantly African-American neighborhoods to infuse African culture in the educational experience of attending students.

Researcher Reflections

Before the completion of this study, the notion was that African-American students were failing academically for lack of receiving a fair educational opportunity in Chicago public schools. The assumption was that African-American students might improve academically if the curriculum was designed to address the cultural interests of attending students.

For one co-author, several years ago, as a seventh grade student in a social studies class with a classroom student population of about 25 African-American students, cultural infusion consisted of learning that Christopher Columbus discovered America and that the African presence began with slavery. This experience led to the idea that learning based on African history and culture would be more authentic than what educators were currently teaching in the schools.

To believe that African Americans sat around in darkness waiting for Christopher Columbus to show up and flip on the light switch or that slavery was the start of a civilized society for African Americans is to ignore the significant contributions that descendants of African people have made to the African continent, the United States, and other parts of the world.

Such realizations provided the impetus for this research and the conclusions we present, which we believe should spur all schools in Chicago and elsewhere to implement appropriate cultural studies for all students.

References

Ayers, W., & Klonsky, M. (2006). Chicago's renaissance 2010: The small schools movement meets the ownership society. *Periodical, 87*(6), 453. Retrieved January 5, 2007, from ProQuest database.

Boutte, G., & Strickland, J. (2008). Making African-American culture and history central to early childhood teaching and learning. *The Journal of Negro Education. 77*(2), 131–142.

Carruthers, J. (1995). African-centered education. *An African Worldview, 2*(7), 1–3. Retrieved, June 16, 2008 from http://www.africawithin.com/carruthers/african education.htm.

Chicago Public Schools. (n.d.). Retrieved from: http://www.cps.edu/Programs/Academic_and_enrichment/Pages/Academic.aspx.

Cholewa, B., & West-Olatunju, C. (2008). Exploring the relationship among cultural discontinuity, psychological distress, and academic outcomes with low-income, culturally diverse students. *Professional School Counseling, 12*(1), 54–61.

Creswell, J. (2005). *Educational research: Planning, conducting, and evaluating quantitative and qualitative research* (2nd ed.). Boston: McGraw Hill.

Davis, P. (2005). The origins of African-American culture and its significance in African-American student academic success. *Journal of Thought, 40*(1), 43–59.

deMarrais, K., & LeCompte, M. (1999). *The way schools work* (3rd ed.). New York: Addison Wesley Longman.

Finkel, E. (2007). African ed. *The Chicago Reporter*.

Marks, J., & Tonso, K. (2006). African-centered education: An approach to schooling for social justice for African American students. *Education, 126*(3), 481–494.

No Child Left Behind Act of 2001. (2002). Retrieved from: http://www.ed.gov/policy/elsec/leg/esea02/index.html?exp=0.

Pai, Y., & Adler, S. (2001). *Cultural foundations of education* (3rd ed.). Upper Saddle River, NJ: Merrill Prentice Hall.

Shockley, K., (2007). Literature and definitions: Toward understanding Africentric education. *The Journal of Negro Education. 76*(2), 103–117.

Swartz, E. (2007). Stepping outside the master script: Re-connecting the history of American education. *Journal of Negro Education. 76*(2), 173–186.

U.S. Department of Education, National Center for Educational Statistics. (2007). *The condition of Education 2007* (NCES No. 2007–064). Washington DC: U.S. Government Printing Office.

Reading 6.4

Black Studies Programs Now Flourishing Despite Early Struggles

Cassandra West

B LACK STUDIES PROGRAMS NO LONGER SEE themselves as the stepchildren of the academy. Eleven top institutions now award a Ph.D. in Black or African-American studies, and 300 graduates have earned doctoral degrees in the discipline over the past 25 years.

Black studies departments on mainly White campuses have survived and matured since 1998 when Temple became the first university to inaugurate a Ph.D. program in African-American studies. As they chart unexplored territories and take their inquiries where no one has gone before, doctoral candidates in Black studies are taking nontraditional approaches to scholarship and transforming academia.

Northwestern University, one of the 11 Black studies Ph.D.-awarding institutions, did just that in May. Over three days, more than 200 graduate students and leading scholars met in Evanston, Ill., for "A Beautiful Struggle: Transformative Black Studies in Shifting Political Landscapes—A Summit of Doctoral Programs." The historic summit, intended to showcase students in Northwestern's 6-year-old doctoral program, also reflected on the discipline's hard-fought struggle to gain legitimacy not only on America's college campuses but also within the broader intellectual community.

That history, many of the scholars assembled said, is important. It often involved "standing on the margins and challenging institutions to change and to become more inclusive," said Celeste Watkins-Hayes, chair of Northwestern's department of African American Studies. "Now we've become incorporated into university life, raising questions about how do we maintain that, being the conscience of the university in some ways."

The summit opened with Martha Biondi, director of graduate studies and an associate professor of African-American studies and history at Northwestern, offering a historical overview of the Black studies movement. Biondi, whose latest book is titled "The Black Revolution on Campus," emphasized students' role in the development of Black studies as a discipline and the risks they took to stand up to stubborn White campus administrations. She called them the "intellectual architects" who confronted "violence, death and conflict."

Figures 6.4.1 and 6.4.2   At the Summit of Black studies doctoral programs held at Northwestern University this past April, scholars debated the future of Black studies programs.

Mary Pattillo, a Northwestern professor of African-American studies and sociology, presented data based on surveys sent to the graduate directors of the 11 programs. A clear picture of Black studies programs emerges. Since the inception of its Ph.D. program in African-American studies, Temple University has graduated more than 150 doctoral students. Yale University's program, inaugurated in 1993, has awarded more than 50 Ph.Ds. The University of Massachusetts-Amherst, University of California-Berkeley, Harvard, Michigan State and Northwestern also have granted doctorate degrees.

When it comes to placing their graduates, most programs report near 100 percent job placement, a critical measure of the field's demand. Job placement for Harvard and UMass Ph.D. graduates is 100 percent; Berkeley, 91 percent; Yale, 88 percent; Temple, 86 percent; and Michigan State, 75 percent.

Casting an eye toward the future of Ph.D. programs, Pattillo said the institutions to watch are Clark Atlanta University, which offers a doctor of arts in humanities program with a concentration in African and African American Studies, and Africana Women's Studies; and the University of Texas at Austin's African and African Diaspora Studies

Department, which is "witnessing one of the major expansions of Black Studies in the country." Duke awards a graduate certificate in African and African-American Studies.

Demand for doctorates in Black studies continues to grow. The five-year trend in applications at Northwestern shows a 152 percent increase. The program also has a "selectivity rate" of 9 percent, which is better than the 11 percent selectivity rate in the university's social science Ph.D. programs.

The summit then moved on to a series of panel discussions. The first, fittingly enough, reflected on the "state of the discipline"—then and now. Dr. Nathaniel Norment, chair of the department of African-American studies at Temple, noted the backlash that met establishing the program at his university and others. But now, "the discipline must become a change agent" and also refocus itself to ask provocative questions, he added.

Dr. Amilcar Shabazz, chair of the W.E.B. DuBois Department of Afro-American studies at the University of Massachusetts-Amherst, noting the historic nature of the summit, began plainly by saying, "we have a lot to talk about." His address, titled "Education for Life," focused on living as a professor of African-American studies. At its core, he said, that involves having "an undying love of Black people."

Harvard's Evelyn Higginbotham, who chairs the Department of African and African-American Studies, talked about how her university's current generation of Ph.D. candidates uses social engagement to advance their academic pursuits.

"Our graduate students are concerned about their contributions to the community," she said.

Ava Greenwell, a third-year Northwestern Ph.D. student, said her concern is that African-American studies stays relevant to the masses, a theme reaffirmed for her in an address by Dr. Khalil Muhammad, director of the Schomburg Center for Research in Black Culture in New York, titled "The Crisis in Black History: Where do Public and Academic History Meet?"

"It's always important to have your work be relevant to the average person," said Greenwell, who spent a couple of decades practicing and teaching journalism before entering the Black studies Ph.D. program at Northwestern. "Going back to school, [I learned] there is so much scholarship out there about African-American people. For me it's so important that there be people who are getting their Ph.D.s who really want to be able to take that knowledge back to communities that are not connected to universities."

Several panels showcased the dissertations of Northwestern Ph.D. students, drawing attention to the diversity of topics they're adding to the Black studies canon. Sixth-year student Zinga Fraser presented excerpts from her research on Black women's politics in the post-civil rights era, particularly Barbara Jordan and Shirley Chisholm. La TaSha Levy, who will receive her Ph.D. this year, read from her research on Black Republicans and the campaign for Black capitalism in the 1970s.

Keenanga Taylor, another fifth-year student who is also a commentator and housing activist in Chicago, in her dissertation looks at how the federal government joined forces with private interests to promote single-family home ownership in the aftermath of the 1960s riots.

The summit occurred at a pivotal moment, Taylor observed. "We're talking about the future of Black studies at a time when the Black population is in utter crisis, and that in and of itself raises real questions about what do we do to [respond] to that. We're trying to deal both with intellectual issues … while in the midst of this war on Black America."

That war hit close to home, when two weeks after the summit, the *Chronicle of Higher Education* published a scathing blog post by Naomi Schaefer Riley that labels Levy and Taylor's work as illegitimate and a persuasive case for the elimination of Black studies. Schaefer Riley admitted she'd never read any of the dissertations and only based her argument on an article she'd read that referenced them. A groundswell of criticism led the *Chronicle*'s dismissal of Schaefer Riley in early May.

Dr. Dwight A. McBride, dean of The Graduate School and professor of African American studies and English at Northwestern, thinks Black studies departments, which took root in student-led activism in the 1960s and '70s, have become part of the fabric of their institutions. The Black studies field, he said, "is at a place in its evolution where it can and has the tools and the ability to re-evaluate and reassess its fundamental premises."

He remembered, not too long ago, when the Black studies department was much smaller, less funded and led by a "small cadre" of colleagues who "were holding up the blood-stained banner."

Where once the field's mere existence dominated conversations, today's Black studies scholars take on topics ranging from Black superheroes to queer and diaspora studies. The summit, as intended, brought home the point that Black studies is changing the way knowledge takes shape in the academy.

Biondi, the graduate studies director and one of the summit's organizers, said it offered an opportunity for those "inside the field" to gauge what perceptions are.

"I feel like it was the beginning [of] something, the beginning of new conversations among the different institutions that grant Ph.D.s," Biondi said. "It helped us create a sense of community. This is who we are. We're changing and we're dynamic and doing important work."

- What is your perception of American education?
- Within the first reading, the authors cited Haney Lopez's (2000) concept of racist scripts. Do you think that racist scripts "are not intentionally or consciously racist?" Please share your thoughts.